The Internet

D0976078

The Internet

An Ethnographic Approach

Daniel Miller and Don Slater

Oxford • New York

First published in 2000 by
Berg
Editorial offices:
150 Cowley Road, Oxford, OX4 1JJ, UK
838 Broadway, Third Floor, New York, NY 10003-4812, USA

Reprinted in 2001

© Daniel Miller and Don Slater 2000, 2001

All rights reserved.
No part of this publication may be reproduced in any form
or by any means without the written permission of Berg.

Berg is an imprint of Oxford International Publishers Ltd.

Library of Congress Cataloging-in-Publication Data
A catalogue record for this book is available from the Library of Congress.

British Library Cataloguing-in-Publication Data
A catalogue record for this book is available from the British Library.

ISBN   1 85973 384 0 (Cloth)
       1 85973 389 1 (Paper)

Typeset by JS Typesetting, Wellingborough, Northants.
Printed in the United Kingdom by Biddles Ltd, Guildford and King's Lynn.

To Debbie, Dennis, Emily, Kim, Mr Dass and
many other Trini friends

Contents

Acknowledgements

Writing acknowledgements is always hard for a work that promises anonymity to its informants. There were many people associated with the Internet Service Providers, the cybercafes and our household surveys and in business who are the backbone of this research but cannot be named. Our thanks go to them all. Several people helped us with the logistics of this project, and they can be named: Bridget Brereton, Terence Brunton, Kathianne Hingwan, Lasana Liburd, Roy McCree, Kirk Meighoo, Debbie Ramlogan and Pearl. In addition we should like to thank the following for making enormously helpful critical comments within a very short space of time: Andrew Barry, Christine Hine, Heather Horst, Kirk Meighoo, Charles Stewart, Nigel Thrift, Nina Wakeford, and Andreas Wittel and, in particular, Keith Hart. We should also like to thank Kim Johnson, Judy Raymond Moonilal Dass, Debbie Ramlogan and Dennis Singh for their unstinting hospitality in Trinidad and also Emily, Liz and Gail for keeping us insane during incredibly intensive work. Our informants online and offline were countless. In every case they gave of their time with extraordinary generosity, no matter how busy their working schedules. What was more they gave us information with such a degree of analytical depth and a comprehensive sense of their place in the larger scheme of internet development, that we feel our contribution has been more a 'writing down' than a 'writing up' of our fieldwork. If we have ended with a worrying prejudice it is a serious respect for (almost) all things Trini.

We would also thank Kathryn Earle for agreeing to be bullied into a very tight schedule and to David Phelps for his conscientious copy editing. The speed of work also transformed into pressure on Rickie, Rachel and David, Jo, Ben and Daniel, all of whom are owed an apology. Daniel Miller would also like to acknowledge the help of the British Academy. His research and writing was conducted as a British Academy Research Reader. It may not be the norm of acknowledgements, but we would also like publicly to thank each other for mutual patience with our respective and many faults, which made for a highly enjoyable and rewarding collaboration. Finally, we share from past experience the authors' frustration at feedback and criticism that sometimes seem to reach everyone but the authors themselves. So comments, reviews and criticisms please to <u>d.miller@ucl.ac.uk</u> and <u>d.slater@gold.ac.uk</u>.

1

Conclusions

Why should we do an ethnography of the Internet in Trinidad, or of Trinidad on the Internet? Because – contrary to the first generation of Internet literature – the Internet is not a monolithic or placeless 'cyberspace'; rather, it is numerous new technologies, used by diverse people, in diverse real-world locations. Hence, there is everything to be gained by an ethnographic approach, by investigating how Internet technologies are being understood and assimilated somewhere in particular (though a very complex 'somewhere', because Trinidad stretches diasporically over much of the world). A detailed focus on what Trinidadians find in the Internet, what they make of it, how they can relate its possibilities to themselves and their futures will tell us a great deal about both the Internet and about Trinidad. Indeed, the premise of an ethnographic approach is not only that each sheds light on the other, but that one cannot understand the one without the other: our presentation should convince you that 'being Trini' is integral to understanding what the Internet is in this particular place; and that using the Internet is becoming integral to 'being Trini', with due sensitivity to the complexity and difference contained in both terms. In this sense, we are not simply asking about the 'use' or the 'effects' of a new medium: rather, we are looking at how members of a specific culture attempt to make themselves a(t) home in a transforming communicative environment, how they can find themselves in this environment and at the same time try to mould it in their own image.

This ethnographic particularity – this focus on Trinidad, on the specifics of one 'place' – is very far from a limitation, either for us as researchers, or you as readers. It is not only necessary – the Internet as a meaningful phenomenon only exists in particular places – but it is also the only firm basis for building up the bigger generalizations and abstractions: quite simply, one can use this particularism as a solid grounding for *comparative* ethnography. Social thought has gained little by attempting to generalize about 'cyberspace', 'the Internet', 'virtuality'. It can gain hugely by producing material that will allow us to understand the very different universes of social and technical possibility that have developed around the Internet in, say, Trinidad versus Indonesia, or Britain versus India. We escape the straitjacket of relativism by recognizing that each of these places is constantly being redefined through engagements with forces such as the Internet. Our presentation should therefore also convince you that there is an analytically rigorous basis for going beyond the particular case, that – paradoxically, perhaps – this is not just a study of Trinidad but that it really is an ethnographic approach to 'the Internet'.

What We Need To Account For

Let us start with a research finding that is both outlandish and yet inescapable in terms of our ethnographic engagement: Trinidadians have a 'natural affinity' for the Internet. They apparently take to it 'naturally', fitting it effortlessly into family, friendship, work and leisure; and in some respects they seemed to experience the Internet as itself 'naturally Trinidadian'. The scale and speed of diffusion was remarkable, and regarded as inevitable. It was a 'hot item', fashionable, and it fitted in with a central preoccupation with being amongst the first to know what's happening and where. It provided a natural platform for enacting, on a global stage, core values and components of Trinidadian identity such as national pride, cosmopolitanism, freedom, entrepreneurialism. This was as evident amongst business people, who felt that the Internet simply suited their natural right and ability to compete at the highest global levels, as it was amongst teenagers, who felt they were the match for any music culture they might encounter in the Internet-accelerated global 'culturescape'. The Internet naturally fitted their intensely diasporic personal relations: being a Trinidadian family has long meant integrating over distances through any means of communication. They also saw various Internet media in terms of conventionally Trini forms of sociality such as styles of chat and hanging around.

We found very little negativity or technophobia. The Internet has reached a level where people can focus on content and ignore the technology, and furthermore there was very little anxiety about either the content or its impact. This is not a book about resistance. Nevertheless we recognize that the effects of this natural affinity need not necessarily be positive. Throughout this book one will find raised expectations and a confidence in the future. We do not deal with the future political economy that may quash many of these expectations, leaving people still more frustrated when their information skills become yet one more unrewarded and unvalorized facet of their lives. We do not discuss this because at the time of our study the consequences of Trinidadians' rapid involvement with the Internet – for good or for bad – are still speculative, and we cannot project our fearfulness upon those we studied. All we can say is that this was rarely the perspective we encountered.

At one level, it is of course absurd to argue that Trinidadians have a special affinity to the Internet, that they 'naturally' take to it, are somehow more at home there than other people, as absurd as the converse argument that media technologies have intrinsic cultural qualities. Nonetheless, if we start from our ethnographic experience of Trinidad online in Spring/Summer 1999, the picture that emerges is of an extraordinarily tight fit: Trinidadians took to the new media in ways that connected to core dimensions, and contradictions, of their history and society. In fact, this is the constant conundrum of studying material culture: that what we observe ethnographically is the ostensibly 'natural' fit of objects within a social order that we are intellectually committed to revealing as constructed and historical. As outsiders we were astonished by the speed with which the Internet has become part of lives. Yet the narratives we encountered in Trinidad were mainly complaints about the unbearable slowness of its development and the forces that were preventing things from changing as fast as they 'naturally' should.

But we are pointing to something that includes but extends beyond studying 'naturalization', the process by which something new becomes mundane, taken for granted, 'second nature'. Rather, we are concerned with a series of 'alignments' or 'elective affinities' between Internet use and particular facets of what being Trinidadian was supposed to mean. These affinities are not just about the idea of the Internet as symbol of modernity, but are more concerned with the practices of Internet use on a regular, everyday basis. This implies that we need to examine not only the specificity of Trinidadian self-conceptions, but also the specificity of the technology, such as email, surfing and chat.

Indeed, 'Trinidad' and 'Trini-ness' are complex and diverse phenomena; not least there are huge differences between Trinidadians at home and those many who live 'away'. And Trinidadians do not consciously spend all their time online as Trini's (though this was far more prevalent than we had expected): they also participate as members of youth cultures, music scenes, career structures, shoppers for consumer goods, etc. In turn, the Internet itself involves many different technologies, practices, contexts: it is no one thing, and our study encompassed a wide range of contexts, from ways of doing business to socializing in cybercafes.

Therefore we do not propose any one general explanation for this 'natural affinity'. We need to look at both the specific and the multiple traits of active agents in creating this overall relationship and at the technology itself as an active component in our account. In the tradition of material culture analysis we are as much concerned with how subjects are constituted within material worlds as with how they understand and employ objects (Miller 1987), a perspective analogous to the writings of Latour (e.g. 1993, 1996) on science studies and technology. Our account has therefore to be multifaceted and not reduced to one dominant or homogeneous notion of either 'Trinidadian culture' or 'Internet culture'. Nonetheless, the complexity and multiplicity of these affinities are precisely what strongly impel us to take as our point of departure the way in which a communicative technology is encountered from, and rooted in, a particular place.

Let's Not Start From There

If the Internet appears so bound up with features of Trinidadian society as to appear 'naturally Trini', then we are certainly not dealing with a case of cyberspace as an experience of extreme 'disembedding' from an offline reality. Nor can we understand or explain this situation – 'denaturalize' it – by treating the Internet as a kind of placeless place, a 'cyberspace', or by taking as our point of departure those features of it that *dis*connect it from particular places, such as its 'virtuality'. In this regard, we find ourselves quite alienated from that earlier generation of Internet writing that was concerned with the Internet primarily through such notions as 'cyberspace' or 'virtuality'. These terms focused on the way in which the new media seemed able to constitute spaces or places *apart from* the rest of social life ('real life' or offline life), spaces in which new forms of sociality were emerging, as well as bases for new identities, such as new relations to gender, 'race', or ontology.

The notion of 'virtuality' has played a key role here: the term suggests that media can provide both means of interaction and modes of representation that add up to 'spaces' or 'places' that participants can treat as if they were real. A virtual reality game should provide a sensory environment, as well as ways of interacting with it, that is 'realistic' enough to immerse participants in the experience and to elicit engaged and 'realistic' responses from them. Similarly, relationships in a 'chat room' can be treated 'as if' they were real. Like the term 'simulation', 'virtuality' points to a representational 'as if' that is separate from but can substitute for the 'really is'. But by focusing on 'virtuality' as the defining feature of the many Internet media and then moving on to notions such as 'cyberspace', we start from an *assumption* that it is opposed to and disembedded from the real.

The kinds of questions that have therefore preoccupied the more high-profile literature, as well as much public discussion and common sense about the net, have therefore assumed an opposition between the virtual and the real: 'All this stuff going on in cyberspace, is it real or not?', 'What *kind* of reality is virtuality?', 'Is it as real as or more real than reality, is it mistaken for reality, or is it a new reality that shows up the constructed, performed, artificial nature of our old offline reality?', 'Is it a good thing or a bad thing, does it spell out doom or liberation for offline life, utopia or dystopia?' On the one hand, a range of authors, sometimes assimilating 'virtuality' to a dystopic reading of the postmodern notion of 'simulation', see the Internet in terms of increasing 'depthlessness' and superficiality, as a poor substitute for the socially essential features of co-presence and face-to-face interaction. On the other hand, often in relation to poststructuralist projects, virtuality provides a kind of social laboratory or even liberation in which the performative character of all social realities and identities can be brought to light, deconstructed and transcended.

In fact this focus on virtuality or separateness as the defining feature of the Internet may well have less to do with the characteristics of the Internet and more to do with the needs of these various intellectual projects. The Internet appeared at precisely the right moment to substantiate postmodern claims about the increasing abstraction and depthlessness of contemporary mediated reality (Baudrillard 1988; Jameson 1991); and poststructuralists could point to this new space in which identity could be detached from embodiment and other essentialist anchors, and indeed in which (some) people were apparently already enacting a practical, everyday deconstruction of older notions of identity (Butler 1993; Haraway 1996). That is to say, intellectuals, like Trinidadians, have discovered their own 'natural affinity' to the Internet, in which their core values and issues correlate quite well with possibilities glimpsed in these new media (for useful surveys of the literature see Crang Crang and May 1999; Kitchen 1998). The point is not that they are wrong in their critiques of simulation or identity, or in using concepts of 'virtuality' or 'cyberspace' in pursuing these critiques. The point is simply that, even if these approaches are valuable in certain instances (e.g. Turkle 1995; Slater 1998, in press a) they are not a good point of departure for studying Trinidadians and many other people. Indeed, in most of what follows in this volume, they simply do not apply.

That is to say, if you want to get to the Internet, don't start from there. The present study obviously starts from the opposite assumption, that we need to treat Internet media as continuous with and embedded in other social spaces, that they happen within mundane social structures and relations that they may transform but that they cannot escape into a self-enclosed cyberian apartness. Indeed, to the extent that some people may actually treat various Internet relations as 'a world apart' from the rest of their lives, this is something that needs to be socially explained as a practical accomplishment rather than as the assumed point of departure for investigation. How, why and when do they set 'cyberspace' apart? Where and when do they *not* do this? In what ways do they make use of 'virtuality' as a feature of new media?

What do *they* (businesspeople, Carnival bands, schoolkids or government agencies) regard as real or virtual or consequential?

Rather than starting from 'virtuality', then, we are concerned to start our investigation of the Internet from within the complex ethnographic experience. If we were to treat virtuality as a social accomplishment rather than as an assumed feature of the Internet, then there would be nothing odd in saying that the Internet is not a particularly virtual phenomenon when studied in relation to Trinidad, but that it might well be when studied in other contexts. By way of comparison, Slater's earlier project on 'sexpics traders on IRC', which was indeed largely confined to online interviews and observation of online settings, could investigate the ways in which participants socially sustained their setting as 'a place apart' and gave it a virtual reality, for example through their use of certain textual practices. 'Virtuality' really was a central feature of this setting, but this itself had to be accounted for: to a great extent, 'virtuality' was useful to participants in order to accomplish their business of trading, and in order to ward off various dangers. On the other hand, participants only accorded serious value to these online realities to the extent that they could be made less virtual and more 'embodied'.

By contrast, we encountered relatively little Internet use in Trinidad that could usefully be construed as 'virtual'. There are few places in this volume where a differentiation between, say, e-commerce and other commerce, playground chat and ICQ chat, religious instruction face-to-face or by email is treated by participants in terms of any clear division between the 'real' and the 'virtual'. Far more evident is the attempt to assimilate yet another medium into various practices (email complements telephone for family contact, websites supplement TV for religious evangelism). Most people were concerned with whether Internet media provided effective or appropriate means to pursue practical projects; and they were concerned to discover what was new or specific about this new set of technologies and practices, given that the Internet appeared to have a huge and inevitable place in their future. New mediations, indeed, but not a new reality.

We can go further here: virtuality – as the capacity of communicative technologies to constitute rather than mediate realities and to constitute relatively bounded spheres of interaction – is neither new nor specific to the Internet. Indeed, it is probably intrinsic to the process of mediation as such. For example, Poster (1995) usefully refers us back to Anderson's (1986) argument that modern nations might be thought of as 'imagined' or virtual communities, dependent on the capacity of newspapers to reflect a singular imaginary back to a dispersed or divided people. This is particularly apt in the case of Trinidad, which has had to imagine national and cultural identity across a complex ethnic mix and a geographical dispersion across the globe.

In much of our research, email communications or websites were experienced as comparatively concrete and mundane enactments of belonging, rather than as virtual.

The relative irrelevance of 'virtuality' in this book, and the fruitlessness of defining the Internet in terms of its separation from offline life, in no way diminishes the Internet's importance or seriousness. Quite the contrary. Trinidadians, like others, may invest heavily in relationships and practices that only exist online: it is as breathtaking here as anywhere to find that the fiancée that has featured in several conversations with someone actually lives in the middle of Australia, and their relationship is based on hours of chatting on ICQ. That is to say, these spaces are important as *part of* everyday life, not apart from it.

The notion of cyberspace as a place apart from offline life would lead us to expect to observe a process in which participants are abstracted and distanced from local and embodied social relations, for example becoming less explicitly Trinidadian. We found utterly the opposite. Trinidadians – particularly those living away – invest much energy in trying to make online life as Trinidadian as they can make it, to see the Internet as a place to perform Trini-ness. Of course, they do not go online solely as Trinidadians. They go online as youth, as religious believers, as businesspeople, as family members. Nonetheless, it was remarkable the extent to which the Trinidadians we interviewed or observed entered into the transcultural networks of the Internet *from somewhere*, as people who felt themselves encountering it from a place, as Trinidadians. A youth living in Trinidad inhabits and enjoys a world of MTV, Entertainment Today, soaps and Nike, and the websites they commonly visited reflected this offline culture and were much the same as that visited by any 'global youth'. Nonetheless, they spoke of themselves as Trinidadians encountering these cultural forms, whether on- or off line: for example, as discussed in Chapter 4, music-oriented Trini youths talking about online cultural resources said that although they respected rap and hip hop, they were concerned to encounter all forms of music in terms of their long-term tradition, in which Trinidadian 'soca' music has been able to incorporate varied musical forms from soul through to rap and techno.

This book is not a case-study of localization or the appropriation of a global form by local cultural concerns. It is not about domesticating a technology. On the contrary, it is largely about how Trinidadians put themselves into this global arena and become part of the force that constitutes it, but do so quite specifically as Trinidadians. Indeed, the significance of studying the Internet is the degree to which it transcends dualisms such as local against global. It forces us to acknowledge a more complex dialectic through which specificity is a product of generality and vice versa. Local Trinidadians do not meet a global Internet. The object we call the Internet actually consists of groups such as the Trindadians you will meet in this volume.

The relationship of our conclusions to Castells's (1996, 1997, 1998) work is necessarily more complex given the extent of his coverage. Much of his work on political economy is not touched upon here. Of the most relevant discussions to our work some certainly ring true. For example, Castells concludes (1998: 340–53) with some ideas on the emergence of 'informational capitalism' and on the importance of rethinking the relationship of skills to education, which finds resonance in many places within this volume, though some predictions made about the implications for future social divisions and power seem premature. However, Castells's primary distinction between 'the Net' and 'the Self' appears to replicate the classical sociological distinction between structure and agency. The result is to separate out the net as a monolithic and reified structure (or 'morphology') whose impact on identity is then investigated. It also seems to run too close to a technological determinism (1996: 1–23). This clearly runs against our refusal to treat the Internet independently of its embeddedness. The problems come out most clearly in his concept of the 'culture of real virtuality' (e.g. 1996: 358–75). Every chapter in this book demonstrates why the assumptions made there about the separation between the real and the virtual are misguided, and why this way of writing about the impact of the Internet seems to us quite wrong for the case of Trinidad.

What is so lacking in Castells is by contrast superbly drawn in the writings of Latour on mediation, in particular, in his exemplary studies demonstrating how one can avoid what he calls the two pitfalls of sociologism and technologism (1991:110) or more generally science and society (1993). Everything that is important is what happens in the mediations that dissolve these dualisms. We would also affirm the Internet as an actant (Latour 1999: 116–27, 303) in the story that is told here. This is not a book about the Internet as a technology that is then appropriated by another thing called society. It is a book about material culture, which can never be reduced to some prior subject or object. We do not start from two premises, that is, the Internet on the one hand and Trinidad on the other. As will become clear in the body of this work, it is more fair to say that both the Internet and an understanding of what it means to feel Trinidadian (e.g. Chapter 4) are seen as the conclusion of the processes we study. In the section (below) on the dynamics of mediation we note examples of new genres such as ecommerce and the norms of Trinidadian Internet chat that cannot be understood except as examples of what Latour terms a hybrid that is irreducible to either its human or its material agents. We trace other dualisms that the embedded Internet renders increasingly anachronistic, especially that of production and consumption.

Furthermore, Latour's work seems supportive of a comparative anthropology/ sociology that eschews simple relativism but maintains a sceptical attitude in the face of glib assumptions about what the Internet 'must' mean or do. We would also wish to see our work building upon prior scholarly studies of the introduction and effects of previous technical developments (e.g. in MacKenzie and Wajcman 1985). Latour also accounts for our sense of ourselves in the production of this work. It is neither some simple expression of our agency nor a simple test of hypotheses. This book is itself a hybrid in which the agency of Trinidadians, of the Internet and of ourselves are we hope combined, transcended and thereby liberated for the purposes of academic understanding.

Comparative Ethnography: An Open Invitation

How does one move between the details of the case-study and the generalities of the Internet at a global level and across contexts? In advocating comparative ethnography, we are suggesting that there are lines of inquiry, linked to dimensions of new media use, that can be usefully pursued across a wide range of settings; and that there are issues about social transformations in new media contexts that generally concern social science and other communities. In this volume we rarely address the question of whether our ethnographic findings are specific to Trinidad or common to many areas. We simply don't have grounds for answering such questions. In the absence of much ethnographic, let alone comparative, material we are offering a limited number of analytical dimensions and issues that have emerged from our own work, along with an open invitation that these either be used in other ethnographic settings to develop comparative understanding; or that they be criticized and modified on the basis that they are either too peculiar to our own setting, or that they insufficiently capture the issues that need to be investigated.

In what follows we will try to clarify both what each category means as a comparative dimension and what it means in terms of the Trinidadian context. This will also allow us effectively to present the conclusions of our research at the outset and indicate the kinds of claims which the rest of the book must substantiate. In the final part of this chapter we will be even more specific, summarizing the particular findings that concern each chapter.

We are offering four such dimensions. They are not meant to be exhaustive. We will characterize them in terms of 'dynamics', a term that directs us to look for both the driving forces as well as the emergent patterns of change. In investigating the embedding of Internet in a particular place, and vice versa, we are concerned with:

Dynamics of objectification: how do people engage with the Internet as an instance of material culture through which they are caught up in processes of identification?

Dynamics of mediation: how do people engage with new media *as media*: how do people come to understand, frame and make use of features, potentialities, dangers and metaphors that they perceive in these new media?

Dynamics of normative freedom: how do people engage with the dialectics of freedom and its normative forms as they are opened up by Internet media?

Dynamics of positioning: how do people engage with the ways in which Internet media position them within networks that transcend their immediate location, and that comprise the mingled flows of cultural, political, financial and economic resources?

Dynamics of Objectification

This dynamic most closely addresses the question from which we started – the seeming affinity between Trinidadians and the Internet – and accounts for the most prevalent results and themes thrown up by the research. People recognized themselves in the Internet in various ways and found that it provided the space for enacting core values, practices and identities. That is to say, there were aspects of these new media environments that allowed them to objectify themselves as Trinidadian, amongst other things (youth, mas' players, computer nerds, whatever) and given the diversity of Trinidadians (Indian, Black, female, elder, etc.). At the same time they were able to mould these spaces to culturally specific shapes and purposes. We are concerned with the ways in which a particular people can recognize or 'realize' themselves through a particular domain of material culture. By 'realizing themselves' we obviously do not mean that people have a natural or essential identity that is then represented or expressed in and through a material culture (though people themselves frequently believe this, and it may be a central feature in their understanding and use of things). But people engage with material culture through versions of themselves that are both articulated and transformed through that encounter.

This dynamic of objectification between identity and the Internet can be thought of in two interrelated ways: In one case, which we have dubbed *expansive realization*, the Internet is viewed as a means through which one can enact – often in highly idealized form – a version of oneself or culture that is regarded as old or even originary but can finally be realized: through these new means, one can become what one thinks one really is (even if one never was). What might be characteristic of the Internet is that this 'realization' is indeed 'expansive': through the global interconnections offered by the Internet, a Trinidadian may feel able to act as the Hindu he or she 'really is' (but could not be within the confines of Trinidad) by participating in worldwide Hindu networks that can be integrated into their everyday local reality.

In the second case, which we might call *expansive potential*, the encounter with the expansive connections and possibilities of the Internet may allow one to envisage a quite novel vision of what one could be, a vision that is often projected as a feature of the Internet itself (for example, transcendence of mundane identities).

Expansive Realization   Here, identity in relation to the Internet is not best understood as novel or unprecedented but rather as helping people to deliver on pledges that they have already made to themselves about themselves. In some cases this was a state that had been realized but then lost; in other cases it was projected but never yet attained. In either case it is imperative to take the two terms – expansive and realization – fairly literally: contradictions concerning one's ability, in practical life, to be who one thinks one is seem capable of being resolved on the expanded scale and terrain of the Internet. This dynamic permeates the entire book, and seems to us fundamental in the Trinidadian context.

For example, as described in Chapter 3, Trinidadians have seen two quite opposed changes to the family as a result of their attempts to embody their sense of modernity. On the one hand, family structures that were previously quite distinctive have tended to move closer to the dominant Western model of the nuclear family. At the same time, migration to metropolitan regions has been so extensive that the majority of Trinidadians live in families that are international even at the nuclear level. In this context, the Internet – specifically email – allows the kind of mundane, constant and taken-for-granted daily contact that enables Trinidadians once again to live in families of the kind they see as natural, to be involved in active parenting and mutual support, despite the diasporic conditions that had earlier been making this impossible.

A second example concerns freedom, markets and entrepreneurship. As noted in Miller (1997), pure competition and entrepeneurship already exist as ideals of social action and personhood in Trinidad, quite apart from any involvement in the market or in commerce. Moreover, they exist as ideals that intersect with but go far beyond simple ideological commitments such as neoliberalism. Trinidadian businesspeople are able to see themselves as naturally highly modern actors within pure market conditions at a global level. But this ideal is very far from the realities that emerged in that earlier book. As described in Chapters 5 and 6, the flow of information and resources developing with the Internet on a global scale allows some Trinidadians to feel much closer to the kind of business practice that they assumed they already followed.

The finest example comes not from this volume but from the brilliant portrayal of this condition by the Trinidadian novelist V. S. Naipaul (1987) in his book *The Enigma of Arrival*. Saturated by British colonial education, Naipaul can only find himself as a Trinidadian by coming to England and identifying himself with a reified image of unchanging Englishness that he finds objictified in the prehistoric monument of Stonehenge and the people who live around it.

A frequent and paradoxical theme is that you could only become really Trini by going abroad: Trinidad itself did not offer the kinds of resources, freedoms and world position that would allow one to 'be Trini' in the sense of cosmopolitan, entrepreneurial, world-class, etc. The Internet may have helped bring the potential for being Trini back to Trinidad; indeed, it worked both for Trinis at home (who could have direct access to global cultural flows, global markets, and world-class skills and technologies) and for Trinis 'away' (who could 'repair' other aspects of Trini-ness such as national identity, 'liming', 'ole talk', family and friendships). A parallel may be drawn with the effects of recession in the late 1980s. As a result of the oil boom some Trinidadians came to assume that a real Trinidadian had a natural affinity with goods of a certain quality. When recession meant these goods were no longer available locally, some Trinidadians declared in the local press that they had to migrate abroad to what in one infamous case was described as the land of 'real cornflakes' in order to remain fully Trinidadian (Miller 1994: 272–3)

The Internet is by no means the first example of new technologies and materials being used by Trinidadians as an idiom for enacting their values and identities. Miller's (1994) previous book on *Modernity* was an attempt to understand the massive impact of consumer culture on Trinidad during the oil boom of the 1970s and early 1980s. That volume concluded that consumer goods were not primarily used to construct new values and ideals, but rather constituted a new idiom, through which Trinidadians worked through core values concerned with freedom (transience) and continuity (transcendence) that had arisen from their particular history, and from their particular relationship to the condition of modernity. Previously, it was kinship that had been used as the primary idiom for expressing the contradiction between these two ideals. In the context of the oil boom, consumer goods took on this role, and could be effectively used to express and sometimes to resolve these contradictions of values. The Internet should be seen through a similar dynamic (or even as a successor idiom for dealing with the same tensions), in which tensions intrinsic to the Trinidadian relation to modernity are worked through using the expansive material culture offered by that same modernity.

Finally, we have stressed a very positive view of both Trinidadian identity and of its projection, through Internet or other means, into global spaces. We do this partly, and paradoxically, in response to Trinidadians' own often very negative sense of themselves, their capacities and their global position. This negativity is often projected on to and through the Internet itself. In countless interviews and chats, Trinidadians would point to their sluggish response to the Internet or to ecommerce. Similarly, the local telecommunications monopoly (Chapter 5) is seen as a symbolically archaic bottleneck in both Internet access and access to the world economic and cultural stage, a kind of symptomatic own goal in which they deny themselves the opportunity to capitalize on their own massive potentials.

Expansive potential   In expansive realization, the excitement is of the order of 'finding oneself' or 'taking up one's rightful place'. In the other dynamic, of expansive potential, people glimpse quite new things to be (or even an escape from what they were). It is about the Internet as a mode of imagining the future, and it incorporates those issues of the Internet as utopia or dystopia that preoccupy so much of the literature but also some of the people we study. The shape of the future may even be thought to be visible in the Internet's own features, as when a Catholic charismatic sees in the infinite interconnectedness of the Internet a vision of the divine and of a new spirituality.

In Chapter 7 an Apostolic Church is striving to discern the latest signs as to the nature of God's purpose for humanity. As a result they assume the Internet was itself created in order that they should come to understand that purpose. It is then appropriated as the medium for accomplishing this purpose, and therefore also as the ideal metaphor for the role of the Church and its adherents. They become the vanguard of the 'World Breakthrough Network' that will establish Christianity anew in the image of the Internet, which in turn is the truest image and instrument of God's purpose for humanity.

Rather more mundane and unselfconscious examples were constantly thrown up by young people. As described in Chapter 3, they seemed to take naturally to a life of MP3s, MTV and chat-room gossip, often merging them seamlessly with playground chat (there was a notable case of fourth-formers calling each other by their ICQ nicks in face-to-face encounters at school). They can constitute new places of sociality in cybercafes and take on new identities as hackers and chatters, with little or no sense that this is something novel and distinct from the school culture of a previous generation. Similarly in Chapter 6 a company called Radical senses that it is now only the Internet that can provide the most contemporary sense of fashion and being 'hot' that is essential for its claims to be in the vanguard of style, and the implication is not so much a change in its clothing range as that it must be seen to be operating in the fullest sense of ecommerce. Jones (1997) provides a general case of such profound assimilation where he notes that our impatience while waiting around for the latest developments in the Internet and computers more generally is based on our constant experience of extremely rapid improvement and change, such that this becomes a kind of 'habitus' (Bourdieu 1977) in which living with the Internet is swiftly naturalized as second nature and our 'common sense' shifts accordingly.

Obviously the line between expansive realization and potential is a fine one: it partly depends on how we and they understand novelty. This in turn involves issues of *time*: it may well be that it is right now at the moment of its inception that the Internet will peak as the prime mode of utopian, dystopian and other images of the future. It may be its very novelty that makes it an ideal idiom for imagining the future. After a while it is quite possible that it will become more mundane and taken for granted.

Dynamics of Mediation

Here we are concerned with how people engage with new media *as media*: how do people come to understand, frame and make use of features, potentialities and dangers that they perceive in these new media. Should email be offered by the postal service, like snail mail? Do advertising agencies see websites merely as a new medium for advertisements or in terms of a fully integrated ecommerce? Which kind of relationships is chat good for, and which not? How should one properly present one's self or one's community on a website, in email, in chat?

For both researchers and participants, a central aspect of understanding the dynamics of mediation is to 'disaggregate' the Internet: not to look at a monolithic medium called 'the Internet', but rather at a range of practices, software and hardware technologies, modes of representation and interaction that may or may not be interrelated by participants, machines or programs (indeed they may not all take place at a computer). What we were observing was not so much people's use of 'the Internet' but rather how they assembled various technical possibilities that added up to *their* Internet. Moreover, all the components that constitute 'the Internet' are changing at a frantic pace. After all, not very long ago this book would have focused on bulletin boards and flaming; it is in fact a book largely about email, chat and websites, and is trying to keep up with its 'subjects' in their understanding of ecommerce. In a year or two's time, when much of the web will be transfigured by high-bandwidth facilities, as well as by completed telecommunications deregulation, the common-sense view of what 'the Internet' is and what one should write about will have again been transformed.

There is not necessarily a lot in common between websites and email. In Chapter 7 it is apparent that the Catholic Church finds one of these pieces of technology analogous to the confessional, while the other acts to represent the community. Again, some businesses are mainly concerned with corporate integration using intranets, while others mainly want to have websites as an adjunct to conventional advertising. This point is particularly clear in Chapter 4, in which chat as a medium has been used to re-create a very particular mode of interaction and socialization full of banter and innuendoes that for many people is the quintessence of being Trinidadian; yet this hardly played any role in email communications. Websites on the other hand go beyond chat as a medium for enacting Trini-ness to become an overt expression of nationalism, but through entirely different means. Very few websites try to evoke the style of chat; instead, they use quite different genres such as those of tour guides and Internet portals. While for some people email, surfing and chat are an integral whole, for others their relationship is merely fortuitous and incidental, since only one of these technologies is of interest to those particular users.

Therefore the various Internet media have to be understood in terms of their particular manifestations as material culture. This is precisely the point of Chapter 6, where commerce is faced by the potential of various new information technologies. Many of the problems of ecommerce development result from difficulties in linking technology and context conceptually. Either commerce fails to respond to the particular potential of the Internet by merely reproducing flyers and adverts on websites, or we find website designers with great technical knowledge of the Internet that they are unable to marshal to commercial ends. What the vanguard users believe is that the future lies in an ecommerce that is neither merely a use of the Internet as technology, nor merely a continuation of prior commercial practice. It has to be understood as a form of material culture that transcends and thereby transforms both the use of the Internet and the workings of commerce. Furthermore, ecommerce as a concept does not take as its point of departure the unity of the technology, but rather the drive to integrate all aspects of a business operation. 'Advanced' thought in this area is concerned with how to use various potentialities in the medium to create 'frictionless' business, in which the firm's relations with its suppliers, its customers and its own departments can take place in a single electronic space. This requires a huge intellectual as much as a technological effort to forge disparate media into coherent schemes within integrated business concepts. Nothing could better refute the idea of a pregiven entity called 'the Internet'.

Yet although we have stressed the disaggregation of the Internet both as a necessary analytical strategy for researchers and as a central dimension of people's experience of new media, a notion of '*the* Internet' still plays an important role. This is particularly evident in public, policy and business discussions in which 'the Internet' collectively labels the juggernaut of social transformations (many of them not technological at all) that is bearing down on Trinidad furiously and with apparent inevitability: 'The Internet will change the conditions of global competition whether you like it or not!' This framing of the Internet as a totality is related to objectifications of 'the net' (whether religious or net libertarian) as a space of utopian possibilities or to other ways of looking into 'the net' and reading the future there. Indeed, in the Trinidadian case (though not here alone) 'the Internet' has come to represent a utopian future conjunction of personal freedoms, market freedoms, global mobility and cultural identity that we will deal with further as a dynamics of normative freedom. Hence it is important to understand the Internet as a symbolic totality as well as a practical multiplicity.

Dynamics of Normative Freedom

Both a premise and a promise of Internet development has been a concept of freedom. Discourse encountered on and about the Internet has been notoriously libertarian: like the Wild West, it has provided a screen on to which could be projected images of freedom, danger, transformation and transcendence. The Internet has both produced new freedoms (of information and of speech) and come to stand as a symbol of potential freedoms. Indeed, two quite contrasting notions of libertarianism have been closely linked to the Internet (Ross 1998), one from free-market ideologies of neoliberalism, the other, 'net libertarianism', from postmodernism. These discourses have been articulated in Trinidad in terms of a correlation between Trinidad itself, the marketplace and the Internet in which each was mapped on to the others in very complex ways. The term 'normative freedom' seeks to capture the apparent paradox by which no notion of freedom is really absolute, but necessarily takes the form of a normative structure, a social order.

Miller (1994) has previously argued that the primary legacy of a history of slavery and indentured labour is the centrality of a project of freedom that permeates a wide range of values in Trinidadian society and is as likely to be expressed in Carnival as in ideals of business. Freedom in Trinidad is ontological, reflecting a basic sense of personhood. So a discussion of the term must be attuned to the specific history of the region and the contradictions that has thrown up. Twenty-five years ago this underwrote the nationalism that led Eric Williams, Trinidad's first Prime Minister, to transform the country from a supplier of raw materials to the developed world into an industrial economy. Today it accounts for an easy appropriation of the language and policies of liberalism. Both government and commerce see the Internet as providing a new form of free communication that will ultimately help Trinidadians to attain their rightful place on the international stage through success in enterprise and careers. As a result, whatever seems to stand in the way appears as an irrational constraint that has to be overcome. This is seen in the prevailing attitude to TSTT, the local telephone monopoly. Even where the company can present itself as effective and efficient, all the other players – government, the ISPs and the public – regard it as the bottle-neck whose restrictive practices are preventing Trinidadians from properly capitalizing on the Internet. Modernization clearly means enthusiastic use of the language (though not necessarily the implementation) of WTO treaties and other mechanisms of global deregulation. Many of the highly reflexive and articulate business community were able to paint a convincing portrait of what they saw as free Internet development. The government shares this ideal or idyll of liberalism, claiming that where possible, as in the licensing of ISPs, there is to be simply no regulation – anyone is free to enter as a player.

Much of the story told in Chapter 5 has to do with specific features of the political economy; but it is important to note that it has strong resonances in other areas also. There was the considerable liberalism in attitudes to online activities, with hardly any debate about pornography on the net (despite people regularly claiming that it accounted for 60 per cent of online activity). Even a Church may see the Internet as largely a step forward beyond the language of the free market in objectifying a concept of freedom *per se*. Similarly in Chapter 3 the use of random chat for engaging in relationships that are anonymous, can come from anywhere and can be ended any time exemplifies the ideal of freedom.

There is generally a remarkably expansive attitude in Trinidad: people see the opening up of markets and the Internet as an opportunity to be grasped, as new freedoms that increase people's potential. At the same time, this needs to be seen in a regional context that has included the ravages of structural adjustment in Jamaica or of 'banana' wars elsewhere in the Caribbean that result from the opening up of unprotected markets. It is hard not to anticipate that freedom in the form of deregulating the telecommunications market might result in replacing a quasi-local monopoly (a company jointly owned by the government and the multinational Cable and Wireless Ltd) with direct ownership by a company such as AT&T. As already noted, our fear is that the expectations that seemed to be rising as we watched will be unfulfilled and quashed. As described in Chapter 2, we can already see some real constraints on the entry into the IT labour market of skilled, deserving and aspiring younger workers, especially women.

Moreover, liberal discourses of unbridled freedom tend to obscure how 'freedoms' are always normative and constructed. In this case, government policies have been as important as any 'automatic' market mechanisms in expanding Internet use, most especially the provision of loans to public sector workers and the removal of customs duties on computers and their parts. Similarly, many of those in business espouse the free market in principle but are looking for all sorts of interventions to secure their interests in practice.

Similarly again, what the Internet produces cannot be understood in terms of the liberation of new and fluid identities. Not only were older identities, such as religion, nation, and family, embraced online, but the Internet could be seen by many as *primarily* a means of repairing those allegiances. This requires special attention to the ways in which freedom and normativity are linked rather than sundered in these newer media of social interaction. In fact, this applies to many Internet contexts. This point was well made by Dibbell (1994; see also 1998) in what is already seen as a near-classic essay on Internet use called 'A Rape in Cyberspace'. Although the people involved in activities such as MUD have strongly libertarian or even anarchistic principles, they turn quickly to the re-constitution of moral and normative order when faced with some action that deeply offends them. Similarly, Slater's (1998, in press b; see also Rival, Slater and Miller 1998) earlier work on 'sexpics trading on IRC' found that various libertarian discourses of freedom (sexual, consumerist, neo-liberal, cyberutopian) were embedded in obsessive practices of normativity and order such as policing, enforcement of quasi-economic exchange rates, and forms of reification.

Finally, we should understand many tensions arising from the Internet not in terms of freedom versus constraint but rather as conflicts between different models of order and normativity. For example, much Internet use involves decentralization and diffusion of authority and power, and hence challenges to both hierarchical organizational models and those whose interests are vested in them. Two examples stood out: the tension within an 'Apostolic' organization between a vertical organization based on elders and a horizontal relation between members expressed in Internet chat; and the organizational models of semi-autonomous and flexible project groups embraced by some younger employees in businesses. In each case, the interconnectedness and flow of information afforded by the Internet gave new powers and autonomy to individuals, which had then to be understood within and disciplined by their institutions.

Dynamics of Positioning

Internet media position people within networks that transcend their immediate location, placing them in wider flows of cultural, political and economic resources. The boundaries of markets, nations, cultures and technologies become increasingly permeable, and require people to think of themselves as actors on ever more global stages. For example, a high-street retailer in a provincial Trinidad town knows that the very idea of a 'local price' is coming to an end: her customers are encountering in the Internet a single marketplace in which they can compare prices and order goods from anywhere in the world. How does she understand this new *positioning*, how does she reconceptualize her business? How do people understand this new landscape of 'economies of signs and space' (Lash and Urry 1994) or 'network societies' or 'spaces of flows' (Castells 1996, 1997, 1998), and how do they try to pilot a course through it?

In Trinidad, these developments are seen as inevitable: the Internet, and particularly ecommerce, is considered central to its position in relation to the rest of the world. However, there was a notable oscillation between excitement and anxiety. On the one hand, Trinidadians feel confident and familiar with competition along international networks: as noted, this is a society that has long been constituted in relation to the global (dispersed families, market orientation, geographical mobility) and sees itself in terms of cosmopolitanism and freedom. At the same time, people are desperately worried that they are already too late or have fallen behind, worries that fit into a long-standing counter-discourse of fatalism and disappointment in which nothing that is Trini can be all that good, and the country constantly has to be 'talked up' through expressions of global confidence.

This is about the local and the global being out of step with each other. For example, in order for provincial retailers to enter the new world market, they need to understand new technologies and concepts for doing business. They also need specific infrastructures such as banking systems that allow online credit card processing and telecommunications companies that provide lots of reliable bandwidth. There has in fact been huge frustration over these bottlenecks in national development. At the same time, both banks and telecomms may be moving slowly because they are dealing with their own positioning problems, as specific industries. For example, local banks are often related to larger banking groups that had always been neatly divided up into non-overlapping geographical regions; the online services that local retailers are demanding can be accessed from anywhere, and therefore set each bank up in direct competition.

Issues of repositioning are evident at the personal level too: for example, a sense of being cosmopolitan, of having the knowledge and capability to act in global contexts (particularly through diasporic experiences of considerable social and material success in education and careers 'away'), has been important to Trinidadian identity. This cosmopolitanism has always run head-on into an awareness of Trinidad as marginal and even unknown. This experience is both replicated and partially dealt with on the expanded terrain of Internet media. For example, in the case of ICQ and Internet chat, Trinidadians who know a great deal about a wider world in which they see themselves as eminently capable participants suddenly discover that most of the people they chat with have never heard of them, and that members of such supposedly metropolitan centres as the US are actually far more parochial than they are. And yet these very same Internet media in which they appear as localized and marginalized also create possibilities for participating in a global cultural space that they thought had already existed. For example, they can engage with world music or global youth culture or pan-national religious communities as cosmopolitan citizens rather than as marginalized observers, and hence are able to 'repair' at this expanded scale a central part of their self-understanding: that the 'natural' stage for being Trinidadian is a global one. Nonetheless, it would be as impossible for online Trinis, confronted by a zillion belief systems on offer through websites, newsgroups, chat, etc., to remain unaware that, for example, their religious identity is a choice within a 'free market' of spiritual possibilities, information, communications, and so on. That is to say, identities have to be positioned in relation to a far wider context and dynamic than before.

Positioning is about strategies for surviving or succeeding in these new flows and spaces. At one level this is a matter of development economics. Trinidadians in government and business are examining their 'competitive advantages' in terms of new technologies: can their level of education, industrialization and entrepreneurialism position them successfully in high-value-added offshore Internet work for Northern corporations, producing software, websites or databases. This also means entering into flows of technology and skills transfer from North to South, and trying to ensure that the extra mobility of the information society does not intensify the historic brain drain of gifted Trinidadians to highly paid jobs in the North.

The idea of websites and a 'world wide web' is a potent metaphor as well as a vehicle for thinking about this repositioning. Following Gell's (1998) work on the notion of 'aesthetic traps' (Chapters 4 and 6), a website can be understood as a form that expands space and time by allowing one to operate on people at a distance. As in the classic anthropological case-study of the Kula ring (Malinowski 1922; Munn 1986), a website in a network of hyper-links can expand the 'fame' of its creator by placing them in an expanded circulation of symbolic goods. In Chapter 6 we start with the case of the Miss Universe website, in which the entire nation seemed to become obsessed with an attempt to project Trinidad on to a global stage that would return to them the new 'fame' of Trinidad. Fame could be reckoned in such things as numbers of 'hits' and reciprocal sponsorship (the site displayed such international names as Microsoft and Oracle, whose sites in turn displayed the banner of the Trinidadian company that produced the site). This placing of Trinidad on the Internet world map also worked in conjunction with leading edge notions of ecommerce, which also focuses on integrating the visitor into a website through appropriate enticements, such as chat, information, photographs of the contestants and multimedia. At a much lower level in Chapter 4 a schoolgirl appears desperate to have visiting surfers (who may be largely limited to the others in her class at school) sign her guestbook, which in turn would attest to her own expanding fame.

A Short Note About Ethnography

It should be clear by now that for us an ethnographic approach to the Internet is one that sees it as embedded in a specific place, which it also transforms. Our four 'dynamics' indicate fields of force or tension between ways of life and potentialities to be found in these new technologies. Moreover, our approach is ethnographic in that it uses immersion in a particular case as a basis for generalization through comparative analysis.

In a more narrowly methodological sense, an ethnographic approach is also one that is based on a long-term and multifaceted engagement with a social setting. In this regard we are both relatively conservative in our defence of traditional canons of ethnographic enquiry. This seems particularly important at the present time, when the term 'ethnography' has become somewhat fashionable in many disciplines. In some fields, such as cultural studies, it has come to signify simply a move away from purely textual analysis. In other cases, the idea of an Internet ethnography has come to mean almost entirely the study of online 'community' and relationships – the ethnography of cyberspace (e.g. Markham 1998; Paccagnella 1997).

We assume ethnography means a long-term involvement amongst people, through a variety of methods, such that any one aspect of their lives can be properly contextualized in others. Slater's (1998) prior study of the Internet lasted 18 months and Miller's prior study in Trinidad was one initial year and three further visits. For the present study, although we each spent only five weeks actually in Trinidad, this volume relies on eleven years of prior research on Trinidad by Miller, which included work on many topics – business, consumption, kinship, identity – that proved critical to making sense of the Internet there. There were also specific advantages derived from this: for example, the house-to-house surveys reported in the Appendix comprised the same four areas described in two previous volumes. Corresponding to this, Slater's long-term involvement in Internet research, particularly chat, laid a basis of skills, methodology and experience against which the Trinidadian case could be more quickly understood. Moreover, the study extended beyond five weeks in Trinidad to 15 months of collecting and analysing Internet data such as websites, interviewing Trinidadians in London and New York, extended email correspondence and participation in chat and ICQ, which could be sustained over time as online relationships. Some of our informants remained in touch for this 15 months. The extension of the work across time and location naturally follows from a general discussion which has problematized the concept of the fieldsite on general (e.g. Marcus 1995; Gupta and Ferguson 1997), and with respect to the Internet in particular (e.g. Hakken 1999: 58–60).

As to the use of multiple methods, the Trinidad fieldwork was divided between several sites and forms of research. Mornings usually comprised several interviews in the capital, Port of Spain, largely devoted to the study of the political economy of the Internet, including businesses, the ISPs and governmental officers. The afternoons and evenings were spent 'liming', that is 'hanging around', in cybercafes watching people go online and chatting with them. We also interviewed them more formally. In addition we tried to become re-involved in the private lives of long-standing friends to see how the Internet fitted within their worlds. We employed students at the University of the West Indies to carry out a basic house-to-house questionnaire, which we followed up with in-depth interviews. We also tried many informal encounters, such as liming with the same friend whose parlour had proved an ideal spot for liming in Chaguanas in Miller's earlier study and who now ran a shop, with an online computer, that became our base in Port of Spain. He attracted countless friends and visitors during the course of the day that we could chat with.

For us an ethnography does include participating, which may mean going on a chat line for the eight hours that informants will remain online, or participating in a room full of people playing networked Quake (both activities Slater is well practised in, and enjoys). But it also includes knowledge of how the Internet has become involved in households Miller has been working with for over a decade. An ethnography is also much more than fieldwork. Just as Miller's (1998a) previous ethnography of shopping turned largely into a study of love, and not, as might be expected, one of spending, so Slater found a study of Internet pornography led on to the study of normative morality and not, as might have been expected, just libertarian freedom. In most ethnographic reportage of quality, the length and breadth of the study allows one topic to become understood as also an idiom for something else. Finally, an ethnography should form part of a comparative project. Slater's prior work and the differences between those results and our work in Trinidad meant that this particular example of Internet use could not be glibly generalized as Internet use *per se*, while Miller's prior work meant that Internet use could be set against other practices in Trinidad. In addition we have tried to contrast our findings with those that seem comparable in other studies.

Summary

(Obviously this short list only includes a sample of the findings within each chapter.)

Chapter 2 – Trinidad and the Internet – An Overview (including Appendix A)

2.1. Access to and use of the Internet is vastly more widespread than might have been expected. Our house to house survey revealed that while around one in twenty households has an Internet account, around one-third of households include a regular Internet user. Even at very low income levels, people purchase top-of-the-range computers, including modems.

2.2. The Internet permeates Trinidadian society as a 'hot' subject. It has become critical to the desire to be stylish as an individual, but also in attempts to launch Trinidad itself into the vanguard of modernity.

2.3. This intense interest in the possibilities opened up by the Internet extends even to settlements of squatters; nonetheless, use of the Internet is strongly correlated with income. While class is expressed in inequalities of IT career prospects, people also attempt to use IT skills to bypass traditional educational qualifications.

2.4. Domestic access to the Internet shows little distinction of gender or ethnicity, but gender and age are reflected in different patterns of use and in unequal institutional attitudes.

Chapter 3 – Relationships

3.1. The Internet has considerably strengthened the nuclear family throughout the Trinidadian Diaspora, allowing closer relations between parents and children and between siblings. It has had an equally strong impact on the extended family.

3.2. The use of random chat, especially within ICQ, has generated new forms of short-term, often anonymous, but also often profound and intimate relationships between Trinidadians and peoples of other countries, some leading to marriage.

3.3. People are very sophisticated in how they distinguish between a serious and a casual online relationship on the basis of shared knowledge and intimacies.

3.4. Cybercafes serve and generate a great variety of new forms of sociality and Internet use, partly reflecting differences in their spatial layout.

3.5. Particularly dramatic has been the impact of the Internet on some secondary schools, where homework, gossip, relationships, and popular culture are rapidly becoming dominated by Internet use.

Chapter 4 – Being Trini and Representing Trinidad

4.1. Trinidadians' national identity and culture is central to their use of the Internet. Contrary to all the predictions about a new global medium, they anchor their encounter with the Internet in their specific place.

4.2. Trinidadians are always aware on the Internet that they are representing Trinidad, and use the net to expound the virtues of their Island. Trinidadians are shocked by the widespread ignorance about Trinidad they encounter online.

4.3. Chat has been turned into a specifically Trinidadian form of communication, and one that is particularly important to the Internet experience of Diaspora Trinidadians.

4.4. Trinidadians' websites are not just about personal expression but attempts to create new forms of exchange, expanding the 'fame' of the individual and of Trinidad in space and time.

4.5. Trinidadian business on the Internet includes a powerfully nationalistic aspiration that translates commercial success into evidence for the presence of Trinidad on a global stage.

Chapter 5 – Political Economy of the Internet

5.1. An ideal vision is emerging of Trinidad as a high-value-added provider of services such as websites and ecommerce to North American firms.

5.2. The local telecomms monopoly is regarded as the critical bottleneck that has prevented Trinidad from achieving this ideal through deregulation. The case of Trinidad thereby illuminates the most important global transformation of the decade.

5.3. The disputes between the local Internet Service Providers, the government and the telecomms company hide a forthcoming battle over the control of key communications technologies and routes.

5.4. We can thereby see in Trinidad central contradictions within global neoliberal and deregulation policies that have been intensified through the advent of the Internet.

Chapter 6 – Doing Business Online

6.1. We provide a three-stage model of ecommerce development, in which The Miss Universe website exemplifies the most sophisticated current use of Internet media for business.

6.2. The advertising agencies have played a unexpectedly muted if not negative role in the development of websites and ecommerce.

6.3. Developments in technical skills and commercial acumen have often been out of synch, which generates surprising new roles for webdesign businesses.

6.4. Sophisticated use of the Internet is increasingly associated with interactive interfaces and with front- and back-office integration that entirely restructures a company's operation.

Chapter 7 – Religion

7.1. Various religious communities are using the Internet to resolve problems of space and location, ranging from the wider Diaspora to their parochial flock.

7.2. The Internet exposes individuals to wider and sometimes unorthodox theological discussion. This may challenge but sometimes actually assists institutionalized religious bodies.

7.3. Specific technologies such as chat and email have been found to have several advantages over face-to-face communication in the process of spiritual dialogue; analogies have also been drawn to other forms of mediated communication such as the confessional.

7.4. The Internet may be read as a divine model of the future of a Church, and several groups interpret the Internet experience as a reaching out to the divine.

2

Trinidad and the Internet – An Overview

In starting this project, we assumed that Trinidad would provide an ethnographic site of limited size and limited Internet development such that we could encompass most Internet use there . This turned out to be presumptuous: the Internet is already huge in Trinidad. Like us, readers will have to get beyond an image of an underdeveloped island economy of sugar and tourism in which an elite minority have access to an expensive technology through which they can communicate with a privileged global fraternity. There are certainly inequalities in access and diffusion, detailed below; but, since the Internet made its entry in September 1995, it has not only grown exponentially, it has also permeated all sectors of society, from 'yachties' to squatters; all social contexts from work to home to school to shop; all senses of the future, whether personal (families are making huge investments in technical education and 'computer literacy') or public (government's plans for education, industrial development and its own bureaucracy focus on Internet); and it is already tied to the restructuring of key economic sectors such as banking, tourism and of course the information technology business itself.

And that is only the part of the story located on the island of Trinidad itself. This is a population in which the majority of families have members at the nuclear level who are living typically in London, New York, Toronto or Miami, most of whom have Internet access and use its many facilities not only to keep in touch with family and friends in Trinidad but also to reconstitute or enact 'Trini-ness' online, quite often with other Trini expatriates. We start with a brief survey of the development of the Internet in Trinidad and of why the Internet is currently 'hot'. In order to establish empirically the extent of Internet use we carried out a house-to-house survey in four residential areas. The details of this survey are given in the Appendix. In this chapter we present a short general introduction to Trinidad, followed by four portraits of households using the Internet drawn from our survey. Finally we consider the relationship between the Internet and a variety of social divisions such as class, gender, ethnicity and age.

Overview of the Internet in Trinidad

Let us start with a snapshot of the state of play at the time of research: The Internet began in Trinidad in September 1995. Officially, the country accessed the Internet via one cable (a second was laid in June 1999) operated exclusively by the local telecommunications monopoly, TSTT. This company also acts as an Internet Service Provider, in addition to five other ISPs that buy bandwidth from it (see Chapter 5). Pricing structures were complex and changed frequently (and there were as yet no free service providers), but were not regarded as unduly expensive so long as one kept to the monthly ration of online hours that normally came free with a subscription. This picture will change radically as a result of both deregulation and new technological infrastructures (notably satellite and other wireless modes of delivery plus cable modems being rolled out later in 1999). Nonetheless, and despite various important bottlenecks, Trinidad had relatively cheap access, from anywhere on the island and over reliable phone lines. At every point in its history, demand for the Internet exceeded supply of bandwidth and points of presence (POPs), causing slowness and busy signals as ISPs 'maxed out' on people trying to connect.

How many people, households and businesses used the Internet? This cannot be reduced to any single set of numbers because of the diversity of what one might mean by 'use' and 'user', and especially as a result of a distinction that is identical to the conventional publishing distinction between circulation and readership. For example, estimates of the number of accounts held across all ISPs vary rather wildly between 17,000 and 25,000. In the vast majority of cases, these accounts represent households or businesses rather than individuals. This is in a population of 1.2 million people, or 350,000 households. To this would need to be added private leased lines and even satellite links that might service many people in a large company, often with a very liberal policy concerning personal use. A number of managers told us that restricting use to company business was impossible without unacceptable levels of surveillance, while it was in any case in everyone's interest to build up Internet skills and confidence through experience. We should probably also have to add on various kinds of piracy. TSTT bizarrely allows multiple simultaneous use of an account, which means that an individual can sell on access to their account to several other people; we heard of a janitor who was running a pirate ISP from the basement of his building.

In addition to access through workplaces, there is also access through cybercafes and libraries and increasingly through schools. As public points of access, these not only increase the number of possible 'readers' per Internet 'copy'; they also point to the fact that pretty much anyone who wants to get on the Internet in Trinidad is technically able to. Indeed, nowhere in Trinidadian society did the Internet feel remote or inaccessible, and it was frequently wrapped up in sociable and familial relations that made it even closer.

So, even if we had an exact 'circulation' figure, it would not represent a 'readership' of single individuals, but rather households, businesses, schools, libraries and in one notable instance an entire residential street that accessed the Internet through one local schoolteacher's account. This is especially important in a place such as Trinidad, where information moves through extended family, friendship and community channels. Hence an account may include a teenager who is chatting online half the night, every night, but also her grandmother's cousin, who occasionally asks her to send an email to their relatives in Toronto. The 'readership' figure is therefore obviously just as significant a number for us to include in any measure of Internet use in Trinidad – maybe more so; but it is one that will only show up through other methods.

Hence we place great stress on the broad range of anecdotes and hearsay that emerged through interviews and ethnographic sites (especially the cybercafes), and on our house-to-house survey (see the Appendix). Since our survey asked about any Internet access on the part of any member of the household it may provide a better picture of how far the Internet has threaded its way into people's lives and homes. Our results indicated that something like 30 per cent of households contained at least one user (which means more than just trying the Internet once or twice). Overall, around 11 per cent of all individuals are users, and around the same proportion of households have computers. These figures varied enormously, depending on the socio-economic levels of the areas surveyed (for details, see the Appendix). This represented a wide range of use from intermittent to constant, and very different levels of integration into everyday life. Where people had their own accounts, we have the impression they were well used, at least by one member of any given household, and at least up to the number of free hours that would come with a monthly subscription. Although there was a lot of 'churn' (movement of customers between ISPs) it was unclear whether any or many people dropped out of the Internet once they had had access. Our impression is that people on the whole stayed connected.

This degree of diffusion was impressive, but does not convey the shock of walking past the yard dogs in front of a squatter's corrugated iron-and-plank-built hut with no running water in order to ask the self-evidently daft question, 'Do any members of your household use the Internet?', only to find oneself in a very well-informed conversation about email, paying for computer courses, career prospects in IT and library access. People know about it, have encountered it, have a sufficiently high level of education and literacy to make very good sense of it and to be interested in the wider world to which it can take them, and have the confidence and ambition to locate the Internet as part of their future.

It should be noted that our research was intended to look at 'ordinary' Trinidadian households, and our house-to-house survey was located in the provincial town of Chaguanas (Plate 2.1), in the same four areas that were used by Miller (1994: 24–50) in his previous research in Trinidad. These comprised four settlements: a residential area, a government national housing authority area, a squatters' settlement and a village being incorporated into the outskirts of a town. We would argue that this would be representative of the whole of Trinidad. We excluded the capital (Port of Spain), as well as 'upscale' residential areas to the north and west of Port of Spain and areas such as Valsayn to the east, where Internet access may well be almost universal. Hence we are not looking at the richest suburbs where, for example, the largest local supermarket chain was intending to pilot an online shopping and delivery service, and where a local company had opened its first US-style computer superstore, complete with cybercafe. Indeed, people in towns such as Chaguanas and San Fernando thought we were very odd for spending our time there when we 'should' have been in the capital, where 'all' the Internet really was in Trinidad. In fact, the Internet was everywhere, so that leaving out these wealthy areas where the Internet is most advanced and widespread still revealed to us extremely high levels of usage and access. Moreover, this strategy gave us a much better sense of how ordinary Internet use has already become. So this book is about typical use, not the most advanced usage we could find.

Whatever its current state and scale, everyone agrees that growth has been and will continue to be exponential, spurred on by factors such as a massive increase in computer ownership and skills, falling prices of hardware, software and access costs, telecomms deregulation, and integration of the Internet into a broad range of activities. Above all, we need to relate this to the general size and quality of the installed base of IT. Probably the biggest factor in the entire story was government policy. Firstly, the government abolished all taxes and duties on hardware and software. This in conjunction with already-existing international facilities such as SkyBox and the Internet itself allowed many Trinidadians to take advantage of massively falling hardware prices in the US. Secondly, the government offered interest-free loans, payable over three years, to all public-sector employees. There was a massive take-up of this offer, as well as of equivalent private-sector employee deals. Finally, there was a government commitment to putting Internet-enabled computers in all schools, libraries and government services. Moreover, investment in computers and the Internet fitted into a wider backdrop of demand for other consumer electronics in Trinidad, both for private and business use: Internet fever was not unconnected to mass purchasing of computers, cellular phones and pagers throughout the population down to low income levels. Pirated games and software circulated at high velocity owing to an increased ownership of CD-write technology. It could be argued that in fact the major breakthrough in the diffusion of Internet media had been facilitated nearly a decade before, when the deregulation of television had introduced people to choosing across a huge range of media in both content and technology (cable TV was hugely popular), as well inculcating a new relation to global popular cultures and media.

One significant upshot was an extremely rapid rise in the number of computers, which not only caused a mini-boom in IT businesses and employment (including training, repair, maintenance and installation) but also resulted in very high levels of specification. Indeed the average installed base, being on average more recent, may well be higher than that in the UK. Most importantly, modems were standard (as were scanners and printers). Computers have rapidly become redefined as machines that must be connected to the Internet, as well as capable of doing word processing, games-playing, etc. Levels of business hardware and connectivity seemed more patchy: while many firms of all sizes were fully computerized, networked and connected to the Internet, we also found many often large and international enterprises with few computers and perhaps only one point of contact to the Internet (a beleaguered secretary or IT enthusiast through whom all correspondence was funnelled, and who might additionally spend many hours researching prices and sourcing goods over the net). This was often due to conservative higher-level management, and a source of frustration to younger employees. This included not only old heavy industrial firms but also advertising agencies affiliated to parent companies that were market leaders in online publicity.

Both business and private users could understand the Internet either as several quite separate or as a bundle of integrated technologies. It was mere coincidence that websites, email and chat were accessed through the same mechanism. The heaviest and most universal use was of email, for correspondence both between relatives and friends and between businesses. Although adoption was indisputably faster and wider amongst the young, the older parents and grandparents quickly saw its potentials and often could use it extensively, even if they had no other computing skills or interest (or got someone else to send email for them). By contrast chat – by which we mean any kind of synchronous, real-time online communication, usually based on the exchange of typed lines by two or more participants in a screen window – was much more prevalent amongst the youth. Our research coincided with the enthusiastic reception given by Trinidadians at home and abroad to ICQ, a proprietary chat system in which each registered participant had a unique 'pager' number. When that person went online, any friends or other contacts who had that number listed on their computer would be notified: hence, you could tell when friends were around (as well as keep altering your list of 'nicks' to reflect your changing friendship networks) and communicate with them through individual and group chat windows.

Most Trinidadian surfing was based around web-based email accounts such as Hotmail, sending egreetings cards, doing research, especially in preparation for overseas education, and surfing popular culture, such as MTV, games, music and sports. People regularly told us that pornography accounted for 60 or 70 per cent of surfing, yet it was hard to find any real evidence of prevalence at anything like that level despite the fact that it was not hugely disapproved of either socially or legally (on the supply side we could find only one adult site run by a Trini). Some web-based facilities such as online games and multimedia are restricted by lack of the bandwidth necessary to make them work properly. Facilities such as MUD and Usenet newsgroups, which are strongly present in much of the previous literature on the Internet, are to the best of our knowledge entirely absent from contemporary Trinidadian use. Some use of Internet telephony, whereby the computer is used as a phone that can transmit digitized voice files over the Internet (and hence for the price of a local call) to anywhere in the world, was noted; video phone was regarded as a facility that might emerge at a later stage. All these Internet media fit within prior practices of communication. Trinidadians consider themselves as strongly antipathetic to letter-writing, but rather addicted to the telephone, principally because the telephone seems much closer to the kind of instant spread of news and gossip that is basic to that foundational principle of Trinidadian life – 'bacchanal' (Miller 1994: 245–55).

The Internet as a 'Hot Topic'

We have built up a picture of the Internet as already widely and deeply diffused through Trinidadian society and business. We will substantiate this picture here, and even try to quantify it in the Appendix. But none of this captures the central point: the Internet has generated great excitement, in which even those with little or no direct experience of it still feel that somehow they are part of it and certainly it is part of their future. While in the last section we needed to consider email and websites as merely contiguous technologies, we have to recognize that they are also clearly transcended by the rhetoric and presence of the Internet as a whole. Critical is the sense that the Internet is 'hot' in contemporary Trinidad. The impetus for Internet use in Trinidad was not coming from the male, student-based nerd culture that marked the first generation of metropolitan adoption, nor from gaming culture. Trinidadians instead adopted the Internet in pursuit of popular and commercial culture on the one hand, and domestic practicalities on the other. Although there was an astonishing investment and interest in upgrading computing skills (conspicuously across the gender divide) this was distinctly careerist rather than based on a fascination with computers in themselves. The work-related impetus came from people recognizing that it would be central to their careers. For youth culture in the widest sense the adoption of the Internet in one apparent gulp came from the desire to access global popular cultures (music, film, soaps, sports and fashion) and to access each other via chat.

All these factors contribute to the current 'buzz' about the Internet; but the sense of its being hot may arise especially from its ability to harness three of the most important aspirations in Trinidad society, and what is more, three that are normally seen as mutually exclusive: First the ability to be in the vanguard of style, second to have excellent career prospects through the established prestige secondary schools, and third the ability to bypass formal education and teach oneself the skills of the entrepreneurial future. In each case, the Internet is style, but in a manner that cannot be reduced to mere fashion, since behind the 'buzz' are profound aspirations and a coming together of deep desires and longings. Irrespective of whether these things actually happen, these were the expectations that had been raised. The experience of researching the Internet in Trinidad was exhilarating, and the sense of excitement generated by the response of those we met to the mere fact that we were writing this book generated the kind of heady aura that might be more expected around an impending Carnival than around something that in other regions is the realm of the 'nerd'.

Obviously the Internet is part of a larger IT revolution that makes it like the crest of a wave of prior interest in computing. But it is not mere froth, since the Internet radically changes the computer itself from something more associated with secretaries and business to something that is associated with the vanguard of style. The Internet becomes crucial to staying in the vanguard of style through facilities such as MP3s that allow free access to the latest music, and provide the ability to use it to make one's own compilations, and the ability to see what is happening on soap operas or MTV before others, and to know about a myriad other fashion-related topics, where being the first to know is critical. In every high street in the country – even in small towns deep in the South and Centre of Trinidad – there are signs offering to teach the population computing, including Internet use, and these far out-number film billboards or other media-related signs. However, the fact that the Internet is assimilated through hype and fashion does not make it either superficial or short-term. As argued in Miller (1994), there is within Trinidadian cultural values a powerful sense that style is much closer to profound aspects of 'being' than elsewhere, since being is viewed by many Trinidadians as manifested on the surface rather than as something 'deep', internal and largely unchanging (see Miller 1994, Chapter 5). As a result, Trinidadians see as profound what others might see as transient events or fashions. Therefore it is important to be in the vanguard of style and to know what is happening. The traditional 'lime', in which people meet at street corners to ask 'wha' happening', the centrality of radio to finding out the place to party also exemplified the desire to know what's happening and thence to participate in international fashion and culture. Trinidadians see themselves as the vanguard of the Caribbean, often in clear rivalry with Jamaica, and as always likely to be the first place in the Caribbean to adopt the latest international fad. The alacrity with which Trinidadians have taken to the Internet is merely the latest instance of the same desire. Naipaul (1962) noted this thirst for modernity in *The Middle Passage*.

The billboards of the high street do not advertise computers so much as advertise computer training, that is, education. In Trinidad education of all kinds continues to command a level of status and respect that is no longer common in most contemporary metropolitan regions. This is not some throwback to colonial values. On the contrary, education in Trinidad is overwhelmingly successful at providing – for those who get into the right secondary schools – the key to their future. A common anecdote was that Trinidadians are *pro rata* the most numerous nationality found at MIT, and it is certainly true that such graduates are prominent in facilitating Trinidadian web facilities such as ICQ networks. There is an international elite of Trinidadians already in place in several metropolitan countries thanks to the sheer level of educational success, so that the Internet inherits as much as it accentuates this route to further prestige.

It is also significant that these billboards are advertising private and often unofficial educational sites rather than established secondary schools and university education. Indeed, they are advertising a means to bypass more official educational channels to provide a skill that anyone can master and use for their own route to success. While some of these establishments are a scam, in general they represent an aspiration that is demonstrably successful. A high proportion of the most skilled and knowledgeable users of the Internet and IT that we met were almost entirely self-taught, or had merely done a course at some cybercafe and, having caught the 'bug', gone with it. One is expected to learn IT through practice: for example, games and software are purchased and mastered without manuals. As several Trinidadians commented, 'we have the best car mechanics in the world', indicating a belief in their ability to teach themselves skills through practice rather than formal education.

We have highlighted these three particular aspirations because traditionally they were regarded as separated and even antagonistic to each other. What makes the Internet hot is that it works on all three fronts and brings them into unprecedented compatibility. Yet these are only three of many instances in which the Internet connects with Trinidadian aspirations. In these and many other cases, those aspirations may not ultimately be fulfilled; but for now they are more than sufficient to lead many Trinidadians to the conclusion that the Internet is hot.

A Brief Introduction to Trinidad

The island of Trinidad is the larger part of the state of Trinidad and Tobago, 4,828 sq. km., and lies in the south-eastern Caribbean 16 km. north-east of the coast of Venezuela. Trinidad's history is clearly presented in Brereton (1981). The original population of Arawak and Caribs encountered by Columbus declined alongside a rather paltry population of Spanish colonists. Most of the colonial impact has come in the last two centuries, mainly under French cultural influence and British political control. Tobago will not be considered in this book, since it has a very different history, population structure and self-characterization. Although some people from Tobago took part in this research, it is not uncommon for them to be subsumed in the cultural term 'Trini' (though they strongly resent this).

Slavery developed later in Trinidad than on other Caribbean islands, and it was also less dependent upon massive sugar plantations, with crops such as cocoa having a major influence. By the time a significant slave population of around 10,000 was established, the slave trade was being abolished, and within forty years came the slave emancipation of 1834. Already at that time there was a significant urban population. Between 1845 and 1917 there arrived around 144,000 South Asian indentured labourers. Other immigrants included Spanish-speaking 'peons' from nearby South America, but also Chinese indentured labourers, Portuguese shopkeepers, French royalists and republicans, economic migrants from the Middle East today known as Syrians, Black soldiers from the American Civil War, settlers from other West Indian islands (e.g. Barbados, St Vincent, Grenada) and others.

The sense of creolization and heterogeneity has been as much assisted by emigration in the twentieth century as by immigration in the nineteenth. Trinidadians have migrated in waves to London, Toronto, New York and Miami. This has taken many forms. There is a vast difference between the migration of relatively low-skilled labour to the UK in the 1950s and current migration to the UK, which largely revolves around training in accountancy, medicine and law. Otherwise Trinidadians today tend to migrate to the US or to Canada, also with an expectation of entry at a high level. Certainly if one inspects the alumni lists that are available on the websites of several of the 'prestige' Church-run secondary schools there is clear evidence that success in the professions abroad is more than just wishful thinking (see Plate 2.2). Although Indo-Trinidadians migrating to Canada in the early 1990s claimed political persecution in order to obtain rights to stay, the essence of this and the other migrations was actually economic and above all educational.

Trinidadians tend to migrate largely because even though educational standards are high the country simply cannot compete with salaries abroad. Once a degree is obtained a Trinidadian is faced with a choice between a higher salary in the host country and returning home to a lower salary and a harder time finding a job relevant to that degree. Almost all the returnees we spoke with saw their return in terms of the sacrifices they have made. In addition, a side-effect of high levels of education is that many Trinidadians have extensive cosmopolitan knowledge that leads some to think of metropolitan centres as their natural home. This replaces a prior but parallel irony explored by Naipaul (1987) in *The Enigma of Arrival*, where, because of the bias of colonial education, Trinidadian culture seemed more naturally located in Britain than in Trinidad.

The elite colonial population has seen its scions depart at various moments of political emancipation. These have included the establishment of the government of Eric Williams, leader of the People's National Movement (PNM) in 1956, the achievement of independence in 1962, and the Black Power struggles of 1970, when a combination of popular protests and demonstrations together with a mutiny in the army came close to overthrowing the government. As a result of these movements an extraordinary number of Trinidadian families are in effect transnational. In a survey of 160 households Miller (1994:21) found that 101 could name a member of their nuclear family (parents, children or siblings) living abroad, 38 mentioned more distant relatives and only 21 stated that they had no relatives living abroad (compare Olwig 1993 for a more extreme case). In 1990 the total population was 1,234,388. Approximately 40 per cent of the population describe themselves as African, 40 per cent as Indian and the rest as mixed or other.

Although Trinidad was originally important for growing sugar, cocoa, coffee and coconuts, today agriculture is a minute component of the Trinidadian economy. For most of this century Trinidad has been dominated by the discovery and export of oil and associated products (see Hintzen 1989; Singh 1989). Oil sustains an industrial base of products such as methanol and steel. In addition the island is an important entrepôt for re-assembling goods such as cars and grocery products for home consumption and export to the other islands in the area (see Miller 1997, and for an ethnography of manufacturing see Yelvington 1995). The capital Port of Spain has been a cosmopolitan centre for two centuries.

If oil took Trinidad to a higher level of development than most of the Caribbean from the 1920s, the island received two further boosts, one being the impact of wages paid by Americans during the Second World War and the second being the extraordinary and sudden growth in incomes and affluence following the post-1973 oil boom (Auty and Gelb 1986). By 1986 most people had seen their wage packet grow by something between a factor of five and eight over the previous decade. For the experiential effects of this even on rural areas see Klass (1991: Chapter 3) and Vertovec (1992: Chapter 3). From 1982, however, the decline in oil prices led to a recession, and the period of Miller's first fieldwork more or less coincided with the bottoming out of this recession. This was also the period when Trinidad had recourse to the World Bank and the IMF. The 1999 fieldwork suggested some modest return to economic development, particularly amongst the poorest segments of the population. Successive governments have tried to lessen the dependency upon oil, but it remains the case that the major factors determining the wealth of the island remain external to the island itself. Unemployment and cut-backs in public services remain a significant concern.

Trinidad is perhaps unusual in the degree to which Trinidadians have themselves been responsible for the development of Trinidadian business. In the nineteenth century it was largely local whites who developed the various import–export businesses that traded plantation goods for high-quality elite consumption items. From around the 1920s, transnational corporations such as Nestlé and Lever Brothers have had an important presence, though, with the exception of foreign-controlled oil companies, they do not dominate (Miller 1997: Chapter 3). On the whole Trinidadian multinationals such as Neal and Massy, ANSA McAl, or CLICO run entirely by Trinidadians have been able to compete with global multinationals for influence in the Caribbean. This matches the self-perception of most Trinidadians of being a successful entrepreneurial people, assisted also by the (sometimes exaggerated) stories of success bought back by migrants returning from countries such as the US, where it is generally believed that Trinidadians are usually more successful than either other West Indians or indeed those born in the US.

The political, social and economic development of Trinidad since independence is fully covered in a series of books by Ryan (e.g. 1988, 1991). The PNM party of Eric Williams dominated Trinidadian politics from the time of independence, remaining in power apart from one period when an opposition alliance, the National Alliance for Reconstruction, held sway (1986–1991). The PNM has always been largely associated with the African population, and a major issue has been the possibility of Trinidad ever being peacefully governed by a party dominated by the Indian population, with uneasy comparisons being made with the political and ethnic strife in neighbouring Guyana. In the event, an Indian-dominated opposition led by Basdeo Panday finally came to power in 1995, and there has been no sign of any such turmoil. Many people today hope that the shibboleth of race in politics has thereby been laid to rest and replaced by rather minor distinctions as to how best to ensure economic development and reduce the crime associated with drug trafficking. Indeed, given that there was never a strong European-style socialist ideology, Trinidadian politics looks today rather more pragmatic than ideological (although not entirely so, as will be seen in Chapter 5). The relation to commerce is much closer to US than to European models, with a largely unchallenged thrust towards entrepeneurialism. Many Trinidadians even when working in the public sector will be simultaneously carrying out small private-sector initiatives in their spare time. The language of free markets and level playing-fields is much accepted even where there is resentment against the strictures of the IMF and the World Bank, which have crushed most protectionist tariffs and currency restrictions. As will be argued later, Trinidadians are not particularly committed to an ideology of neo-liberalism, but much the same effect has arisen from the attraction of an ideal of freedom in economic policy and in flows of information and goods, alongside a powerful commitment to personal freedom that is a legacy of slavery and other forms of oppression. Trinidadians in business are, however, aware and resentful of the degree to which the liberalization of trade has not actually created a level playing-field. Trinidad can no longer do much to prevent US and European imports, but many of its industrial goods are discriminated against by US and European protectionist policies.

The economy of Trinidad and Tobago is relatively healthy. Over the past five years GDP has shown a fairly constant growth rate of 3 per cent, while inflation has remained between 3 per cent and 5 per cent. Unemployment in 1998 was at 14 per cent. Recent years have seen under the tutelage of the IMF increasing divestment of public-sector enterprises. A key factor is the fluctuating oil price, which looked very low at the time of our fieldwork, but has risen to a much higher level since. The Trinidad and Tobago dollar floats freely, but at the time of research was worth around 6 US dollars. Overall life expectancy is 73 years and 72 per cent of pupils continue to secondary school. Literacy is very high, at 99 per cent. Although 29 per cent of the population live in rural areas, agriculture counts for less than 2 per cent of GDP. Along with the Bahamas and Barbados, the country probably has the best long-term prospects in the Caribbean.

Trinidad is important in that it defies most generalizations that till recently divided the world between areas of considerable Internet access and those with a dearth (e.g. Cairncross 1997:22). While it does not possess all the attributes of a developed country, it nonetheless has little in common with most underdeveloped societies, for example those in Africa (Wresch 1998; compare neighbouring Latin America Everett 1998). As such it is a place where we may reasonably ask whether the Internet is going to exacerbate global inequality or in some cases provide a promising developmental strategy.

Four Households

Having given an overview of both the Trinidad and the Internet in Trinidad, we need to turn to the experience of individual Trinidadians. We can do this by looking at some case-studies drawn from interviews conducted following our house-to-house survey. Our survey comprised two hundred households, divided into four residential areas in the hinterland of Chaguanas, a small but flourishing town in Central Trinidad. Here we introduce just one house-hold from each of the four areas, in order to give a sense of how the Internet connects with the lives of Trinidadians from very different class backgrounds. The names of these areas are fictional (for details see the Appendix and Miller 1994: 24–50).

A Meadows User

The Meadows exemplifies what in Trinidad are called 'residential areas' which are built as 'up-scale' enclaves, in this case the wealthiest residential area in Chaguanas. Plate 2.3 reveals some quite grand housing, as well as more ordinary suburban forms. Nevertheless even the richest inhabitants of Chaguanas would tend to be disparaged as relatively provincial by people in the much wealthier residential areas around Port of Spain inhabited by the country's elite. In our first case-study, knowledge and use of the Internet is quite extensive in the household, because both the father and son have a profes-sional involvement in IT. The Trinidadian husband and his Indian wife met while students at the University of London. Indeed, recently there was a twentieth anniversary of their peer group, which resulted in the re-establishing of links through email between students all over the world. Both parents have siblings and many other relatives living abroad in countries including Kenya, Canada and the UK, and the wife in particular keeps in touch with them several times a week. They also encourage their 12-year-old daughter to exchange emails with her Canadian cousin about school, friends and such like. The cousins also meet occasionally during reciprocal visits. The Internet is viewed as an 'unmitigated good'. Although the time spent online means that phone bills have not actually gone down, they feel they are doing a vast amount more correspondence for the same amount of money. The wife, however continues to write letters to her mother.

An older son is now working as a systems analyst looking to be promoted to the kind of job that would pay around tt$10,000 a month. He used to do some chatting, but doesn't really trust it, though he is impressed by a friend who is marrying a Canadian whom he met online when she made enquiries about Trinidad for a vacation. He spends a couple of hours a day online. He uses e-commerce for goods such as Japanese car parts and software, and buys from Amazon.com and other firms. He surfs mainly for work-related material, though with some other regular points of call such as CNN. He also downloads MP3s, mainly to play at his office. He has seen portable MP3 players in Trinidad, but they are too expensive for him. At the moment he is thinking hard about a new personal web-page. He had done one as part of a course, on which he published his résumé and a photograph, but it hadn't been very interesting; and this time he wanted to make a more serious job of it. He has been looking at many other personal web-pages. He is struck by the way Trinidadians put themselves forward as Trinis, and he feels their sites are often as sophisticated as those of foreigners. He has been borrowing/ taking what he regards as interesting pieces from such web-sites, for example clocks and counters or animations of moving water. This is in preparation for his own new site, which will be hosted on a free provider, although he knows this will limit the size. He wants to give some personal information, but beyond that he simply can't decide how to give it any further character. He has friends who have their own web-sites, one of whom runs the local pitbull terrier club, with many pictures of the dogs on his site. But for his own part he has no particular hobby, and is so far without a theme, which is perhaps why the site has not yet been created.

A Newtown User

Newtown is an example of the many settlements constructed by the government's National Housing Authority, and often largely inhabited by public-sector workers or supporters of the previous PNM government. Plate (2.4) shows that the originally identical houses are now being personalized by their tenants. Emily is a confident largish woman in her sixties, with a hearty laugh, and a strong belief in her own common sense. Although already primed by her sister in Canada, it was the government loan scheme put forward in the last budget, and for which she was eligible as a schoolteacher, that was the catalyst for her recent purchase of a computer with all the trimmings from a store in a nearby town. She took the full tt$15,000 loan, calculating that she could match a monthly payment of tt$415 dollars over three years, and noted the advantages she gained as a cash purchaser. Notwithstanding the fact that the typical income of the civil servants and policemen that dominate the area would be around tt$3,500 a month, with taxes at 28 per cent and rent at tt$350 a month, Emily suggested it was no surprise that most households in the area were about to embark on the same purchase, indicating the high priority given to gaining access to computers and the Internet. More surprising to us was one purchaser who had also taken up a loan to purchase a highly specified computer (justified as a business investment) despite having no regular income and being unable to pay his electricity bill. Emily was probably not the retailer's favourite customer, in that she not only used her trade union training to bargain hard on the original purchase but since then has phoned up with all manner of enquiries about using the machine with the expectation of pretty rapid home servicing for all problems. She used the Internet for research and coursework material in relation to both her teaching and trade union work. She also saw the Internet as crucial to Trinidadian development, and was actively involved, through the teachers' union, in pushing for increased computing facilities in schools.

A particular incentive is communication with her daughter in the US. As she puts it, 'Girls need to know they have their mother's love, and they will have little things where they cannot ask their father, or their stepmother, and they need motivation, just words of inspiration.' As a result she seems to know what her daughter is doing every single day. She has sent each of her three children for computer courses, but had not had the time for one herself. Her passion is e-greeting cards, which she finds on the websites of firms such as Blue Mountain. But she enjoys being creative, with extra messages and effects. She also feels the scanner and printer makes the machine an effective tool for her primary school teaching, and was delighted when surfing led her to material on 'attention deficiency hyperactive disorder' which she feels gives her both the diagnoses and the solutions to some of her most difficult pupils. She also uses a site that specializes in financial advice for women, but not the fashion sites that fail to cater for her self-description as 'Cinderella's sister'. Without an international credit card she cannot use e-commerce.

The computer and the large fan she uses to cool it dominate her bedroom. The large computer table and its hovering clipboards on either side are already filled with her notes of things to ask the retailer or ideas for greeting cards and for school. The computer's presence radiates beyond her house to include children in the street, who come and are allowed to download information for school or to share her other passion for joke sites. They are not allowed to download games, which she restricts to solitaire. Sometimes this can become a more sociable event, as when many of the kids came to see the Miss Universe site and went on to the associated information about the contestants and the chat between them and the public. 'It was fun', but may also be why her husband complains that he doesn't see much of her these days.

A St Pauls User

St Pauls, the only one of the four settlements to have existed more than 25 years before this study, consists of a village that has since been incorporated into the town. It has had more time to develop the diversity of housing that can be seen in Plate 2.5). It was therefore less likely to have a 'typical' user, and no such claim is made for Brian, a senior scientist who lives with his wife and three of his four children aged between 16 and 25 (one has now left home). Brian is unusual in that he has had a computer at home since 1983 and email from the early 1990s, though then only by going to a computer lab. For the last three years all his Internet access has been at home. He receives at least one hundred emails a week, the majority connected with his work but many from friends and relatives, almost entirely those living abroad. This has been important in reinvigorating his relationships with his brothers in Scotland and Canada, and with several old friends he had grown out of touch with. He goes online twice a day to check these emails, at which point he usually finds that one of the ten or so people who typically make up his ICQ list will also be online. Most days he will at least say hello to one of these, but not necessarily engage in any long chat.

He had been on a twenty hour per month contract, but his daughter's involvement with an American boyfriend drove this up to forty, sixty and eventually one hundred hours per month. Another of his children is studying computers, despite which there has been no domestic discord over access to the home computer, which is dominated by his professional concerns. All the family surf the net, and use email, chat and ICQ, including his wife, who at first opposed ICQ. As far as he knows, however, the net is used to continue relationships with people they had met in person, rather than anyone they had initially encountered online. He and others do use random chat, but this is specifically for short-term encounters. He is circumspect about such relation-ships, since he uses his real name online and, as he noted, 'the woman making advances might just be your own wife in disguise'. Also one of his friends is heading for a divorce owing to his wife's finding another man online whom she wishes to marry. On the other hand he is quite liberal about what his children encounter in their surfing, feeling they are quite old enough and mature enough to avoid any bad consequences – 'I know they can't get cocaine over the net.' He is aware of pornographic use by them, but then he is open about his own use, noting at one point that he would not use his credit card for such purposes, because of the dubious nature of the firms concerned. In general he feels his family, like most Trinidadians, would be drawn to the sexual material on the net.

He is quite prepared to use ecommerce with established firms, and recently managed to obtain a supersaver British railway ticket in advance for a visit to the UK. Indeed, checking out places he is about to visit is an important part of his surfing. He has only stopped buying himself and his wife books on Amazon.com because he feels they ended up buying far more books than they were actually reading. He also took readily to e-greeting cards, and recently sent twenty Mother's Day cards to 'friends who happened to be mothers'. He was fascinated by the possibilities of the net when these first emerged, whether chatting, surfing or at one time playing chess, and at least had an initial look at all the 'weirdness' that could be found there. But one has the impression that much of the novelty has worn off, and the main usage is now seen as largely mundane.

A Ford User

Ford is part of an extensive settlement of squatters, one of many such around the country. There has been some improvement in recent years, and although wooden shacks can still be found (in one case with an Internet user) larger concrete housing is developing, as can be seen in Plate 2.6). Colette is a sixteen-year-old girl. Her mother has four children from three different fathers, and is married to the father of her last two children, who also has two children from a previous marriage. He works as a plumber while her mother does an occasional 'ten days' (the government unemployment relief scheme). They live in a wooden house on stilts, but are about to lay the foundation for a concrete house. Colette herself is a clearly articulate, well-informed pupil with a keen interest in reading, but also watches cartoons and films on TV. She obtained good marks in her common entrance exam, which allows her to attend a school in Port of Spain, from where her prospects would be good if her family can find the funds to pay for the next stage of her education.

At present Colette's main access to the Internet is through a relative who lives in The Meadows. But she is still very much a 'newbie', primarily dabbling at surfing rather than email or chat. We watched her surf at a local cybercafe. Her primary interest was in the sites devoted to cartoon characters, such as those that have emerged from the original 'dungeons and dragon' style, where each character is designated as having various personality traits such as 'given to beheading their opponents' and presented in colourful graphics. At one point Colette appeared keen for us not to help her, and was trying to turn off the computer. It transpired that a friend had given her a web address to look up which was said to be 'interesting'. It turned out to be a porno site, and every time she tried to get out of the site it merely duplicated itself on her screen.

Our sense of Colette's involvement in the web meshes with that of Ford as a whole. If her family find the resources to keep her in education, she clearly has the ability to move from being a squatter to joining the middle class if not the elite within a single generation. She is not in any way intimidated by her experience of places such as The Meadows. Her family have relatives in the USA and she shares the self-confidence of most Trinidadians that the USA is a relatively easy place to succeed, both educationally and financially. But Miller has seen many people in her community over the years with similar high levels of skill, information and entrepeneurialism who have simply never had the capital to gain that education or set up that business, and remain for their entire lives in the precarious world of partial and temporary employment and limited access to facilities such as the net. In that case the Internet may well remain little more than something to have occasional fun with.

The Internet and Social Divisions

We began this chapter by noting our surprise that access to the Internet in Trinidad is so widespread, as is the sense even amongst those who do not use it that this is the direction in which the Trinidad world is going. This produces another kind of surprise: that the Internet does not appear to Trinidadians as exclusionary and divisive; it seems to cut across rather than exacerbate social divisions. In this regard, Trinidad breaks with common preconceptions of a developing countries, in which new technologies are supposed simply to increase inequalities and stratification. Although Trinidadians' optimism has to be qualified in some respects (see below, on employment), nonetheless in looking at the Internet through the grid of classical sociological categories of division (class, gender, age, ethnicity) our first finding was that people saw the Internet in inclusive rather than exclusive terms, and that in many respects they were right. Whether these potentials are realized will depend on many future developments.

Most people we encountered clearly connected the Internet with the idea of 'the level playing-field': it represented relatively low entry costs in terms of both skills and money to markets, information, contacts and culture. Via the Internet, a small businessperson could sell to an international market on the same terms as a multinational, any schoolchild could use the largest library in history and get access to news about jobs, courses and scholarships, and anyone could know 'what's happening'. Thus Henry, a young computer whiz running between at least three different jobs and businesses:

> The whole thing is level playing-field. Everybody starting from the same level . . . I have a company called the MiniWizard. If you check any register of businesses you will not find it. If you check anywhere, hard copy, paper, government offices, you will not find it. But if you go on the Internet, it exists, it's there. Because it's a name I wanna register and everything but I have already started gathering my information and doing my trading and being known as – that's what the Internet has allowed me, without financing of my own, whatever, whatever, you just get up and do it.

This ideal was taken very seriously, and contrasts with the expectation shared by much of the literature (e.g. Cairncross 1997:22; Eisenstein 1998; Haywood 1998; Holderness 1998) that the Internet would exacerbate differences of class and country. It also tallies with Trinidadian ideals of entrepreneurialism and free competition, and this is crucial to the way it is being adopted: people see the Internet as overcoming traditional barriers and divisions and try to use it in this way. This is very clear in the case of education, where there has been an enormous embrace of the Internet as a study tool and children are encouraged to use it as a homework tool (indeed children from a prestige girls school informed us that they will only research topics they can pursue over the net, regarding books as redundant). This could be perceived as a huge levelling force in a country that focuses intensively on education as a primary means of social mobility yet has an education system strongly skewed towards selection. Almost without exception parents want their children to gain a place in the prestige secondary schools through the 'common entrance' system. Three-quarters of those who attend such schools end up with a successful career in a foreign country, where they will certainly regard themselves as middle-class. In aspiration at least this is a middle-class country through and through. Since, however, most people do not go to the prestige secondary schools and a place in the rest of the education system has been a barrier to such international prospects there is every reason to consider Trinidad as having an entrenched class system (see Henry 1988; Ryan 1991). In addition, there is a close articulation with ethnicity (going back to a time when class and ethnicity were largely synonymous (e.g. Braithwaite 1975; Ryan 1991)), in that certain minorities – White, Syrian, Chinese and Portuguese – will tend to assume that their children will find places in these prestige schools, while at least in proportional terms few of the African and Indian populations can be quite so sanguine. Furthermore, the education system and its consequences will tend to be reflected in income levels, so that The Meadows is found in the census to be as clearly differentiated from the other areas surveyed by income as it is by educational background.

Obviously, the Internet could either help overcome the relation between education and social division or could be central to reproducing and exacerbating it, given the close relations between information access, schooling and class investigated by Bourdieu (1984) amongst others. Although access to the Internet is wide, and surprisingly so in the poorer areas, our survey clearly shows massive differentials (ranging from 62 per cent of households with Internet users in The Meadows down to 14 per cent in Ford), which can translate into further entrenching of educational and therefore career inequality. In the end, despite all the knowledgeable interest in the Internet, computers are expensive, even with interest-free loans, as are domestic phones, online time in a cybercafe and so on. Hence, a great deal depends on maximizing access through the schools themselves, as well as libraries. The school system thus far exacerbates differentials in access: despite government promises to get all schools online, this will take some time, whereas prestige schools can (though often with difficulty) raise funds from parents, sponsors and benefits. There are further inequalities even within the prestige school system as it intersects with gender: the attitudes of staff and the facilities provided in a boys' prestige secondary school as opposed to a girls' that we visited could hardly have been more distinct. The lack of facilities for girls was regarded as an act of fate, the slightest lack of facilities for boys was a challenge that all efforts would be made to overcome. And yet, despite lack of facilities, the girls were heavy users, and these gender distinctions are not found in the survey of home use. The public library service was very quick off the mark in providing free public access to the Internet throughout Trinidad; but this provision is heavily criticized as inadequate in numbers of usable computers, limited facilities and insufficiently trained staff.

The same relation between skills, education and social mobility is crucial in another aspect of the Internet's entry into Trinidad: jobs and careers. Again, as the quote from Henry indicates, jobs in Internet services or in selling goods via the Internet appeared to be a route to a wide range of new and professional, middle-class employment. This looked as plausible in Trinidad as elsewhere in the early days of the Internet: for example, with a computer, a very little knowledge of HTML – and very rudimentary codes – and maybe some design sense, one could set up as a webdesigner. Many did, from schoolkids to hobbyists to serious entrepreneurs (see Chapter 6). Already in two years an atmosphere has been generated in which skill has been radically separated from formal education. People with Internet skills are as likely as not to be young self-taught enthusiasts. Moreover, precisely because schools have not been up to speed in producing IT skills (and indeed there is much criticism of the University for not generating suitable graduates), there has been a huge investment on the part of even the poorest people not only in computer hardware but also in private tuition, as we have indicated. This is part of a broader investment in education as a mobility strategy that has led Trinidadians to buy into many kinds of private education in recent years, but is quite spectacular in IT and the Internet. More specifically, private Internet training is part of wider investment in IT skills such as basic computer literacy, programming and systems administration. There has been a particularly impressive take-up of courses certified by international organizations such as Microsoft.

Globally, IT businesses have been more likely than most to favour enthusiasm, youth and demonstrable skills – even if acquired by unconventional means – over mere credentials. Even non-IT firms, when hiring new staff and filling IT gaps in their organization, need to acknowledge that an Internet whiz-kid might come out of a place like Ford rather than from a prestige school. Yet this picture is fraught with problems and countervailing tendencies. As indicated in Chapter 6, few small webdesigners make a living, partly because there is too little money in it; partly because getting jobs depends on good contacts and networking. Many of the young whiz-kid designers were sons (not daughters) of small business owners or advertising executives, and were often in fact *en route* to more lucrative professions by way of a foreign degree. In any case the skills and knowledge demands are already escalating out of many people's reach. The days in which a smattering of HTML would suffice are being rapidly left behind in a whirlpool of Oracle and XTML, of both more sophisticated ecommerce concepts and more advanced programming technologies. The kid from Ford may not get this kind of knowledge unless he or she is already inside a corporate or educational hierarchy. At the same time, both the kid from Ford and the university-trained graduate are as likely as not to go abroad for real opportunities.

This issue also intersects powerfully with gender, where there is an apparent diffusion of access and knowledge around the Internet, and a buoyant sense of opportunity. Many young women are either investing in the courses described above, or are self-generating formidable programming, design and user skills through their own encounters with the Internet. There was very little sense that women shy away from technical learning or tasks. Certainly if we stuck to our house-to-house survey or cybercafe observations we would offer a strong picture of the Internet as an equalizing factor in terms of gender: equal numbers of men and women used it, and women were particularly involved in email and chat. And yet workplace observation typically finds women in secretarial positions. In the main, women may collect and collate the email, but the ecommerce and contracts are passing from male to male. A graduate woman systems analyst and programmer in the US, facing a forced return to Trinidad at the end of her visa, recited an honour roll of returned women engineering graduates from the US Ivy League who were making cups of coffee for their male bosses. Her point was clearly substantiated by the following male member of the elite Miss Universe design team (see Chapter 6):

> The women who are involved on our team are involved more along the line of project co-ordination and PR and marketing . . . At the beginning of the project when we really thought we would need forty HTML programmers, we had tons of schoolgirls who knew HTML and just wanted to come in, and we had a lot of women who were in that field. It was only when we saw the scope of the project and involving all these people only caused more damage and we said let's keep the team we have and just bring on one at a time as we need them. So none of them came on board.

The tightly co-ordinated core team that remained was not only male, but male graduates of UWI, though 'only two or three of them graduated in the field that they are in now . . . Most of them are self-taught and most of them see it as a kind of hobby.' That is to say, they might fit the profile of an unconventional career route outside credentialist hierarchies, but they were nonetheless as unlikely to have come from Ford or even Newtown as they were to be women. So, as indicated in this quotation, a radical shift away from a reliance on traditional credentials does not mean an end to conservatism with respect to gender.

Similar points could be made about ethnicity and employment. Although it is one of the dominant topics in the social science literature on Trinidad (e.g. Yelvington 1993; Rheddock 1999), ethnicity was generally almost absent from our study in that unless we raised the issue there would be silence: most Trinis did not regard it as a salient division in relation to the Internet. Although people constantly foreground ethnicity in relation to ownership and control in other economic sectors and occupations (cf. Miller 1997: 84–90), it was not regarded as relevant here: people of all ethnic mixes were caught up in the general fever of Internet use, training and desire for employment in a dynamic, expansive and apparently hierarchy-upsetting sector. And yet in reality, this is again mediated partly through access to higher levels of prestige education (where certain ethnicities are over-represented), but also through access to higher levels of capital and entrepreneurial skills and connections: it is no accident that amongst the biggest players in the emerging telecomms battles (Chapter 5) were both Chinese- and Portuguese-descended entrepreneurs.

In other words, although we have no doubt that the Internet has opened up many opportunities in terms of both jobs and access to skills with which to increase mobility for all sectors of the population, at the same time it is quite capable of throwing up new and escalating hurdles – necessary social capital (networks and connections), educational capital (ever higher necessary levels of design, programming and ecommerce skills), and financial/economic capital (investments needed to launch Internet-based enterprises).

One rather more problematic area is age. As everywhere, Internet skills and practices are a young person's (man's?) leverage against older heads in business and other hierarchies. It was clear from many meetings and interviews that older managers and owners were regarded as not understanding either the use or the implications of new technologies (though this sometimes turned out to be quite untrue), and were regarded as barriers to implementing them. IT would be represented in the organization (including religious organizations) by young and frustrated Turks who felt they could deliver the future if given half a chance. They were also generally clear that introduction of the Internet would lead to the kinds of further organizational changes (devolution to flexible work groups, horizontal connections on the basis of skills) that would reduce vertical lines of power and hence diminish the authority of age. However, in talking about age we are simply talking about those who have already passed the hurdles of class, gender and ethnicity.

If we shift our consideration of social division from education and jobs to a wider sense of usership and content the picture of widespread diffusion and inclusion is rather more positive. As our survey reveals (see the Appendix) access and use are skewed to the more prosperous strata; nonetheless, for the purposes of use as opposed to employment it is not hard to get some access, for example, to get emails sent or to get information. Similarly, even if the level of skills required to be marketable is escalating, nonetheless the skills necessary to send email, build a personal website, conduct web searches and so on seem already to cut across class, gender, ethnicity and even – though to a lesser extent – age. Moreover, information and experiences garnered on the Internet could break through the parochial limits of these social divisions, as with a 16-year-old schoolgirl in a provincial cybercafe finding out about forms of employment she had never heard of before and consequently re-examining her skills and qualifications in quite new directions.

While our survey shows no significant difference in the degree of private use by males and females, this is not to say that men and women are developing identical patterns of usage: for example, in school discussions about use of the computer at home, male versus female usage seemed fairly equal, and the Internet was equally welded into boy and girl youth culture, and yet the genders may divide in stereotypical ways (see 'male hackers and female viruses' in Chapter 3). In our study of home use amongst Trinidadian couples based in the UK a regular motif was the gradual emergence of the female as a kind of social secretary of the Internet. Much of the routine emailing and chat devolved on to females, even to the extent that they became the conduit for information between their husband and his family. In some cases women were searching websites for their husbands' professional training in medicine or law. For example:

Q So what about your husband, how much does he use it?
A Not much at all, I do all his work for him.
Q So basically you are much more into it than he is?
A Yes, I done all the researches for him and we use it for the classifieds when applying for jobs.
Q Do you write to your parents?
A Both parents, my husband's and mine. I will get them, I do all the writing, I do all the emailing and he will say 'Tell me the gist of it.'

On the other hand, men seem more ready to complain about the expense incurred by wives' use of the Internet, to makes jokes about their wives' 'Internet boyfriends' and to complain if Internet use gets in the way of domestic duties such as cooking dinner. Women might find the online experience of Internet use liberating, but there were clear constraints on their ability to translate this into offline changes in gender relations.

Gender difference is also hugely important to organizing online behaviour. The prime example is chat and ICQ: in the vast majority of cases, users made it evident that chatting with same-sex others was either rare or very low in interest compared to chatting with members of the opposite sex. Even public chat is dominated by the canons of flirtation and competitive insult that are the mainstay of liming and similar gender encounters (see Chapter 4 for details, and compare Yelvington 1996). This kind of observation brings Trinidad well into line with general findings that Internet behaviour often involves reproduction of conventional sexual difference (Wakeford 1999; Slater 1998; Springer 1996; Bassett 1997), but with a very particular Trinidadian spin.

Ethnicity was an area in which we would have expected some differentiation as to usage or content, given that in almost every other aspect of life, and certainly in politics, ethnic distinctions are the paramount parameter of social and personal identification in Trinidad and one of the main topics Trinidadians tend to talk about. Yet ethnicity did not arise in interviews or observation. There seemed to be an extraordinary absence of ethnicity from mundane areas such as online relationships (Chapter3) and identity expressed in personal web-pages (Chapter 4), where we would certainly have predicted it. The main factor that may account for this is the overwhelming emphasis upon a superordinate level of identity, that is, nationalism (Chapter 4), combined with the relatively apolitical nature of Internet use as against the importance of politics to general discussions in other contexts. It is possible that the apolitical nature of Internet use in Trinidad may foster a depoliticized and therefore conservative ethos, as is implied in a recent article on nearby Venezuela; but it is too early here as there to be at all sure (Lejter 1999).

There is one major exception to this picture, discussed in Chapter 7, in which ethnic and political implications of the Internet are fundamental to the Hindu community. Furthermore, after our study was complete a website was founded that is clearly intended to interpret all Trinidadian news from the perspective of a clear Indian position. Most of the articles in their online newspaper, 'Trinidad News', represent Indian interests alone. With articles attacking the government for spending any tax money on Carnival, and one writer describing himself as 'a secondary school graduate who is deeply concerned about the emasculation of Hindus in all respects', it is not surprising that opponents (one of whom is represented on the associated bulletin board) clearly regard the site as representing a paranoid and racist sector that has resorted to the Internet because it failed to find any place within the conventional media. It would be quite wrong, however, to allow the single case to contradict the general direction of our evidence.

Just as online ethnicity seems submerged within a more global Trinidadian nationalism, many other differences are filtered through a sense of the Internet as being overwhelmingly about popular culture, and indeed that it is itself a form of popular culture and style, as indicated earlier. Just about anybody can send e-greetings, go to the MTV site, download MP3s and chat on 'de Trini Lime' in ICQ. At the same time, because Internet content is dominated by popular culture we might expect this to do no favours to the middle-aged, let alone the elderly. Terms like MTV, MP3, Nike that might build bridges across gender, class and ethnicity may produce social exclusion by age. Formal statistics gained by other research (e.g. the demography of users of free Internet services in libraries, and the register of users of cybercafes) would suggest that age was perhaps the most important category of discrimination for Internet use in Trinidad. But this needs much qualification. In the house-to-house survey age distinguished type of usage rather than access. For example, many users in The Meadows are middle-aged businesspeople and professionals who use the Internet at work and have extended this to the private sphere. They pay the bills and assert their priority rights when it comes to using up the monthly free hours from their ISP. The differences are rather that the young dominate the area of chat, and certain topics such as

MP3s and games, while older people tend to surf for commercial and family concerns. Although it is school-age children who most fully inhabit a world where Internet usage diffuses through the playground and permeates their daily society (see Chapter 3), nevertheless they may have their access limited at home. Furthermore, Trinidad is not a country where people slip easily into age-bound roles. There are plenty of wrinkles generated by the smiles and laughter of Carnival and associated partying. In general, however, it is probably the elderly who feel most isolated from and least able to or even desirous of 'keeping up' with yet another new technology. But there is some evidence that the centrality of email to family relations is being grasped by some of the elderly. Moreover, the rest of this volume deals with topics such as religion and commerce, which are by no means dominated by the young.

Conclusion

The Internet cannot paint itself on to a blank canvas. Trinidad is not a homogeneous society, and in it the Internet fits into a wide range of distinctions and meets many social barriers. We have shown that in certain areas such as the world of work these may result in Internet access and use becoming an expression of class and gender inequalities. Even the enthusiasm and entrepreneurship we saw in many individuals may not be able to overcome entrenched distinctions of gender, class and ethnicity, although it is rather early to tell. It would be quite wrong, however, to reduce the Internet to a mere symbol of prior social divisions. The main lesson from this chapter is that the Internet is already becoming an integral part of how Trinidadians perceive and reproduce these divisions.

We were however wrong in some of the assumptions with which we started the research. Internet culture is mass culture here, and bright-eyed technical whiz-kids and avid users are coming from almost any background. A study we expected would be of certain relatively wealthy communities turned quite clearly into a study of Trinidad – a study that ought to include groups such as squatters precisely because they have already struggled to include themselves. As the means towards style, towards knowledge and towards expanding one's position in modernity the Internet is remarkably inclusive. Nonetheless, we are presenting a snapshot at a very particular moment in time. Some of the technologies described, such as ICQ, have been in common use in Trinidad for less than a year. Already these technologies are lending themselves to different uses; indeed, these diverse uses rather than the technologies themselves are now the driving force, as we will be discussing through the rest of the book. The following chapters deal with very different topics, from commerce to religion to nationalism. We simply cannot predict the future impact of the Internet except to suggest that the impact is likely to be different in each of these diverse areas.

3

Relationships

A recent advertising campaign for a British beer company proclaimed that real men go out to the pub and relate to females, not just to emails. It reflected a widespread assumption (shared by some academics) that the Internet generates a culture of 'nerds' who substitute virtual relationships for 'real' ones, a charge that is inadequately met by the opposite argument that virtual relationships are themselves real. The opposition of real and virtual in both cases completely misses the complexity and diversity of relationships that people may pursue through the communicative media that they embed in their ongoing social lives. The point is made clearly by thinking back historically to the times when 'old (media) technologies were new' (Marvin 1988). Worries about the reality of telephone or telegraph relationships and their impact on 'real' (i.e. face-to-face ones) may have been rampant at the time of their introduction (Stein 1999), but it is no surprise that the bulk of present-day telephone advertising can take it for granted that the telephone is widely accepted as a means of enhancing and developing relationships, not for replacing them. Where public concern re-emerges – as with the introduction of mobile phones – it is articulated in far less global, far more contextualized terms.

Hence, we will pursue the present discussion as if the Internet technologies were older, reflecting the alacrity with which Trinidadians have indeed embedded them in relationships, ignoring the issue of 'real' versus 'virtual'. This is particularly evident in looking at the family, especially the diaspora family, with which we begin. The second section examines the use of the Internet in friendships, including those that develop into love and marriage, and the third section deals with the immediate spaces in which Internet use and relationships take place, using as examples our studies of cybercafes and of Internet use amongst schoolchildren. Finally, in the conclusion some of this evidence will be considered in terms of the history and theory of Trinidadian society.

From Diaspora Family to Internet Family

Prior to the arrival of the Internet, the family was indeed under threat as the core institution of social life in Trinidad. The Caribbean family is highly distinctive, as is indicated by the anthropological literature discussed in the conclusion to this chapter. Most anthropological accounts have been conservative in emphasizing continuities or a well-established normativity in expectations about the family. To understand the use of the Internet, however, we need to focus on a radical disruption that has been of huge importance for more than a generation: the impact of widespread Caribbean emigration on the Trinidadian family (see Basch, Glick Schiller and Szanton Blanc 1994; Chamberlain 1998; Ho 1991). Migration from Trinidad has been very extensive, even if it has not matched other Caribbean contexts where the majority of those who identity with an island now live abroad (e.g. Olwig 1993). Miller (1994: 21) found in his earlier survey that in the majority of families at least one member at the nuclear level (that is either parents, siblings or children) was living abroad. Therefore the following discussion of the use of the Internet by diasporic families[*] actually applies to the vast majority of Trinidadian families overall.

Email was taken up readily as an intuitive, pleasurable, effective and above all inexpensive way not only for families to be in touch, but to be in touch on an intimate, regular, day-to-day basis that conforms to commonly held expectations of what being a parent, child or family entails. It appeared as an obvious way of realizing familial roles and responsibilities that had been ruptured by Diaspora, and even of reactivating familial ties that had fallen into abeyance. Email contrasted on the one hand with letter-writing, which was seen as proverbially problematic to Trinis (perhaps the most common generalization people made during fieldwork was that 'Trinidadians hate writing letters') and stymied by what was regarded as an inefficient postal service. In practice letter-writing was important to some of those living in the UK, but they were a minority.

---

[*] The term Diaspora here is used to include not only Trinidadian families that live overseas but also families that are split between residence in Trinidad and overseas. Obviously this does not accord with the usual definition of the term Diaspora, but we feel the text would lose rather than gain clarity by trying to specify the degree of transnationalism in each case. With respect to the issue of Internet use we are concerned with all situations where some members of a family that was once from Trinidad now live outside Trinidad. It would also seem to be pedantic to try to be too precise about the semantics of migration, since most accounts show just how fluid identities and residence can often be for Caribbean migrants (e.g. Basch, Glick Schiller and Szanton Blanc 1994; Chamberlain 1998).

On the other hand, while the phone has dominated contact amongst family members it was viewed as inordinately expensive. It tended to be associated with less frequent use and therefore with a very different temporality, appropriate for the exchange of news rather than casual communication. Telephones were also considered to be more suitable than email for special occasions and lifetime events such as births, marriages, deaths and other rites of passage, but as far too expensive for enacting what are held to be the more 'Trini' forms of communication, involving liming, banter and ole talk, which were pleasurably performed through email and chat (as discussed in Chapter 4), where time could flow more naturally without an eye on the phone bill. But this connects to a wider sense of why email and chat could so easily serve the purposes of re-establishing normal or normative family relations: conversation could be mundane, everyday, intimate in a household way, in both style and content. Internet communication could shift contact from once a month to three times a week. This was sufficient to turn these into quite different types of relationship, because of the sense of the present it allowed. Email could allow constant, taken-for-granted communication, engaged in without great thought. It was informal or playful in style, and filled with everyday trivia (what we had for dinner, or bought at the shop, or who said what to whom) or with nothing much at all except a sharing of each other's 'voices'. Email could also encompass the exchange of mundane 'objects' such as scanned photos, addresses of websites the other might like, jokes found online and forwarded to a family member with the thought – clearly expressed by informants – of bringing a familiar smile to the other's face. Indeed, it was rare for people to talk about email without a smile.

This use of email extended into the hugely popular practice of sending each other e-greetings or virtual postcards (as well as electronic flowers and chocolates). This applied to many relationships besides family ones. Websites offering greeting card services were amongst the most frequently visited by Trinidadians, who invested a lot of time in finding ones that were animated, multimedia or simply unusual, often sentimental. This use of cards was interesting not only as an extension of a long Trini tradition, but also in making explicit the latent sense that an email was in some ways itself a gift, though one that could be offered at any time, not merely special occasions. And yet it demanded a response, and therefore created the conditions for sustaining relationships through reciprocity (see Carrier 1995; Mauss 1954).

Approximately half the Trinidadians we contacted in the UK primarily used the Internet for such mundane and constant email contact with their families. Given the nature of the Diaspora this could as well be family living outside Trinidad as within. If only one side of the family had online access they often exerted considerable pressure on the other end of the family also to go online, in some cases buying and sending the equipment. For example, several older people came into one of our ethnographic sites (a little shop with an online computer) brandishing letters from relatives abroad instructing them to set up an email account, and giving their own address. Someone in the shop (sometimes one of us) would help them register on a web-based email site. The ability to engage in routine contact through the Internet had two primary effects: the first was to re-establish the kinds of family contact that would have existed in a non-Diaspora context and the second was sometimes to actually expand the family as a viable unit of sociality. Ann-Marie may exemplify the first point. Perhaps the important relationship that emerges in Trinidadian discussions of the family is mother – daughter relations, and the sundering of these in the Diaspora family had often been a cause of anxiety, especially for the mothers. But with the Internet Ann-Marie reports the following norms of contact:

> Q: So your mother emails you every day? What kinds of things does she talk about?
> A: Nag.
> Q: What kinds of things does she nag you about?
> A: Motherly things – like eat properly, dress well and she checks out everyday the weather in London. And she would say all right you are going to have a little bit of sun next week. And then she will talk about whatever she has done. . . . My dad is not into it at all, you will not get a letter from him at all. But Mummy she is home and she got time to sit down.
> Q: How long has she been doing this for?
> A: For a year. She likes to know everything that is going on so she can tell you how to take your vitamins and how to do this. It is almost as if you are talking all the time because she is always giving advice, she would do a paragraph at a time.

Others who reported such regular connections with parents revealed how this re-constructed the common ambivalence of living together as a family. For example a UK-based student noted on the one hand:

> By speaking to my family every week, I do feel that they still have quite a strong hold on me. I feel that they do need to know where I am and what I'm doing. For instance I wanted to quit my Ph.D. about 6 months ago. I felt that I needed to consult them as it was common that I did when it came to big decisions. They were not very happy about the decision and used the guilt factor to make me continue. I'm still doing the Ph.D.

On the other hand a moment later she notes: 'I do feel that it's keeping them close and despite differences in opinions at times, I don't feel alone here in

England knowing that I could contact them at any time.' Just as when people are actually living together within a household, parents could be regarded as oppressive and constraining, but this co-existed with the sense that one had returned – thanks to the Internet – to the security and support of this fundamental family relationship. It was also not uncommon for the relationship to work the other way around, so that a Trinidadian parent who had left her or his child in Trinidad used the Internet to continue to provide support to their children, though in most cases returning at times when more support was required, such as exam-taking. The Internet assuaged some of the problems and sense of guilt of leaving the children behind, since it made possible a new mediated parenting.

The impact of the Internet is not restricted to the nuclear family. In the case of the extended family, and in particular in relationships between cousins, there is the possibility not only of repairing the rupture caused by emigration, but also long-term relationships between cousins are made viable in a way they had not been before. For example George has settled in the UK for many years, but keeps in contact through the Internet:

A: The only person I contact with in Trinidad is my cousin. Every weekend Saturday five p.m. in UK time we hook up and have a little chat. ... We speak for about three hours. All my aunts and cousins and everybody coming down. They want to speak to this one, that one. I will call my cousins and they will come to him. They are of the same household. But everyone will speak. Some of my cousins who can't afford PCs in Trinidad will come on weekends and have a little chat.
Q: So you are quite close with that family?
A: Yes. What we do as well is that all of the cousins, I got most of my cousins as well in Canada, we do link up together on weekends and all of us have a little family reunion every week. It's just an hour. Just a family thing.

As in this case it was common for an online relative to then communicate news to other relatives who are not online. Group cousin chatting could also take place through chat sites: 'I met six of them and we chatted. We were on the chat site for about three hours on a Sunday. It was quite good though – everybody use a different colour.' As well as this collective sense of family, cousins were also very often the 'friends' one confided in, confidants for discussing intimate problems such as reactions to the death of a relative. Equally for those in Trinidad the most common use of the Internet for contacting people abroad was related to aunts, uncles and cousins. Of course not every cousin turns out to be a natural friend. As a UK-based Trinidadian noted: 'Stephen would send email, but he has got a weird sense of pornographic humour, I do not reply. I don't even open the attachment because I did once and I said O God! He sent about a hundred disgusting jokes.'

In general Trinidadians found that their 'cousinhood' is now viable as a much larger phenomenon, bringing back into the fold relatives that would not otherwise have been included. Discovery of a cousin in New York they had not heard from in ten years would re-create the relationship, or on returning for Carnival they might meet a cousin settled in Japan who had also returned to Trinidad. They would then exchange email addresses and strike up the relationship on their return to their respective homes. It is possible that these contacts will decline as the cousins grow up, just as one would expect in the conventional developmental cycle of the domestic group. It is also possible that one result of the Internet will be a longer maintenance of such relationships, since the factors that often break up 'cousinhoods', such as moving away, will no longer have the same effect. However, the time depth of our study is too shallow for confident predictions.

The possibilities for actually expanding the family were most dramatically illustrated by George:

A: Both my parents split up twenty-eight years ago. I had contact with my Mom but I never had contact with my Dad. Twenty-eight years and I never what he look like, I never knew where he was, what he did, or anything. And through the Internet I decided, I saw these search engines. So I was going to fiddle around and see to try and get a world-wide one, which there wasn't. Then I thought America is the biggest country on the Internet. I'll try a search there. I came up with nothing. I then tried one in Canada, and half an hour later I came up with twenty-five names and I thought every week I would send out one letter and see what happens. So the first name I pick from the list and four days later, about four o'clock in the morning the phone rang, and it was my Dad. He couldn't believe it himself, I couldn't believe it too. I thought it was a joke or something. But what happened about this letter I send out. I sent a photo of me and I send a photo of him. His wife phones me back, and that caused a bit of problem there.

Q: She never knew . . .?

A: She never knew if I existed. That was a shock to her.

Q: So he is in Canada?

A: He is in Canada. He phones me every two weeks.

Q: So he phoned you first to check it out?

A: She phoned me and she thought it was a joke as well. Because she is looking at my photo and she is looking at his photo and she is saying to me where did you get this photo from? This is my son and this is his Dad. I said no, it isn't. That's me and that's my Dad and she thought it was a hoax and I thought she was a hoax as well.

Q: Did you ever meet?

A: We met last year. One of my brothers or sisters were suppose to come but financially they weren't able to. I think I am going to make an effort go across to them actually.

Internet use by the elderly is more rarely encountered but is perhaps an important pointer to the future. One example was a widow who seemed to have lost much of her reason for living when her husband died. In order to keep in touch with a particularly close grandchild who had gone abroad, she was persuaded to educate herself in Internet use. Subsequently she contacted many other relatives abroad and in Trinidad, and has taken to the net to such a degree that the younger members of her family swear it has given her 'a new lease of life'. This might offer a partial resolution to the increasingly common problem of elderly people who had previously tended to live in the homes of their descendants but are now being encouraged to live by themselves: the Internet keeps the new physical separation but in some other respects can keep them in the heart of family life. However, this is currently rare, and there are worries that the effective family might become restricted to those that are online, which would particularly exclude the elderly. On the other hand, a UK Trini noted that although the Internet tended to determine which of his cousins he continues to be close to, it would in no way affect the close personal relationship he has with his grandmother, who happens not to be online.

Friends and Partners

In contrast to family relationships, friendships, acquaintances, and chat partners point to less well-defined relationships that can be more ambiguous when pursued online. Establishing their character and status as relationships may need more reflection, since they may take novel forms that have to be assessed in terms of new normative concepts of friendship. Moreover, in addition to being a means for pursuing established relationships (school friends, boy- and girlfriends, colleagues), the Internet – particularly chat and ICQ – routinely opens up the possibility of engaging online with people from anywhere in the world whom one has not and probably will not meet face-to-face; and these contacts are likely to be made through interests or even through random meetings and coincidences.

The situation is made more complicated by the dynamics of internet mediation. People tend to experience the Internet as a battery of related but separate possibilities for pursuing relationships, which they assemble in different ways according to their particular preferences. One individual who has his own personal website abhors the use of chat-lines and makes all his new friendships through signing the guestbooks of personal web-pages that happen to appeal to him. He will make a comment about that website, and hope for a reply from which further contact can ensue. Another uses chat but hates using email, while a third only uses email and extends his range of contacts by being put in touch with friends of his current email friends. Sometimes this is just conservatism; an individual is 'taught' one method, takes to it, and is resistant to alternatives. A UK Trini suggested that he continued to phone friends where the relationship predates the Internet, but emails those who have become friends through the Internet, though this was a rare distinction.

Chat and ICQ, however, are the Internet media that were most fashionable in pursuing relationships, and ones that corresponded more to what we have called 'expansive potential' than to the 'expansive realization' that marked family relationships. Especially for the young within Trinidad, Internet chat and ICQ marked their entry into an expanded possibility of new encounters, including immediate, unexpected and volatile styles of encounter. Chat can be used as a straightforward extension of pre-existing relationships, or of ones related to the immediate locale (as with the schoolchildren discussed below), or it can be a vehicle for developing relationships that were initially made on ICQ itself. Or it can be a mixture, as in the case of one teenage informant who carried with him a list of fifty ICQ friends, most of them from other parts of Trinidad but all first encountered online, some of whom he then met offline, some not. ICQ software includes the ability to make lists of ICQ contacts and categorize them as one wishes (e.g. home versus away, work versus personal), a feature that recognizes the desire to be flexible in ordering, or even separating out, the variety of possible relationships.

In fact, many people claimed that they only put a very few people on their lists. This generally indicates that people make strong distinctions about which relationships are valuable and therefore should be closely integrated into their online activities, and which are not. This distinction – which we encountered across many observations and interviews – was closely tied to the issue of time, of dividing online relationships between those considered short, casual and 'light' and those that are more serious, enduring and emotionally weighty. This tallied very closely with Slater's (1998) previous observations of 'trading sexpics on IRC': chat comprises a larger number of short-term casual encounters, which can be exciting, interesting, boring or lunatic, but are treated as relatively weightless as relationships. They may be valued and sought for many reasons, but they are in a different category from the serious relationships into which a very few of them will develop, which are characterized by the kinds of trust, investment and intimacy that are only possible over a longer term: 'Every time you go online, you'll always find some crazy fool out there, talking rubbish . . . there for theirself, just to be on the net, that's all they're there for. You talk shit to them and that's about it but you don't take them on, you don't get down to anything. With a long-standing relationship you talk to them for *loooooooong*, [i.e.] you start to share stuff between each other.' In Trini chat, just as in the chat studied by Slater, 'long term' is not necessarily all that long in comparison to offline relationships of a similar seriousness. Because of the dynamic character of these social settings and because of their intensity, three months is very good going, but this might mean three months of spending as many hours of the day as possible locked into the highly internalized modality of chat. This intensity also means that chat very much takes place in the moment: people frequently talk about current relationships as if they were several years rather than weeks old, while earlier similar relationships are all but forgotten.

Short-term encounters of a largely random nature are primarily a form of mutual entertainment. Their essential characteristic – that the other person could turn out to be more or less anyone, and one can never know – already gives it something of the *frisson* of gambling. In addition it commonly has the additional *frisson* of sexual banter. While this is no difference in principle from non-Trini chat (again see Slater 1998) the role of flirtation and sexual language in Trini culture (see the next chapter and Yelvington 1996) gives it a very particular salience for Trinis who use it. While some users will talk to same-sex others, most readily admit that almost all their chat is with opposite-sex others (reflecting a pervasive assumption of heterosexuality offline). For example a man notes he chats to: 'Mostly women! The only time I would chat to men is when I want information on music, games and stuff. When I want to download something form the Net and they might know where it is.' Once a partner has been located then the encounter sets up a challenge where there is relatively little to lose, given the cover of anonymity, but much to be gained:

> Yes, you learn a lot from them, especially the different types of expression for stuff. . . . It's like when you go on, the first time, uh talking to a female over the Net, it's kind a like if you meet a female on the street, uh tackling her. You're not seeing what she looks like unless you have video conferencing, but she sounds good. What she said really catches your attention and you're able to hold that attention. It's kinda like a thrill, the longer you could talk to this person, keep them excited as well as they keep you excited and sometimes the things they say to you, well. . . . It surprised me the first time. After a while I started to get used to it.

Quite apart from this art of banter, at which Trinis know they are particularly proficient, for many users the experience of playful sexuality is clearly a major part of the pay-off of the time spent online, even if some of the stories are apocryphal:

> There was one time we actually got a girl sent us twelve different video clippings of her while she was talking and then she started to take off her clothes. She stopped when she reached half way. And I bet you it was real. There are chances it might not have been real but it was fun. It's like you being able to do what you want and knowing that the person doesn't have to know who you are, because you could never meet them at all.

For women, in particular, however, there is the problem that Trinidadian forms of sexual banter can be quite different from many of the societies of those they are chatting with, so the scope for being misconstrued is endless. A girl who went by the 'nick' Miss Sexy simply could not see why she kept having such problems:

> I know, it does: it simply does attract a lot of people, because basically most of them come on and say 'what your name goes with, why are you calling yourself Miss Sexy?' and I simply tell them, that to me, I'm very beautiful and to me, I think I'm sexy, but it's nothing more than that. Most of them think I want to do stuff. I simply said, no my name is not Miss Sexy, just my nickname 'cause I'm friendly, I'm kind-hearted and understanding. Basically I want to chat with them, and there where the conversation goes they find I'm intelligent and what they think I was with my nickname is not what I am.

While sex dominated, there are other concerns in short-term chat. These include simply the interest in each new person. For example, 'every time I go on ICQ it's somebody new, something new, some different story, some guy claims he's having family problems or with some woman, this sort of thing. Each time I get ICQ it is a unique story.' There is also a kind of mediated but personal tourism, where the interest is in meeting people from different countries and learning about the countries. The implications for Trinidadian identity are discussed in Chapter 4. More female chatters seem to follow this route, and they often seem particularly interested in interleaving it with discussions about personal problems such as dealing with their parents. The result confirms for them the general sense that 'underneath our differences we are all the same', so that an aura of global sentimentality can be one product of these kinds of encounter.

Given the 'lightness' of these short-term encounters, when did Trinidadians ascribe them 'weight'? We argued in Chapter 1 that 'virtuality' needs to be treated as a social accomplishment rather than an analytical assumption, that we need to understand when, why and how particular people come to treat online relationships as 'real' or not. Slater has previously argued that, in the apparently extremely disembedded context of 'sexpics trading on IRC', this was crucially related to the ways in which one could establish sufficient trust in the authenticity of the other to warrant the risk of investing in them emotionally, and that this was related to the persistence of the other's online presence over time, as well as to ways in which they could be 'embodied' through encountering them through additional media.

Similar dynamics were clearly at play in Trinidadian chat relationships, and a range of social and technical possibilities were used to sort out which relationships mattered and how they should be conducted. Firstly, just as with email in a family context, there was a great stress on sharing a mundane life with the other both on- and offline. That is to say, people could spend a great deal of very intense time chatting online, over the course of which they felt that the other had a clear idea of their daily lives, thoughts and attitudes. One informant, Jason, had some unusually long-lasting relationships (one of over two years' duration), which he placed at the same level as face-to-face relationships on the basis that they knew him well, were stitched into his everyday life and had been tried and tested over time by a variety of means:

A: Yeah I would say I take them seriously. 'Cos they ask me, how ya going today? They knew when my baby was born. They all got the news that my baby was born – send cards of congratulations, everything. When I go online they say, how's ya baby going today? What's she doing da? It's like regular people, regular conversations. . . . they're just a part of your friendship group: you still consider them the way you consider the friends who you see everyday.

Q: They feel part of your everyday life?

A: Yeah – also part of your everyday life, 'cos basically I get an email from them every day, chat with them every day . . .

This sharing of mundane life included everyday exchanges of electronic jokes, pictures, e-greetings and postcards, electronic boxes of chocolates and bouquets of flowers that people scoured the net to find for their friends. Sites for e-greetings were amongst those most commonly visited by Trinidadians, and are offered by Trinidadian companies and found on Trinidadian portal sites (Plate 3.1). These new electronic gifts are indeed new material forms that constitute relationships in new ways: that is to say, they should be treated seriously as mediations or material culture (Jaffe 1999). Virtual postcards, as noted, extend to the Internet the immense and long-term popularity of such cards in Trinidadian society generally. However, in going online, postcards have now slipped out of their previous more formal frame of being used for marked events and special occasions. They have become a regular means for maintaining general contact, acquiring – like email – the informality of a gesture or spontaneous moment of acknowledging the other. Moreover, people seek out cards with animations, music or other such accompaniments so that they can also feel they are part of a 'coolhunt', and they accept the gift of cool (one teenager talked with zest about the recent receipt of: 'the frog in the blender swimming, and he's insulting you and you have to press each knob on the blender and in the end, it just blend him up . . . cool!').

Stitching the other into a shared everyday world rapidly extends to the sharing of intimacies, problems, perspectives and values, so that you not only feel that the other really knows you, and vice versa, but also that they reliably 'there for you' as a persistent and embodied ethical other.

Q: How much do you value a [long-term] relationship like that; how real does it feel?

A: You have to think about how well you know the person, what you talk about, things like that. . . . we exchange ideas about what's going on her life and what's going on in my life, and we put together what we think about it and how it should be and how it shouldn't be. We learn from each other.

Q: So part of being a real relationship is getting into real issues?

A: Real issues, yeah. Because I tell her what's up with me and she tells me what's with her. I know her family, what's going on with her. How she handles going to school and her family, being with them. Her mum is separated from her Dad so she tells me how different her life is from living with her Dad from living with her mum 'cos I'm the same, I'm living with my Dad and I told her about it.

Q: You feel she understands you and shares your values? You trust it?

A: Yes, everything, yes.

People could describe this sharing in nearly therapeutic terms, as in the case of one woman who actually was a counsellor and transferred her listening skills and values to ICQ.

This intimacy can be treated and treasured as something that is largely detached from offline consequences and costs and at the same time differentiated from 'the usual stupidness' of casual chat encounters. Although we encountered almost no talk that corresponded to cyberutopian expectations about a radical break between offline and online identities, Jason talked about his serious online relationships through a notion of 'just communicating':

A: Sometimes it's more meaningful, right, 'cos they know you're not taking them on any other level but the mind, it's like a kinda brain to brain kinda thing . . . yeah, just communicating, looking out for each other. Talking, being friends, without the hangups.

Q: So there's almost something pure about it?

A: Yeah, yeah [he agrees with that]. That's the exact term: there is something pure about it.

The nature of the 'impurities' from which his serious chat relations released him in order to be treated as 'real' relationships were quite clear:

A: Even though we try not to be, we all have our prejudices, right, and there will be people who automatically on sight you see them and you categorize them. On the Internet it is not like that. Right. Especially the chat sites or whatever: you actually see into people's minds, their personalities, right there.

Q: But you can be wrong about people, taken in by them?

A: If you're stupid, yeah. You are what you type. Especially the way people type in the chat groups you could actually get a hint of their accents, of the way they speak, everything from the way they type, the word structures, everything. You got good feeling for people. And you know if they are lying , hands down – 'cos a lot of them saying, well I am 5'11", the usual stupidness . But when you get, like you meet people seriously, and ya talking to them, it's a whole different level. You don't consider what they look like, whatever: it's a mind-to-mind contact kind of thing. It's entirely different, and you actually find yourself making a good few friends online. 'Cos I got four or five people that I can really kick with regularly. And I just met them over the net.

Jason – like most people who take seriously any online relationship – felt he had reliable strategies and instincts for assessing these relationships. In fact he was pragmatic in sorting out the real – trustworthy, serious, weighty – relationships, and therefore in deciding where to place his trust:

But the way I'm made up, I always give everybody, no matter who, right, that comes into my space and touch my life, they always get a chance to screw me up – but they only get one chance to screw me up. You tell me this and you say this is the truth, I take it as ok. But when you're online and you're getting to learn somebody you do proceed with a little more caution. In this case you can see somebody's eyes and you know – well yeah, he lying to me, or – he pulling a fast one. Online you track what they say – me, I track what they say. The trust comes from normal banter, because when you first meet somebody online you're usually talking some stupidness or the other. You're not really into anything serious. Most of the times it's a lot easier to trust someone online because they can't hurt you as much as someone who you trust face to face.

Finally, Jason not only sorted the light from the heavy relationships, but he placed them in quite different ethical universes of responsibility and commitment. As we have argued previously, the issue here is in no sense a distinction between the 'real' and the 'virtual', but rather the ways in which

Jason chose to frame online relationships as significant and what consequences he then attached to them:

> The thing is when they say stuff, say in the general chat rooms, etc., stuff is said, whatever goes. But when you're on a one-on-one with somebody, and [when] you get past the bullshit and the jokes, people really reveal a lot of their soul to you. And you are entrusted to keep what you have there as sacred property, 'cos they share a piece of theirselves with you. And if you sharing you expect that they return the sentiment, and they do.

Whereas Jason tended to see chat relationships as a potentially very pure form of what he valued in offline relationships, a surprising number of people framed special chat relationships as very literal forms of the most conventional primary relationships. They talked to us of boyfriends or girlfriends or even fiancées who turned out to be entirely online correspondents living in another part of the world. In an even more surprising number of cases we could confirm that these relationships, formed through random chat encounters, had in fact been pursued into serious offline encounters, including living together or marrying. For example, in one family visited, the daughter, a university student, had met a Buddhist from Brazil online. The relationship developed, and the Brazilian twice visited Trinidad; but finally the religious divide from the staunchly Catholic daughter proved too great a barrier to a permanent relationship. While the daughter has since fallen in love with a Trinidadian, she has also managed to develop a sufficiently deep friendship with a Danish male that he also planned to visit her in Trinidad. So common is this kind of occurrence that we would predict that for the young the tradition of anonymous tourism may increasingly be replaced by holidays being taken on the basis of a previous long-term Internet-based friendship.

Serious relationships and indeed marriage developed from online meetings. These can be framed in quite diverse ways, as could be seen in the case of several relationships within one family. The mother had actually married an American whom she originally met online. However, she still not only expressed worry about the online relationships that her children were concurrently developing, but also doubted the reality and seriousness of their relationships as opposed to hers. She pointed out that although there were several months of purely online communication before she met her husband face to face, she did not and would not characterize it as friendship, let alone as developing on to love, until they had actually met in person. It was not 'real', and there was too much possibility for deception. In this and other respects, such as her distaste at the very idea of cybersex, she clearly distanced her own actions from her children's, who fell in love and got serious without meeting the persons concerned. A further irony here was that her children's practice was condemned mainly on the basis of her own ideals, that a couple should live together before marriage. It seemed in talking to her own children separately that one of them had internalized his mother's strictures and was clear that the eight-month relationship he had had online was only to be understood within the confines of the medium. It was also clear that his brother and sister were much less constrained or influenced by her scepticism, and saw their online relationships in terms of love and possible marriage. This is a clear example of the different ways in which people can construct or assess the 'virtual'; not as an assumed property of Internet relations but as a criterion by which they understand them.

On the same day and at the same cybercafé at which these interviews were conducted, an 18-year-old girl had just announced to us that she was getting engaged to a man in Australia whom she had never met, on the basis of almost daily ICQ contact supplemented by occasional phone calls to him and to his parents. As one of the company pointed out, it is 'mostly girls and those who are rather sheltered at home. You know they have problems, they don't agree with their parents, and they are looking for getting out of the house and maybe out of the country.' It was implicit that this remark particularly applied to Indian girls living in the local villages. As in this case, such relationships could be unusually public in their development. Another large group reported eagerly awaiting the first visit to Trinidad of one of their friend's ICQ correspondents from Dominica, and their delight when the couple subsequently married.

Sometimes these relationships start as unintended consequences of short-term random chats, with conversations about their respective countries and common popular culture leading to an exchange of photographs, and then a mixture of flirting and discussing personal problems. In most such cases the Trinidadians have a clear normative model of how such relationships should develop, and a rich language to describe this. Their correspondents are commonly accused of being too *maco* (nosy) or too *fass* (fast); they give one the horrors and fail to keep cool. In short Trinidadians do not like people who come on too fast and too strong. Many users had stories about dropping people from chatlists because they were incapable of taking things at the pace the Trinis wanted. On the other hand there are some who go online with the specific intention of looking for long-term rather than short-term relationships, which they expressly state on the information forms attached to their names on ICQ. Since already many Trinidadians know of others who have found partners this way, the Internet has quickly become a specific option for those in search of love, with the additional implication of leaving for another country through marriage. This is a possibility that many

Trinidadians, young and old, view with what might be termed an interested ambivalence. Another option is to establish long-term online relationships without either partner's having any particular expectation of this ever turning into a face-to-face relationship.

Once established, these relationships can have many of the characteristics of any other long-term relationships. When those involved discuss them, often with rich details about quarrels and making up and issues of different degrees of commitment, it is very hard to discern any tangible difference from their discussion of offline relationships. When a woman storms into the room in a fury of 'God that man drives me to . . .', the man in question may be in the room she has just stepped out of; but equally he may be on the screen in that room. Sometimes there is an online version of a common offline scenario. For example, one woman noted that: 'I have this boyfriend and I caught him sweet-talking somebody else in a next chat room. I dumped him. I don't remember her name, but I found him out. Well, I tell him it's over. I stop talking to him.'

This implies that those involved do not perceive as problematic what to outsiders might be the 'obvious' constraints of online romance. This is important not only in new relationships with those living abroad, but also to ongoing relationships between Trinidadians. Internet use in respect of long-term friendships follows a similar pattern to that with relatives: partly recovery, partly maintenance, partly expansion. Indeed, there is a close similarity in the use of the Internet to 'repair' the specific problem of relationships that would have been sundered when one partner went abroad to study and the other remained at home. A common speculation was that a particular relationship would have subsequently broken up, but thanks to the Internet was maintained until the couple could be together again. It was very common for those who had not gone online while at school to purchase a first computer or to go to a cybercafé when their school friends went abroad to study or work. So here the Internet comes across as the saving of such relationships. For example, a married couple had known each other since they were 15, but had had to spend three years apart, as she was in the UK and he remained in Trinidad. During this time they would email every day, and go on a chat line every 2 or 3 days. As they noted this was: 'Fantastic. It was more effective than a phone call. It was harder to say goodbye than when I was on the phone. Strange enough, it was as good as actually sitting down and talking to the person. When you are on the phone you just don't get that sort of . . .; probably because we write and that sort of triggers off all the emotions. We get more time to think, I guess.'

This was a rare statement; most couples wanted to complement their online chat with telephone calls, and ideally with visits. This was a clear difference from short-term use, where the other is viewed specifically as an online correspondent. But for long-term relationships the medium does not define the partner; rather, it is merely the means by which the partner is encountered. Some users never seem to be that comfortable with chat and email as a means to express deep emotions; but it is striking that most users have quickly taken these new media for granted as entirely appropriate for expressing emotions, running the gamut of love, anger, jealousy, guilt, and intimacy. This is evident not only from discussing online relationships, but also from watching people online getting riled by but also intensely involved in their communications, or waiting around in agitation (particularly at cybercafés) when there is a technical problem that delays them from finding out if the significant he/she has left a message.

Chat and ICQ lend themselves to floating and unstable populations; ICQ encounters are commonly fleeting. However within the institutional facilities created to make chat possible there are provisions for photographic and personal archives and message boards, which may be used to support relationships in a more enduring, visible and material form. A more formal and perhaps more socially consequential example of this would be the lists of alumni posted on their websites by some of the prestige schools (Plate 3.2). These often list names, email addresses, websites and graduation years of any school graduates who are online. This was clearly a significant resource for a body of alumni that largely disperses to further studies around the globe immediately on graduation. There remains a strong sense of 'old boy' and 'old girl' affinity with their 'alma mater' fostered by the schools. Perhaps the most conspicuous example of this Diaspora effect was Fatima College. Because of its long-term association with computer and Internet teaching, this school seemed to have a presence on the Internet well beyond its relative size. As well as the alumni listed on its own site, there is a separate website developed in Canada. Broken down by current place of residence, this reveals the following spread of ex-students, which in turns explains the immediate significance of the Internet: USA 170; Trinidad and Tobago 148; Canada 87; UK 13; country not entered 10; Jamaica 3; together with 2 each for Australia, Grenada, Scotland and Venezuela and 1 each for Bermuda, Botswana, Brazil, Denmark, Ireland, Japan and Switzerland.

The significance of such lists goes beyond renewing friendships. Simply by hyperlinking between the websites of all these graduates, the Internet comes both to represent and to replicate a key aspect of Trinidadian social structure. The Internet not only maps it but plays a part in reproducing it through the practical interconnections it enables. Some of our research developed by following such links and email addresses, which have become an effective means of tracing the Trini elite.

Places of Sociality

In so far as Internet studies have shifted their gaze from what happens online, they have started to investigate the microsociological contexts of Internet use, such as cybercafés or domestic spaces (Crang, Crang and May 1999; Furlong 1995; Wakeford 1999). The immediate social locations of Internet use both frame and set limits on the kinds of relationships that take place through them. For example, workplace access could range from minimal to extensive, and from extremely liberal attitudes to personal use to a restrictive, 'business use only' policy. Hence some people could treat their office as a place for pursuing family contacts on behalf of their entire household, for chatting and even for cybersex; others could not relate workplace access to any kind of sociality.

Just as important as the impact of social spaces on the way relationships were pursued through the Internet was their impact on relationships around the computer. Two places of sociality that brought out quite different possibilities for relationships were cybercafés and secondary schools.

Cybercafés

The global usage of cybercafés is diverse, as Rao (1999) has noted. In Trinidad, they were largely unstable and in most cases unprofitable enterprises. They were generally either adjuncts to other businesses (computer sales or maintenance, private IT courses) or on the verge of transforming into other businesses (webdesign and Internet technologies). They also ranged from scams (one charged people TT$5 for each email sent or received) to dynamic community centres.

In the event, we were able to visit six operating cybercafés, each of which was very different in style and in the kinds of sociality it generated. For example, of the two in which we spent a good deal of our research time, Café A had a strong emphasis on an informal and convivial ambience. There was always music, loud conversation, bustling activity. It was also literally a cybercafé, in that it served food and drink. The eight computers were placed along the outside walls of the main rooms so that anyone sitting at the spare tables in the centre could see what was going on at the monitors. It was a very public space and a friendly liming spot. This reflected the personality and strong beliefs of the couple who owned it, especially the husband, who was regarded by many users as a kind of father-figure, who calmly dispensed advice, support and encouragement, as well as keeping both order and excitement. He combined entrepreneurialism and nationalism in typical Trini measure (see the next chapter), doing his utmost to develop his users' Internet expertise and enterprise. He also gathered about himself talented and enthusiastic young people who could use the facilities to develop commercial projects in webdesign and programming.

The second cybercafé – B – was an adjunct to a computer retail business that also had an extensive programme of computer courses. This was distinctly a business premises, with white and undecorated walls. Partly for teaching purposes, the computers were sited in three different rooms, and within them machines were positioned to give much privacy to the user. There was no area for general liming, and the consumption of food and drink was forbidden. Despite the different style, the social ambience was very friendly and supportive, but this was entirely due to a core of employees, their relatives and some regulars.

In each case there were probably a majority of people who used the spaces as individuals, without much apparent connection to the cafés as institutions beyond finding them more or less congenial. This included people stopping by to check their email or research a particular topic or just surf or chat for a while. The population was mainly, but not exclusively, young. They related to the staff mainly for technical support and help in using software.

On the other hand, both places had a core of one or two dozen regulars who came in very frequently and spent a lot of time there. One person we knew seemed to live there, chatting non-stop to her cyber-fiancé in Australia, to a degree that staff expressed some concern to us. Hourly charges were laxly enforced, and in some cases the most regular visitors paid for little of their online time, but in return helped the employees sort out 'newbies' and generally added to the ambience of the place. Even though Café B had little in the way of atmosphere, and certainly did not put itself forward as a liming spot, regular users still strongly identified with it, and another cybercafé noted that most of their Christmas decorations were put up by users. Café A went much further. A few people said that they came there even though they had online computers at home or work; others hung out after school with no apparent desire to use a computer at all: 'Nearly every day after work I come up here, even if is not to use the PC, if I buy something from the cybercafé downstairs and I'll come up and eat, or just chill. People come up here to study too. It does be a real nice lime.'

Sociality comprised a wider variety of collective uses of the space than simply hanging out. At this point, the styles of the two places diverged more markedly. A lot of the activity in cybercafé B was oriented to chat. Partly because of the privacy afforded by the room and monitor arrangements, people could both pursue their own activities and at the same time form small groups, sharing their experiences. This might mean that regular users found their on- and offline worlds merging in interesting ways: for example, they might pass chat friends on to each other, or gather round a screen as a chat progressed. The girl mentioned above, recently engaged to a man in Australia, encouraged him to find Australian girls who would chat to a boy she had come to know at the café. Equally his interests in certain games led him to make friends both with café regulars and with some online contacts. Often young users would want to make sure there were friends around to appreciate some sexual adventure or the excited danger of encountering a hacker online. Regulars would rush over to a friend's screen to take over their keyboard and latch on to some event, in between juggling half a dozen open windows and conversations on their own machine.

The private spaces possible in Café B (especially, but not exclusively, its 'back room') also allowed looking at pornography, alone or in groups (pornography was banned at Café A, because of the public view of all monitors rather than for reasons of principled disapproval). For example, a group of gay Trinidadians collectively used the back room to look at sexual material – an important opportunity in Trinidad, which has tended to be highly homophobic. The staff are clearly aware of the pornographic material being used, and themselves suggested that this represented some 70 per cent of all usage (we felt this was an exaggeration, although some users claimed the same figure); but their concern was primarily to ensure that such activities be carried out in privacy and not be directly exposed to chance encounters with schoolchildren and others who would be offended. Our observations would then certainly support Wakeford (1999: 188–94) in noting the importance of spatial order within the cybercafé to understanding the kinds of interaction that take place there.

Coming into the café as a group generally tended to have an impact on machine use, creating the bravado for illicit activities. In addition to porn, this might include schoolchildren who would impress each other with their ability to work as hackers. Another example was:

> Sometimes me and my friend will come as a group and just sit at a computer and go into ICQ and just diss everybody and get thrown out from the chat room. Well, we just like to interfere with people. Like harmless, just embarrass, just jump in, listen to a particular conversation and then we chose this one and decide that we going to harass this one. Out of kicks and then everybody just get involved. Only as a group, until we got banned, restricted, eventually: got kicked out a couple of times, then we got banned.

Sociality in café A was rather different. As opposed to the groups huddled around monitors in Café B, people were either liming at the tables or engaged in more purposeful (but still sociable and pleasurable) development of their skills or projects. There was a great emphasis on helping each other learn ever more ambitious skills and on projects. Finally, and rather unusually for Trinidad, where computer game culture is not as important to Internet use as in North America and Europe, there were a number of people at Café A, many of them core staff and regulars, who were heavily into networked games such as Quake. There were occasional all-nighters, and some investment of time in downloading the paraphernalia of Quake clans.

One final case of cybercafé sociality that indicates how unexpected the relationships formed around the Internet can be: a cybercafé recently opened up in an up-market mall by a young woman turned into a kind of virtual crèche. She started by offering basic training in Internet use to younger children 7and found that not only did the children love it, but their mothers loved leaving them there, in safety and worthy educational pursuits, while they shopped for several hours. One particularly wealthy family regularly left their son there with his personal bodyguard, and both would play for hours.

Secondary Schools

One of the traumas of Trinidadian life is the common entrance exam, which separates children between the more prestigious Church-founded secondary schools and the ordinary government schools. The striking difference between the two was that the Internet had already become an integral part of school culture for students of the prestige schools. This was as much a reflection of the fact that they tended to come from wealthier families with Internet access at home as from the much improved online facilities at school (clearly evident in their school websites, e.g. Plate 3.3). As was indicated in Chapter 2, provision for boys and for girls was radically unequal, though this did not seem to make the Internet any less of a feature for girls' school culture or schoolwork, at least at the schools we visited. Home use was more equal, with several individuals and groups suggesting a figure of around a third of schoolchildren having online access at home, though those without access might come and use the computers of those with. Schoolchildren with online computers at home tended to receive 5 to 20 emails a week. There was much sharing of online culture, with people forwarding jokes and cards but also friends to each other. Chat and ICQ were very common for younger children. One noted how she had stopped using ICQ, since she had found it so addictive during the four months she had used it. For boys music was the most common use after chat and ICQ, followed by email, and then porn, with rather less use for sports and games.

Perhaps in schools more than anywhere else one has a sense of the Internet as something that already has a history, and also a relationship to the school as a life course. For example, there is the sense of a pre-ICQ phase or a pre-personal webpage phase. There is already the expectation amongst schoolchildren that members of a certain school form would go through a phase of heavy involvement in Internet pornography or cybersex, but that by the next school year this was already seen as immature and not really cool. In one year children might come into school and call each other by their ICQ nicks instead of their real names; but again this would be scorned by the more senior year. As one pupil put it: 'Some get out of the phase faster than others, others are still into it. They are the minority. The other forms are in it right now. When we were in lab in Computer Science everybody had their own porno section. I had 300 pictures, a friend had about 400 pictures. Now if you go back only the lower forms have their porno sections. The school doesn't really know.'

Schoolchildren constituted one of the only groups that extensively exploited the Internet for socializing with other Trinidadians in Trinidad. One example of this was the extension of playground gossip and interaction. ICQ seemed to have replaced the telephone as the privileged medium for continuing school conversations after school, letting each other know about or comment on events that day, in the privacy of their one-to-one chat. Already the patterns of spitefulness, cliquishness, sentimentality and making-up that are familiar genres offline were finding their online equivalents. Also there was the concomitant rise of the particularly Trinidadian sense of bacchanal and *commess* (disorder caused by gossip). For example schoolgirls relished the story of a boy who published gossip about his friends on his personal web'-site. News of this event spread quickly, so that they too had visited the site. During the one week before the boy's mother closed the site down, it had been hacked – we were told – by some of those concerned to publish counter-accusations about the website author. Another story concerned a boy watching a screen with his girlfriend while gossip about this girlfriend was being relayed. A more direct relationship was established in San Fernando, where there is a concentration of secondary schools. Many pupils used an IRC-based chat room where they tended to congregate online, especially on Friday nights continuing through into the morning hours while the parents were asleep. They also arranged to meet occasionally for a group lime at the food court of the local mall. Email and ICQ might also be used to plan a weekend lime or other gathering.

The Internet was also providing schoolchildren with a major conduit to offline relationships. Chat was seen as an ideal precursor to dating, since both boys and girls could be less reticent and feel their way towards a relationships while staying relatively anonymous:

Before, the girls are shy kind of way, so it would take a fellow to go over and meet a girl and talk. But with ICQ it's easier. You speaking to them like you know them kind of thing, before you actually know them. And when you meet you already know them.' Another boy noted of a friend: 'He met her on one of the open chat lines and then he met her in real. They going strong now, haven't had a fight yet. It's a good way of meeting girls. It's easier than walking up to someone and talking.'

Internet content becomes common school culture as easily as television programmes such as South Park. In the morning people would report new sites or software. The Internet could be used to constitute the non-school sociality of children, as: 'A place to get away from school, that's what the Internet is for my class. They look at it as liming on the net. They are all in one big chat room and lime.' But this was the least academic class in the year. For most students the relationship between the Internet and school culture clearly integrated both sociality and also educational activities, such as sharing Internet resources for schoolwork. One group of schoolgirls laughed at our adult naivety when we discussed using books for essay-writing, since they pointed out the great store of previously written essays existing on the Internet that could be mined as the basis for their own essays. They all claimed that they themselves (of course) only ever used ideas and snippets of these essays, but that others in their class had submitted entire essays taken from the web without as yet ever being caught out by the teachers. One group did suggest, however, that their teachers were asking more obscure questions in subjects such as literature partly in response to the threat of their pupils' merely presenting public-domain essays. Books and libraries were seen as *passé*: according to the girls, even teachers accepted the inability to find information online as a reasonable excuse for not handing in a homework project.

Almost all these children will at least investigate the possibility of further education abroad through researching the net; indeed throughout Trinidadian society this has become a far more frequent use of the Internet than pursuits such as sports and games. This was confirmed by inspection of many 'histories' recorded on web-browsers in cybercafés. At Fatima College around half the students were expected to take SATS exams for US colleges, of whom around half were expected to obtain full scholarships to prestigious universities in the US. The evidence from the alumni lists on the school websites suggest this is not unrealistic. The schools themselves clearly recognized that Internet skills were becoming an integral part of general education. Some were quite liberal in opening up their banks of computers to after-school use, even when finding on occasion that a schoolchild was still online when they returned for school the next morning! Fatima funded its computer laboratories partly through putting on annual courses for the public. IT remains integral to the social relations of its alumni (see Plate 3.4).

The personal websites of schoolchildren are themselves clear expressions of school culture. They also make far more inventive use of the technology than even the most expensive commercial sites. 'Maria's So Called Life', with the address 'sullengirl' (plate 3.5), has words like 'pathetic' and 'wasting away' that come and go within a frame. Instead of the simple 'about me' found in most personal websites (see Chapter 4), this one states 'Stuff on me, WARNING! – Before you proceed to waste your time by reading this page I should warn you . . . it SUCKS!!! I don't know why I'm doing this really, guess it's because I have a lot of time on my hands.' Sullengirl thereby illustrates the effectiveness of a website in conveying the typical sense of the teenager as alienated: even visually, she mainly appears on the site as an alien. Other teenage sites also present themselves as stupid and pathetic and tell us how they really shouldn't be working on this site one week before taking their examinations but . . . (e.g. Plate 3.6).

What is impressive is not just the sheer dynamics and creativity of these sites, but the techniques they use to entrap surfers and draw them in. For example there is the brilliant way one site (Plate 3.7) exploits a conventional form of computer link to suck in the passing surfer. The crucial factor in all these sites seems to be not just the ability to attract surfers but also to engage in the act of exchange represented by the (usually mutual) signing of their guestbooks. It is this that attests to the fame/name of the website creator (for examples see Plates 3.8), and is analogous to the circles of exchange that create the name and fame of those who transact Kula (Munn 1986). Surfers are drawn to share the offerings of the site, for example their jokes, their MP3s, their friends, or their links to other sites as long as they sign the guestbook and attest thereby to the fame of the creator (Plate 3.9).

The Internet was also at the centre of school cultures of heroes and outlaws that focused on technical feats and knowledge, generally possessed by boys (this was not confined to schools, but certainly prevalent there). While some of this involved relationships formed between technically proficient boys who were developing small website businesses or helping manage school IT facilities, the thrilling stuff involved various kinds of organized outlawry, often mythological, directed against school or each other. One school had allowed a highly skilled 15-year-old to develop their website and other computer facilities for the school. The fact that the same pupil was reputed to then hack into the system at will led to a subsequent parting of ways. All the students had a repertoire of stories about master hackers and hacking feats, of particularly devastating viruses and ingenious 'trojans' that could take control over anyone's computer. It was hard to confirm any of these stories, and many of them were pretty outlandish (the shared ultimate ideal was for some schoolboy to hack into the Trinidadian banking system); but it was clear that reports of such exploits were a guaranteed addition to peer status. As one 15-year-old put it:

> Normally they brag about how good they are at hacking, or blowing up somebody's system, shutting them down. Some instances – they are true. People that they do it to come back and talk about it. They does be real vex. They quarrel a lot. Why you do me that? They have this fella, he left school now, he was in form five with us, he could shut down somebody even on the net, or disconnect, he's real good.

Hacking involved competitive bravado between the boys. By contrast, a 15-year-old schoolgirl noted that girls would commonly send viruses to each other, often in the belief that they were already victims of a virus sent by the girl in question. Girls would come to school also moaning about how their computer had been messed up and how they would wreak revenge on the girl they believed had sent the virus. Again, the mix of truth and lore is both undecidable and revealing of school culture, but the comment that 'this is their mentality' strongly suggested that the stereotypes that are developing about how schoolgirls and schoolboys respectively use their skills closely follow older gender stereotypes.

Continuities

Much of the first half of this chapter could have been written under the rubric of kinship studies. At first glance the material appears very different from what one might expect to encounter in kinship studies; but we want to suggest that there may be much more continuity here than meets the eye. This becomes more apparent when it is recognized that the relationships discussed throughout this chapter are, like kinship itself, an idiom for the expression of core Trinidadian values. The central argument of Miller 1994 was that there existed a historical logic that could confer on Trinidad a vanguard position in arguments about the nature of modernity. It was suggested that the relevant values – termed there 'transience' and 'transcendence' – were historically first developed and expressed through the idiom of kinship. After the oil boom of the 1970s the same contradiction in values was also expressed through the meanings given to the objects of mass consumption, perhaps now through the medium of the Internet.

The key author for understanding the distinctive character of West Indian kinship is R. T. Smith (1988, 1995). Trinidad had equivalent norms of kinship to those Smith describes for Jamaica, although they have recently moved closer to international norms and ideologies as a result of affluence and cosmopolitan aspirations. Smith (1988: 49) found that Jamaicans typically recognized a large number of people as relatives (a mean of 284 in 51 cases). As in Trinidad, these became a kind of potential network rather than, as in other countries, a series of concentric circles representing decreasing degrees of contact and obligation. Closeness or affection is almost an independent variable one establishes with some kin but not with others. Connections with kin are rather less tied to a sense of obligation based on relative closeness of blood than would be true elsewhere. As a potential network these connections grow in particular ways. For example, in Trinidad the birth of a baby signifies the creation of new bonds irrespective of the continued presence of the baby's father. This relative separation between a sense of connection and a sense of obligation may be understood in part as an act of resistance to historical pressure from groups such as the Church to develop more institutionalized norms of kin. For example, there was resistance to marriage prior to demonstrating the ability to have children and most especially the ability to own and run a house.

Instead, kinship included a strong element of pragmatism. One might be only vaguely aware that a particular relative lived in a locality until the decision to send one's son to school in that area, in which case that relative's house becomes the obvious place for him to live. Similarly if one wanted to extend a business link to a new region. The same applied to affection in general. Cousins were more like a pool of potential close relations; but only through mutual attraction does a very close friendship develop with one particular cousin. So what mattered was not the distance between any two relatives, but rather the realization of particular pragmatic and affective relations out of a pool of possible relationships. Even in the practice of sexuality there is a stress on the mutual act of exchange, for example of giving one's labour in clearing the yard of one's sexual partner as part of mutual recognition of the relationship. There is also an antipathy to forms of marriage in which partners can take each other for granted in providing either sex or labour.

In effect kinship represents a potential pool of people, while circumstances are allowed to determine whether or not there develops a bond of affection or whether or not a relative becomes an important node in solving some logistical problem. In Miller 1994 (pp. 168–93) it was argued that all of this expresses the value of transience, in which institutions are prevented from limiting the sense of freedom and voluntarism basic to what are seen as authentic relationships. Its roots in the particular history of the region are therefore clear.

Such a perspective is very different from the 'baggage' that usually comes with terms such as 'community' and 'family' if used as models for Internet use. Usually such terms tend to assume a commonalty of sentiment in which community as a symbol and focus of commitment transcends the relations that constitute it. If, however, West Indian kinship of this transient variety is taken as the model for Internet use, other possibilities arise. The first analogy is found in the way people use the Internet to create networks. One common concern is simply to expand the number of people one knows or knows of. Once one has had a communication with them it could in future be extended if that were mutually desired. This evolution occurs through a number of different routes. These include creating networks of potential correspondents, for example through contacting distant kin on the Internet, developing a list of 'nicks' on one's ICQ link, or signing a website's guestlist. A prime example of this would be the 'de Trini Lime', an ICQ list that grew as we were doing fieldwork to 2,215 people. The only criteria that mattered as far as most people were concerned were that the other person on the lime was a genuine Trini and then also usually that they were of the opposite sex.

As in the transient family, one finds with Internet relationships that larger appeals to sentiment or obligation on the basis of nearness or proximity often have little authority. Rather, there is a large pool of potential contacts that can be realized for either or both of two main reasons, one being to create bonds of affection, sometimes including deep intimacy and acts of confession. The other is to engage in mutual communication in order to fulfil some largely pragmatic and perhaps fortuitous need, such as a common desire for computer games cheats, though such a need might also be represented by something one might think of as more personal. Many of the random chat links are based around discussions of such things as how to deal with nagging parents or teachers, or persistent ex-boyfriends.

As a result the presence of the correspondent cannot be taken for granted. It follows that there is a constant need to recreate the mutuality of the relationship. This works for both short- and long-term relationships. As some young men noted in trying cybersex, they simply had to show more sensitivity and concern for the pleasure of their female partners than they had in offline sex, since otherwise their partners would just leave them standing (as it were). So, as in transient kinship, Internet relationships are more dyadic, voluntaristic and based on the continuity of their re-constitution through constant acts of exchange. This is not to say that the relationships are more superficial or less normative or lacking in the possibility of affection; but rather it makes these compatible with using relationships to objectify a project of freedom as a central value of modernity. This argument thereby exemplifies the dynamics of normative freedom as discussed in Chapter 1.

The final point is that contrary to expectations such uses of the Internet are not to be opposed to 'traditional' forms of relationship and especially kinship (Castells 1998: 340–51). In this case, by contrast, such attributes would make the Internet strongly continuous with those values that were developed first in kinship and later through the experience of mass consumption (see Miller 1994: Chapter 5). So while it is too early to know to what degree these Trinidadian uses of the Internet are highly specific, if they are, there will be a local historical trajectory that might help us account for that specificity. Once again there may be elective affinities at play; but most importantly, the argument suggests that the relationships outlined here cannot be assumed to mere creatures of the Internet developed in opposition to or replacement of something else called 'traditional kinship'.

Conclusions

The evidence in this chapter suggests that online and offline worlds penetrate each other deeply and in complex ways, whether people are using the Internet to realize older concepts of identity or to pursue new modes of sociality. With respect to the family the Internet is used largely to roll back changes that were dissolving some family relations. It is used to bring people back to what they think of as 'proper' family life. As such it is a prime example of what we called in Chapter 1 the expansive realization. Chat and ICQ can further new kinds of social contact, which then have to be assessed and related to a normative sense of what a 'real' relationship is. They may also be reframed as, or even literally lead to, the most traditional forms of sociality, such as marriage. Apparently quite mundane new media, such as virtual postcards, can both transform older gifting practices and materially reconstitute the relationships in which they are embedded. Spaces of sociality emerge around Internet use in cybercafés and schools, with their own norms and variations based on a complex interweaving of online and offline worlds, frequently more significant in their intensification of offline rather than online relationships, or in the way they integrate the two.

'Virtuality', as we indicated in Chapter 1, is unhelpful or even misleading as a point of departure in sorting out this complexity. Ethnographically, it is at best a special case that emerged in Jason's valuation of 'just communicating' in chat relationships – yet even he did not use the term 'virtual'. Rather he stressed that the value of these relationships hinged on the way in which they were stitched into his everyday life, exemplified in their knowledge and participation in his family life. Similarly, although it is tempting to treat the alumni lists of prestige schools as a kind of virtual social structure, they evidently arose from and maintained an intricate relationship with a quite conventional sense of social structure, and had an eminently practical function in reproducing that structure, alongside other modes of formal and informal practices (for example careers, travel, and business contacts).

As in other chapters, these conclusions are tied to local circumstances. It need not follow that ICQ will necessarily have the same consequence for another society or Diaspora. The 'elective affinity' by which a particular Internet technology can be developed to enhance a particular genre of relationships is highly contextualized. Indeed, it was suggested at the end that there may be strong continuities with earlier forms of kinship, partly because both kinship and the Internet are being employed as idioms to express particular values that connect with what we have termed normative freedom. To try and separate our material into the 'real' and the 'virtual' would thus seem to us to lose almost everything that can be learnt from studying relationship on and through the Internet.

4

Being Trini and Representing Trinidad

Most discussion of the Internet has emphasized both the abolition of distance – a theme we found to be very important – and a consequent dis-embedding of relationships from particular places, a conclusion that we found to be very misleading. The Internet media are very capable of bringing dispersed things into immediate, virtually face-to-face, contact: prices and commodities, families, music cultures, religious and ethnic Diasporas. However, there is no reason to suppose that these encounters dis-embed people from their particular place; or that they come to treat their real-world locations as less relevant to their encounters or identities; or that they construct new identities in relation to 'cyberspace' rather than projecting older spatial identities through new media and interactions. In fact there is a better *prima facie* case for the opposite conclusion: that people would hold to older senses of self and place in their encounter with a sudden, immediate incursion of 'the global'. The Internet would be used to help them in expansive realization – to become what they already wanted to be, partly in the face of the more global environment they are exposed to by the net. This was indeed what we constantly found in our particular case-study: being Trini was crucial to people's encounter with the Internet.

We will certainly not argue that 'Trini-ness' was left unchanged by this encounter; but we will argue that the encounter cannot be understood without understanding Trini-ness and its various meanings for participants. The centrality of place is captured in the two phrases that make up the title of this chapter: 'being Trini' and 'representing Trinidad'. Participants routinely went to great lengths to make the Internet a Trini place, a place where they could be Trini and perform being Trini. Indeed, in the case of diasporic Trinidadians, this was often put forward as the major reason for being on the Internet in the first place: to make contact with Trinis, talk about Trini things and also do Trini things online – to lime, banter, talk music, food, drink and sex. However, because 'being Trini' on the Internet involves perform-ances in public spaces and the production of material cultural artefacts (websites, chat rooms, archives), there is also a hyperawareness that one is also constantly 'representing Trinidad': one is both a representative of Trinidad, and hence responsible for presenting it well by being personally successful, and one is producing representations of Trinidad, and therefore constructing it as the thing known by both members and outsiders. 'Being Trini' and 'representing Trinidad' were not always the central or most conscious aspect of Internet activities, but we rarely found an Internet experience in which they did not feature. This might be peculiar to Trinidad (island culture, culturally and economically ambitious but on the periphery of North America, and so on) but then that would be precisely our point: that we cannot exclude spatial and even national identities from Internet studies, either on the basis of theoretical assumptions about dis-embedding or on the basis of extra-polations from exclusively US and European experiences of the Internet.

Trinidadians, then, seemed highly aware, whenever they were online, that they were meeting the rest of the world *as Trinis*. They might be aware of this in either a nationalistic, patriotic sense (they were Trinidadians encounter-ing other countries) or through a broader sense of the cultural specificity of their tastes, ways of doing things and communicating things. It would be hard to imagine mid-Western American students including in their websites links to the local chamber of commerce or to government information sources, as Trini students would normally do by prominently linking to TIDCO's site. And they were equally online as Trinis when chatting, informing people about the country, and putting its music or sports on the global map. This was not always part of an explicitly nationalist project or orientation (though it was so to a massive extent). They were also seemingly continuously aware of themselves as Trini in terms of thinking through their difference and identity in everyday discussion: it is part of every encounter that one both has to inform the other as to who one is partly by explaining Trinidad to them, and yet at the same time to explore the commonalities of one's global participation.

It should not need saying – but we will say it in any case – that we do not assume that there is a uniform, let alone a natural, national character, a 'Trini-ness' that generates a unified culture or identity, on- or off line. The term masks the extraordinarily complex issue of ethnic identity. Quite apart from the more obvious and homogeneous ethnic categories in Trinidad the recent literature has shown an extensive ability for the category of mixed ethnicity to engage with a diverse set of political, economic and social issues (e.g. Khan 1993; Rheddock 1999; and more generally Yelvington 1993). It has become almost axiomatic in contemporary anthropology that one should not discuss ethnographic material in terms of a homogenized entity called 'culture', nor should one homogenize groups around categories such as Trinidadians. As Thomas notes, it is often facile to talk of 'the Samoan view of . . .' (Thomas 1999 263, though see also Sahlins 1999). Yet it is one thing to avoid an unwarranted projection of a simplistic or ideological category upon a group of people. It is quite another to deny to a people the integrity of a category they apply to themselves and spend much of their lives living in respect of. Moreover, much in line with more sociological accounts of 'new ethnicities' (Hall 1988) or diasporic identities (Gilroy 1993), we are reading Trini-ness as a project defined and pursued over a particular history, not as an origin nor as a nature. What we *are* saying, *contra* current cyber-literature, is that the Internet is being understood and used to an unexpected extent in relation precisely to those projects that might be understood as 'being Trini' or 'representing Trinidad'. Our inclusion of an entire chapter on these issues does not in any way reflect our own attitude to questions of nationalism or national identity. Rather, it is a reflection of the overwhelming evidence from our fieldwork about their importance to those we are studying. This chapter will therefore show, amongst other things, why throughout this volume we use the term 'Trini' as a generalizing category – indeed, why we must.

Being Trini

Trinidad-Online.org (Plate 4.1) was intended as an exemplary representation of Trinidad as well as providing a range of facilities for being Trini online and for bringing together otherwise dispersed diasporic Trinidadians. On first sight, Trinidad-Online appeared to be a corporate website that included in its highly designed look a range of Trinidad-related facilities: bookshop, music store, penpal and personals service, postcard centre ('Where Emotions and Technology collide'), web-based email facility, a chat room (de Rumshop Lime) hosted on Yahoo with accompanying photograph archive and member-ship list, the Trinidad-Online webring, and an email list (Trinbago-Now) as well as an offline, hard-copy magazine called *Kalypso*.

In fact, the site was run entirely by a 22-year-old woman, a recent graduate of a top New England college, now working near New York in systems analysis and maintenance. Patricia had started her online operations while at college (where in fact she studied mainly liberal arts rather than computing), setting up one of the ambitious early Trinidadian sites that offered huge amounts of history and other information about the country. She seemed to pour vast amounts of her personal time into Trinidad-Online, and felt a dual responsibility: her mission was both to connect up Diasporic Trinis (and keep them connected to home) and to ensure that they were represented well to the rest of the world. Moreover, the site was both a mission and a business:

in addition to keenly and sincerely feeling her responsibility to promote and organize Trinidad online (and offline through the magazine), Patricia was intensely entrepreneurial, with several jobs, enterprises and projects always on the boil (itself a trait often said by Trinis to be typically 'Trini'). Business and mission were very far from incompatible; on the contrary, it was the professionalism with which she ran and projected her mission and her business that she felt would best bring Trinis together and promote their identity – hence, the corporate look and feel.

The webring was a way of formalizing links, including 76 Trinidad-related sites covering everything from business to politics, culture and personal websites. The chatroom facilities and mailing list extended the ways in which Trinis could connect up with each other, find each other. However, Patricia's project of organizing and presenting Trinidad online is not just a matter of information and connections. It is also a matter of providing the facilities for 'being Trini' online, for performing Trini-ness, making Trinidad manifest and indeed objectifying the participants' connectedness through hyperlinks, spaces in which to meet and styles of communicating. Internet facilities – above all the chat room – provide places in which to be Trini, and as part of this they become Trini places. That is to say, bits of the Internet become assimilated as Trini, indeed as part of Trinidad itself, in the process of using them to be and to represent Trinidad.

The chat room, 'de Rumshop Lime', had a membership similar to that of the largest dedicated Trinidadian ICQ list – 'de Trini Lime' (Plate 4.2). Here Trinis (and a few non-Trinis with some connection or affection for the place) place their nicknames and a few details as a basis for contacting Trinis online either individually or via a collective chat room. The webmaster (a Trini living away) proudly proclaimed them to have come from 40 different countries (though massively dominated by North America). As is detailed in Table 4.1 they were also mixed in terms of gender (though with more men), leaning towards the young, dominated by home-based Trinis and with Trinis abroad roughly equally split between the US and Canada.

The names of these chat rooms – de Rumshop Lime, de Trini Lime – evoke central aspects of Trinidadian culture. The 'lime' especially evokes the street

Table 4.1 Breakdown of Participants in 'de Rumshop Lime'

Location				*Gender*		*Age*		
Trinidad	Americas	UK	Other	Male	Female	0–18	19–23	24–90
1190	791	22	56	1176	879	668	575	613

corner, where males traditionally exchanged innuendo and banter with passing females and aimed to hear about whatever was happening (Lieber 1981; Eriksen 1990). The rumshop is a local, down-market drinking place, in the old days dominated by dominoes and rum, today often filled with ear-splitting music and Carib beer, another favourite place to lime, filling one's time with skilled banter, dancing and drifting onwards to other places (a street corner, a club, someone's house, another island). The term 'lime' is regarded as quintessentially Trini – both peculiar to the place and definitive of its people – and was regularly cited as the Trini pleasure they most wanted to recover on or through the Internet. In fact, 'liming' was the word generally used to describe chatting online and other non-serious uses of the Internet, as it would describe any similar hanging out. The Internet comes to be seen simply as liming extended to just another social space. Indeed, Trini youth could pursue their lime from school to home to street to ICQ (either at home or in a cybercafé, which was also a place to lime face-to-face) to fête.

So the internet as a place to hang around constituted a most obvious 'natural affinity' to Trini-ness (Plate 4.3). Even to a non-Trini, 'liming' could perfectly describe the flow of time and banter in a chat room (in Slater's previous work (1998), North Americans would use their own idiom to describe IRC as the world's biggest cocktail party). Of course, people from all around the world fill Yahoo chat rooms and ICQ in ways that might with futher study appear similar or different to the way Trinis hang out on the net. But to describe a chat room as 'liming' was to place it squarely in the centre of Trinidadian identity and to frame what one was doing online as a valued enactment of Trini-ness.

The term 'lime' highlights the free-flowing sociability of chat sites. An observer could look inside to find no one there; all of a sudden someone else spotted them and joined, a crowd would gather, people would drop in and out, regular characters were described and discussed. Characters were important: individual eccentricity plays out the stock Trini types found in literature such as Naipaul's (1959) *Miguel Street* and in Carnival characters. So in the chat room BriantheLover performed the most outrageous version of the red-hot, flirtatious predatory Trini male (and was constantly, affectionately, described to us as a real Trini 'type'), but every chat room had its equivalent SexyMan or similar, who was essential in keeping things going in what was seen as a specifically Trini way. There was endless talk of how hard one had partied last night, or wanted to party but couldn't because of work or being stuck in Toronto, or even how late de Rumshop Lime had gone on the night before. Indeed, given that so many people were liming from North America, with its very different lifestyle and time structure, they might lime online at some personal cost.

The most definitive feature of this liming is the 'ole talk', which variously refers simply to endless talk about nothing in particular, to talking a lot of 'shit', whether it be bragging, telling tall stories or – and this was the crucial thing – endless banter and ridicule, almost inevitably of a sexual nature. Trinis pride themselves on verbal dexterity typical of what Abrahams calls *The Man of Words in the West Indies* (1983), but here shared by women who are just as proficient at the ambiguous innuendo or the withering put-down. A second vital trait is the ability not to 'take things on'. This depends on a sense of 'cool' that means that traded insults are kept on the surface for batting to and fro like ping-pong balls, and there is a pride in the fact that they therefore do not hurt, cause resentment or penetrate into the wider being of those taking part. Trinis see this ability as differentiating them from other regions whose people would be seen as hot-tempered and unable to cope with such insults, especially in the area of sexuality, which is their richest field of production (for more detailed analysis see Miller 1994: 227–31). The third trait is the basic shared nationalism that means they can together praise but perhaps more often disparage Trinidadians (politicians, institutions, websites, etc.), but with an underlying affinity to Trinidad that would make the same negative comment by an outsider seem highly offensive.

There are two crucial points about Trini sexual banter that were lovingly recreated in all chat rooms (compare Yelvington 1995, 1996 on flirting in Trinidad factories). Firstly, that women give as good as they get, and indeed that a central theme be a woman's demonstration that she is far too much for the man in question (or her husband) to deal with either verbally or sexually ('boy! you cyan (can't) deal with me, it would give you a heart attack'). Secondly, that although the banter can be – indeed, should be – more outrageously suggestive with every additional remark, there is a complete ban on swear words or indeed any explicit sexual reference: the skill and pleasure is entirely in the use of the most extensive and creative range of metaphors for sexual acts, desires and body parts. In this, ole talk is quite the opposite of cuss outs, which are seriously heated and where the virtuoso filth of the language has nothing to do with sexual pleasures.

Both these points were routinely replicated to perfection on de Rumshop Lime, quite consciously and with repeated asides (to us as observers or to each other) pointing to precisely what they were doing (for examples of chat, see Plate 4.4). For example, Patricia, seen by herself and the others as a benign control freak, played the role of matriarch, keeping everyone in order. On countless occasions, the banter had gone way over the top (though still without a swear word) when Patricia entered the chat room: everyone would jokingly tell each other to hush up because the boss had arrived, and she would equally jokingly guess at what kind of mischief the playfully shamefaced chatters had got up to in her absence. We see here the dynamics of normative freedom, in which a sense of themselves as open and outrageous is transferred to the Internet alongside those normative structures and indeed the policing that renders it a meaningful and enjoyable enactment of a particular cultural identity. This kind of policing makes it Trini, both in replicating the role of the powerful woman, and in the policing of overt sexual crudity, which forces participants into replicating exactly the linguistic prowess that is considered archetypally Trini.

The idea and ideal of a specific genius of Trinidadian sexual linguistics was often explicit, as in an email list where a newbie (to Trinidad, not the Net) expressed appreciation of the use of innuendo in soca lyrics, but made the mistake of putting soca in the same sentence as rap. One of the angry responses was:

> Our music is suggestive but we have what rap and other modern music [don't] have . . . respect for the listeners and class.
>
> We can talk about sex and other forms of sexual innuendoes but we twist the lyrics in such a way that it won't offend the delicate and corrupt the young mind. there is a French phrase for it i cannot remember. . . . Patricia probably knows. [They agreed it was *double entendre*.]
>
> Think of that the next time you listen to Biggy, little Kim and the majority of the artist today before you compare our slightness with there blatant porn.

The policing of crudity was also connected with other limits that were seen as equally Trini – however intense the badinage, as we have noted, it should never get 'too hot', or touch too close. Hence there was a particularly Trini dislike of flaming as outright aggression, which was quite compatible with the almost continuous tone of disputation and bacchanal. The same features characterized Trini websites: they were clean, however obsessively they talked about bacchanal, sex, drink and fêting. The language was always proper (whether 'proper' English or clean 'dialect'). Moreover, the Internet was perceived as a public place with a foreign audience, and it was therefore deemed essential to maintain dignity, respectability and what was deemed a proper place in the world. Trinidadians showed a total fluency in switching between 'proper English' and patois, the latter written with complete orthographic and syntactic regularity. The two were mixed in highly conscious and playful ways on websites and in email too. As might be expected, the pattern depended on far more complex features than whether one was addressing other Trinis or not, rather involving context, matters at hand, displays of status or cultural capital and so on.

In these and other performative modes there was a great deal of unanimity about just what were the essential Trini traits and tastes that should be enacted, valued and spoken about in online contexts. In the cases of Trinis both home and away there was also an equal idealization of Trinidad (discussed below). The obvious difference was in the longing, nostalgia and pathos expressed by those away. There was a great emphasis on portraying oneself as 'a true Trini', and this involved above all an inexhaustible capacity to lime, as well as an appreciation of music, food, sexuality and being open to new people and experiences ('love meeting people from everywhere'). It also must include a deep love of Trinidad (and Trini sports teams of all sorts). The following quotes from self-descriptions posted on 'de Trini Lime' exemplify these points:

> *Some home-based Trinis:*
> A true true trini who loves to ole talk about any and everything under our beautiful island sun!
> Abigail: As a doubles eating, red-solo drinking, Maracas bathing, Nuts going, mango sucking, man gaping, sunday sleeping, card knocking, bar hopping, nice car driving Trini, of course I liming every weekend.
> I live for West Indies Cricket, love to listen to David Rudder, love all things Trini liming, drinking, feting and did i mention liming, drinking, & feting? And lets not forget the trini-woman dbest in the world!

> *Some Trinis away:*
> Ex-convent San'do girl, going to school here in Canada. Love liming, feting, bake and shark and plain ole talking. Want to come home real bad.
> If there is anyone who can tune my pan, contact me.
> All alyuh boy up here studyin' in dis cold ass country. Ah real missin' de limin on de block, eatin' doubles dong by UWI wit ah beastly cold [beer] in meh hand, alyuh drop meh ah line nah and make meh feel like ah home again.

These mailing list messages and fragments of chat bring to mind what Mary Douglas and Baron Isherwood (1979: 75) refer to as 'the enjoyment of sharing names'. Because the meanings of consumption goods and activities are central 'for making visible and stable the categories of culture' (1979: 59) they can be treated as an information system that is strategic in mapping out inclusion and exclusion with respect to a culture; access to and facility in using this information system is integral to reproducing one's social membership. There are serious senses in which 'being Trini' really is about the ability to use and share terms such as Carib, doubles, Maracas, bake and shark, and so on, and the Internet seems to offer particularly appropriate facilities for doing this. Although Douglas and Isherwood emphasize how class and gender inequalities in access to the sharing of names impact on social inclusion, the analysis works well for cultural identity, particularly in relation to Diaspora.

While all this adds up to something like a 'common culture', a minimal shared agenda for being Trini, it also adds up to a very idealized way of representing Trinidad (see the section on websites below). But whereas for home-based Trinis there was a strong desire to present an ideal Trinidad to the rest of the world both through one's online behaviour and one's websites (and a very strong desire to insist that Trinis away should do the same), the Diasporic Trinis clearly wanted to recover through re-enactment what they were missing. Perhaps the word 'warmth' – of climate, sociability, food, friendship, jumping up to music – captures this best.

The Diaspora View – Being an Online UK Trini

Part of our study focused specifically on UK Trinidadians, involving interviews with 25 informants, ten doing courses in the UK for around three years and the rest resident there. The total Trinidadian population in the UK is not large. Peach (1998: 210) gives 10,204 for London in 1991. Along with additional sources (email questionnaires, address books, ICQ chats) we could estimate that around half of all UK-based Trinidadians were online and used the internet, which in part would reflect their largely professional niche in British society. In almost every case there was a clear sense that the Internet had changed their relationship not only to individuals, as discussed in Chapter 3, but also to their sense of being a Diaspora Trinidadian.

UK-based Trinis, though far smaller in numbers than those in North America, fit exactly the model described above in their use of chat as a stage on which to perform Trini-ness. For example, the liming, ole talk and sexual banter may be seen as either a relief from or an antithesis to the UK host society. The banter, insult, and flirting that is seen as intrinsic to their being Trini would most likely be misunderstood or misconstrued (for example, as sexist and racist) if it took place within any context not specifically framed as Trinidadian. As with the traditional 'lime', there is a sense that people can relax, or be themselves, while engaged in this activity, free from the stress of having to watch their behaviour and conversation, except in terms of the normative version of freedom that is accepted as intrinsic to the activity (such as no swear words). Given the centrality of spontaneity in the definition of the traditional lime this kind of activity almost disappears when living within the UK, where it would be seen as intrusive and rude. At the same time the online lime thereby became a shared affirmation of what they see as the skills and delights that come from being Trinidadian *per se*. UK-based Trinis also enjoyed using localized dialect in chat, even if they would use a more standard English for their private e-mails. This also has the effect of making people feel inclusive – for example, it eliminates the class distinctions that might otherwise be associated with the difference between dialect and standard English. Anyone taking part can easily – if they have a mind to – move to standard English instantly, but as one person put it: 'I feel that only another Trini would be able to relate to d' ole talk and ting!'

This creation of a specifically Trinidadian internet space is a particular moment in the local history of the Internet itself. Five years prior to this research the relatively few Trinidadians that went on line abroad tended to be involved in user group culture, with its own traditions of flaming (attacks on opposing opinions) and such like. Sanpath gives an example of this (1997). At that time the identity of users tended to be given in terms of 'Caribbean' or 'West Indian', and an observer might have seen the Internet as a means for transcending local or national identity and creating a supranational regional sense of community. But as soon as new technologies developed, such as ICQ, and the numbers online permitted it, we see the regional community of users almost entirely disappear without any kind of legacy, to be replaced by this highly nationalistic category of Trinidadian. Although some call themselves Trinbagonian, most of those from Tobago either have to form their own chat group or accept the label Trini, with the occasional protest at the semantic exclusion of their island from the national label.

Clearly this also forms part of a sense of being able to remain 'Trini' while living abroad: 'The "talking" (via e-mail and ICQ, mainly) to people in Trinidad and reading more information, and more up-to-date information, on what's happening in Trinidad, have led me to feel closer to Trinidad, almost as if I'm living there – except no hot sun, no hot food and no cold Carib [beer].' While chat and ICQ only appeal to some of those living in the Diaspora, the one almost ubiquitous feature of internet use was reading the Trinidadian newspapers online. Both the main daily newspapers, *The Express* and *The Guardian*, have websites providing daily updates of a sample of their contents, and most Diaspora Trinis said they used them. Only one of our informants regularly used the other newspaper on line – the *Catholic News* (see Chapter 7), which he told us was also read by some of his friends.

Other uses are more partial or seasonal, such as the interest generated by Carnival. Carnival is a time when many expatriate Trinidadians would like to return to Trinidad to *play mas'* (join a masquerade), and quite a number had visited the TIDCO site that provides coverage of a wide range of Carnival activities, as well as the websites of individual mas' camps on which their costumes were displayed. Indeed the website most commonly favourably cited for both aesthetics and content was a mas' camp (Hart). Several UK Trinis had at least tried to look at the live webcam that TIDCO had set up over the Savannah (the high point of the parade). Indeed, one enterprising Trinidadian who had gone back to play mas' that year subsequently went through the archive on line in order to find and download a clip of him and his wife crossing the Savannah stage! Carnival was also the time of year when people might look at a wider range of Trinidadian websites, as part of a general feeling of nostalgia. Overall UK-based Trinis reckoned that around 50 per cent of their surfing was directed to Trinidad-related sites, which might include personal web-pages of friends, or a particular hobby such as philately. The Miss Universe site was also much visited at the time of the competition.

There was less than the expected interest in using the Internet to find other UK-based Trinis, which accords with the evidence that, compared to immigrants from other parts of the Caribbean, Trinidadians do not seem to form communities in the UK. If they do come together it will tend to be around Carnival, the recent growth in the Soca Fete scene for dancing and music, or to a lesser extent politics. In conclusion, the factor that makes the Internet so appropriate to UK-based Trinis is that it allows them to retain a strong sense of the specificity of Trinidadian culture and practice while not attempting to form any kind of UK-based Trinidadian community, or associate particularly with other Trinidadians in the UK.

Dealing with Difference

Trinidadians at home, as we have seen, used chat and ICQ to perform Trini-ness, and they made these media into Trini locations. Indeed, they could do this in more obviously grounded ways by virtue of being in the same physical locale: some could flow from schoolroom to ICQ to fête and back again (Plate 4.4). This extreme localization of the net exemplifies the distinction with which the chapter started between the Internet as something that overcomes distance as opposed to something that spatially dis-embeds social relations. For example, when talking of how chat or email allowed them to re-establish everyday contact with friends or family away, two boys in San Fernando might talk interchangeably of ICQ girlfriends in California or in the Trinidadian town of Arima. Both have intimate online female friends in the US, which involves frequent and long contacts on ICQ. These are treated as real and valued for all the reasons discussed in the previous chapter: trust in the reliability of the other party, excitement about the contact, sharing of intimacies – both everyday and long-term – about current problems and emotions – for example, divorced parents, hatred of school or work, etc. – and their effects on the self. But in both cases – and particularly in relation to the last point about intimacy – the boys felt that their friends' understanding of their Trini-ness was essential to understanding both them and their lives and problems.

Typically, when one of them chats to his online friend in California, who plays in a band, he feels that he is way behind her in global culture (TV schedules and soaps, film or music releases), which she fills him in on. But he is not intimidated, since he feels that Trinis do everything a whole lot better, if given half the chance (which they might not get in Trinidad). There was one big Alanis Morissette concert, happening near his friend, that he was desperate to go to. It was covered by a website, but that was nothing compared to the possibility of his friend's relaying the event to him via chat:

> I like [say] to her, You make sure you go to the concert and come and tell me all how it was, I wanna know how it was. What she seen and how she dressed and everything . . . I know I have found the site, and they show you the dates and stuff like that, but she can tell me how it was. [His voice goes expressly dull talking about the site; thrilled when talking about her account.]

In return, he relayed to her the Miss Universe experience, describing what was going on. This is all about exploring the world through each other's eyes at the level of very mundane social life. Central to knowing and being known through chat, as well as being the natural consequence of this process, is an exploration of difference that is construed entirely in terms of local cultures, for example through the difference between a Trini lime and that of Southern Californian youth culture:

> Q: Sounds like you know a lot about her everyday life
> A: Yeah – how it's the same, how it's different. . . . How she feel: like after they did this concert they didn't feel much tired, so they went liming and they went to the cinema in the middle of the night, and I'm like, whey you did *that*? After concerts? Our version of partying and their version of party is like two different things. When we party – when we come out, we like go to the mall, we spend a couple of hours in the mall, we come here, we chat online, check our email, we go to the movies and lime, 11.00 then we go home. A basic lime, you know. That's ok with us, you know, that's our lime . . . First time someone told me that they went to a concert then this happened, then this and this – How dey do all *dis*??? Their type of concert they will go and listen to one song, scream with them and then go and chill in the back for the rest of the night. *We* go in for the whole night, six hours straight we'll just be jumping up and screaming, six hours straight. Carnival is two days straight jumping up: jump up, scream, run to the next one . . . I can't understand you pay all this money to go in a concert and just static, do nothing. When we go to clubs on the weekends, we jump up, run around.

He is completely articulate about how the Internet places him into new, yet quite familiar, encounters. Like most Trinis, he feels he is open to a wide range of music. 'I have all kinds of music from the start. Had some appreciation of all music. But like hard, hard core metal I didn't really like it all too much. But I heard some and I kinda like it now. . . . Music on the net, it exposes it some more so they get the public to understand and give it appreciation.' The issue is respect and openness ('appreciation'), and this was always deemed to be intrinsic to Trini music, which moved from calypso to soca (soul – calypso cross-over) years ago and now mixes with anything from rap to techno. Online these encounters are seen in terms of an extension of this tradition of appropriation into Trinidadian-style music rather than as being submerged under a tidal wave of MP3s. Taste continues to discriminate. Though he likes rap mixed with progressive rock, he finds rappers too hardcore:

> With rap they have how life is hard for them and what they go through with the cops ... about their experiences, but it's totally different [he talks about New York or Rodney King which denote different experiences from 'quiet places' like Iowa or Arkansas]. In gangsta there is violence everywhere, in school, streets, etc. ... that's their way of life, that's how they are, that's how they grew up and that's how they know life as, that's how they think, that's how they experience life.
> Q: But it doesn't mean too much in terms of life down here?
> A: No, no, life down here: as with soca so with our culture, we take a little piece of everything and just mix it up. We have fun, yeah ... the racial issues doesn't come up that much – it's almost non-existent, we cannot afford to be racial because everyone's so mixed up ... You'd be racist against yourself.

But the difference is precisely what he likes on the net, 'it exposes you to what's out there, makes you value what you have more'. The technology allows them to go anywhere, 'besides watching the news, I learn from the sites and all, I find out what's going on here and there and all over the world and I like feel at home all over the net'. Unlike the Diaspora Trinis who are looking for other Trinis, most of those at home are using the net to be Trini in the wider world – talking to anybody and everybody, and being 'open-minded'. They constantly stated that they went online to engage in what were seen as global cultures (being where it's at in music, film, style). But this experience is then returned to Trinidad in the form of debriefing their schoolfriends and others on what they had seen that afternoon. The circle was squared by virtue of the fact – which we have constantly raised – that being cosmopolitan and 'open' was considered as intrinsic to being Trini, as was a powerful sense of the local, the trading of local knowledges and styles of interaction.

It made perfect sense that intrinsic to enacting one's cosmopolitanism was the urgency of informing the other about Trini-ness (especially given the public conviction that Trini-ness really was the best thing in the world). At the same time, exploring one's Trini-ness in these cosmopolitan spaces was clearly part of a process of defining and refining it, thereby understanding who one was and how one related to others and elsewheres. To repeat the boys' clear statement of this: 'it exposes you to what's out there, makes you value what you have more'.

There are precedents to this construction of identity in relation to difference. Much circulated on the net are the endless 'Ten ways to spot a Trini?' jokes (for an analysis of these see Miller 1993). There were many ways to 'spot' a Caribbean or Jamaican, and one list that hilariously detailed how to spot someone from Central Trinidad as opposed to the North-west Corridor (where the really rich live) as opposed to the South, etc. The point would seem to be that it is precisely through exploring differences associated with one's place, culture or nationality that Trinidadians deal with or position themselves within the potentially vertiginous space of endless difference that Internet media can open up. We now turn to the background to this encounter, which is the realization that most people in other countries have little or no knowledge of or interest in what, where or who the hell a Trinidadian or Trinidad is.

'What is Trinidad?'

> What I usually find with new people, they don't know about Trinidad. Their reaction is where is that, or what is that? It is some *thing* to them not some *where*. I think especially with what happened last night. The Miss Universe Pageant it has opened up a lot. I think from now I should be getting a different response from people when I say Trinidad. "Was that where the Miss Universe was held, we thought the culture was nice and everything." I think that is the exposure we have got from last night.
>
> Some of them have the idea that Trinidadians live up trees and swing from branches. I am big real world fan from MTV and tell them we have real world. Our schools are different, we wear uniforms. I don't show them specific websites or anything, I just tell them about it. They think the Caribbean is natural rain forest like the Amazon.

Trinidadians have already had plenty of exposure to the wider world, but this has tended to be with certain metropolitan areas in the US, the UK and Canada that have Trinidadian populations and at least some knowledge of Trinidad. As the two introductory quotations above illustrate, most people are not prepared for the sheer lack of knowledge about Trinidad as they encounter the more global reach of Internet chat, summed up in the form of the question 'What is Trinidad?' Partly because with high education levels their own knowledge of geography tends to be very good, they are often quite shocked at the constant ignorance that Trinidad is even a place, or, if known, what kind of place it is. In fact they tend to see this as part of a general lack of geographical knowledge held by some others. In particular they often note the parochialism of US residents, claiming they know more about other parts of the US than the Americans they chatting with, even though they have never been there.

At the same time, then, that the Internet opens the gates to a potential cosmopolitanism it also exposes a global parochialism that makes them feel insecure as to whether their own nationality constitutes a recognized place in the world at large. As we have noted, a large part of Internet chatting is about establishing points of sameness and difference: most Trinis seem to enjoy spending much time learning about other places such as Latvia or Argentina through the personal experiences of their correspondents. They also almost without exception take upon themselves with pleasure and alacrity the task of becoming personal ambassadors for Trinidad, telling the tale of Trinidad in their own terms, which is also the way they were learning about other places. With the exception of the TIDCO site (Plate 4.5), they made almost no use of existing Trinidadian information sites, such as the many portal sites discussed below; and indeed, Trinidadians living within Trinidad hardly ever looked at Trinidadian websites. The only frequently visited sites were those of the mas' camps, but they never directed others to these sites. It seems, then, that, in marked contrast to offline tourism, the online experience is almost always that of meeting a place through the person. As the case of chat, above, it is most often the intimate details of how that person faces problems with, for example, parents or life at college that is the preferred mode of encounter with another society. The closest analogy to experiencing life in another country (and explaining one's own) through the Internet is therefore penpals rather than (virtual) tourism.

The defining event in these encounters was the Miss Universe Pageant website (see Chapter 6). The site and the event itself were generally believed to be something of a turning-point in Trinidad's relation to the rest of the world. This was the first time that Trinidad had hosted an event that they believed would be watched on television (and to some extent the Internet) in almost every country in the world. It was also a competition in which Trinidad had traditionally done particular well, and were the current title-holders. This was seen as reasonable, in that Trinidadians tend to assume that Trinidadian women are particularly beautiful and stylish, and there was hardly any whisper of criticism, feminist disdain or worry about vulgarity that could counter the tide of national enthusiasm. There was also a general awareness that the associated website was of the same international standard as the competition itself, so that it represented the first wave of nationalist sentiment that had ever been addressed to a website as such.

The highlighting of nationalism in their representation of themselves to others went with a tendency to engage with others as members of national cultures and to engage with them through popular cultures. Of course, many of these conversations are conducted through common reference points in specifically North American popular culture. With the expansion of cable TV there had been a reinforcement of an already enthusiastic and knowledgeable immersion in American music, television and film. Compared with only a few years earlier, Miller noted a major increase in concern with designer labels, with American pop music and with television serials that occupy the main cable stations. This means that, for example, comparing which episodes of a soap opera have played in their respective countries provides chatters with that same sense of 'same yet different' in online encounters that people commonly report in traditional forms of tourism. Trinidadians would often aggressively assert their knowledge of this common popular culture to their correspondent in order to combat any suggestion that they are an unsophisticated 'third world' country.

But there were other elements of popular culture such cricket and soccer that had no US base and pointed to other regional associations. Overall, if there were preferred nationalities for correspondents and for potential relationships they would seem to be Canada and Australia. For example: 'I think Canadians have a similar education to us, compared to people in the US who are very low, they can't carry very good conversations. Canadians are the most intelligent. I have invited a few Canadians for the Miss Universe pageant, I would like to meet some of them, they are very interesting people.' Overall, it would be misleading to assume that experience of the net in itself leads either to nationalism as it was previously constituted or to cosmopolitanism. Rather, the primary advantage of the net was that it became yet another means of reconciling and preventing contradictions between these two ideals. Trinidadians could, for example, the more easily follow a British football team they supported. In one conversation in a taxi, a young woman from a conservative Muslim Indo-Trinidadian village said she could pursue her passion for a British team by buying football shirts and other paraphernalia from catalogues ordered via the Internet. Using the net to obtain CDs at US prices or MP3s for free aided anyone following the music scene. The fashion scene – particular sports labels – could be followed on key websites. But in every case they are following these cultural forms as Trinis. For example the most sustained use of fashion sites was schoolgirls downloading patterns to help inspire a local seamstress design their graduation gowns. This confidence in their ability to appropriate the world was partly based on a sense of unity ('one love') created defensively in relation both to Trinidad's smallness and marginality in relation to the rest of the world and to its internal ethnic divisions. Hence, there is a huge disapproval of any show of disunity, of putting down Trinidad in any way, and a great praise of anyone who represents Trinidad well.

In Trinidadian email lists, the question of Trinidad's relation to the world – how it was perceived and how it was doing competitively – was central to virtually every message over the six months we monitored it. For example, in May 1999 a list member wrote, overwhelmed by the peak of national awareness that had been reached because of the convergence of Miss Universe, Manchester United's European Finals football triumph and optimism about the upcoming cricket in Australia: 'It's such a nice feeling to be proud of your people's achievements', which he then thoroughly discussed. The simple fact that Dwight Yorke from Tobago plays for Manchester makes them as much an expression of Trini success as the national sports team. As one offering put it:

WE WIN, WE WIN GOOD GOD ALMIGHTY MANCHESTER UNITED
WIN . . .
yes folks in one of the greatest matches in history and i'm sure
for a long time it was the best. Imagine Bayern was 1 goal
ahead, Manchester was struggling, time had ended and it seemed it was all
over as they went into the final minute of the match, when in a flash two
goals were scored one after the other by Manchester. WOO
HOOOOOOOOOOOOOOOOOOOOOOOOOOOOO
YES!

We can attest to this ourselves. Standing in the Port of Spain bus terminal, it took us a minute or two to realize that the eruption around us really was a Manchester United goal and not an imminent riot.

One effect of this complex space of identity is that Trinidad was not necessarily deemed the ideal place to enact Trini-ness. Miller found in earlier research that after the oil boom was followed by recession, many middle-class Trinis felt that a certain level of consumption had become intrinsic to who they now were. When they migrated (in one notorious case to what was described as the land of 'real cornflakes'), it was with a sense that Trinidad no longer had the resources to be properly Trinidadian (Miller 1994: 272). This meshes with a constant doubt about whether Trinidad itself is so unified or supportive of its own people. For example, Patricia, the manager of Trinidad-Online, experienced the familiar paradox that she might not be able to be Trini if she had to return to Trinidad and pursue her Internet- and IT-based career there. She feared her positive achievements and abilities might be quashed or devalued back home, firstly because she was a woman, and could recite countless stories of Trini women with MIT engineering degrees now making coffee in Port of Spain offices. Secondly, she felt that Trinidadian firms would always offer work first to non-Trinis; and thirdly she and others felt there was a mistrust reserved specifically for returning Trinis, who are viewed as being both cynical and patronizing of those back home. Many examples were given of the 'Trini' heroes who had only been respected back home once they had been honoured abroad.

The Internet can not only bring these issues to the fore as topics, but can also be the actual location in which the same dramas are acted out. The only flame war we observed was typically over Miss Universe, and the suggestion that perhaps Miss Trinidad and Tobago could have been an Indian woman this year. In the ensuing discussion of ethnicity, list members had two responses: firstly, everyone vied with each other to demonstrate just how many 'races' were mixed into their blood; and secondly, they argued that race doesn't matter: 'one country, one people, one love'. Somewhere in the mayhem, someone suggested that they might support Miss Venezuela, which provoked a torrent of abuse about how typical it was for Trinidadians not to support each other. There is the common Caribbean accusation of 'crab antics' (Wilson 1973), that people would rather pull someone down than help them out of the barrel.

> Why do we as a people spend so much time and effort searching for weaknesses and faults (real or apparent) in our heroes instead of being thankful to them for what they have accomplished for our country? I mean, geez, yes we have a l'il oil and gas but our biggest resource is and will always be our people. Men and women whose dedication and effort have put our tiny 5000 sq. km. country on the world map. And what do we do in return? Reward them with negativity and dredge into their private lives just to find something to bring them down. Jealousy at its worst.

Indeed, faced with a barrage of critique the original supporter of Miss Venezuela replied:

> I have supported my country when all others like you have left it behind to seek your fortune . . . never to return because 'Trinidad doh have what foreign have.' I have worked hard, prayed harder and loved my country the hardest while Trinidadians continue to adopt other cultures other than their own like a pack of fools, oblivious to how they look to a world that does not accept copy cats.

This last sentence should be read in relation to the two boys encountering rap. There was, bizarrely perhaps, relatively little xenophobia in Trinidad, and only a secondary worry that the country was being swamped by foreign cultures (for example via cable TV or the Internet itself). If anything there was – to us – an almost unrealistic confidence that they could remain open to all cultures and remain themselves. But that stated precisely the problem of being Trini, either online or off: how to become more oneself through this openness, rather than less.

Some of the material in this chapter has touched on the contemporary literature on globalization, in particular the contrasting yet complementary dynamics of the local and global (although this theme has played a surprisingly small role in literature on the Internet). Much of globalization literature (e.g. Waters 1995) has connected the increasingly symbolic and informational content of economic and other flows to a bifurcated dynamic. On the one hand there are strong pressures to globalization in the sense that cultures and economies are dis-embedded from local contexts, in particular making national boundaries redundant as political, cultural or economic borders. On the other hand, the nation also disaggregates downwards, as it were, into more local or regional entities, into new re-embeddings and re-formations of identity. The connection between the two is often made, especially in relation to consumption, through the term 'glocalization': the assimilation of essentially transnational or global commodities and processes into local contexts whereby they are made sense of within grounded cultures (Howes 1996).

No doubt these are real and important processes, but they do not quite describe how Trini-ness and Trinidad are being reconstituted here. 'Glocalization' in particular focuses on the reception of global goods in a local context; what we have been describing is a projection of nationally-conceived projects and identities into a newly available global context. Moreover, Trini-ness in particular is an identity that in crucial respects has been conceived of as naturally global and cosmopolitan long before the Internet appeared. Trinis, as we have constantly argued, participate in this space to a surprising extent specifically as Trinis. The relation to world music culture may well be emblematic: there was very little indication, for example, that Trinis – unlike repressed minority groups in many countries around the world – were interested in subsuming themselves within Hip-hop nation; rather they confronted rap in terms of an assertion of their own national music culture.

Representing Trinidad

The Website as a Trap

The preceding sections have tended to focus on 'being Trini', and hence on chat; in turning to 'representing Trinidad', the focus is rather more on websites. There are generic differences between Internet media (though also a definite overlap). Moreover, we will be moving from a focus on Trini-ness in the broad sense of cultural specificity and identity to something much closer to overt nationalism (though again, the difference is hardly total). In turning from email and chat to the topic of websites we are not simply moving to another technology, but rather to something that has already emerged as a series of cultural forms with their own aesthetic and normativity. As is argued in more detail in Miller (2000), much of the efficacy of these sites may be captured by borrowing from a recent theory of art by Gell (1998). Two of his points in particular seem borne out by our material. The first is that websites are an expansion in space and time of their creators corresponding to what Gell called 'the distributed mind'. On analogy with the anthropological study of the Kula ring (Malinowski 1922; Munn 1986), much of the concern is to expand the fame and name of those who place themselves in this expanded realm. The second and related point is that the aesthetic of the medium is designed as a trap, something that will entice and bring into the circulation of exchange those web partners that are desired out of the entire pool of possible surfers.

It is hard to imagine an experience of surfing that does not include both the sense of flowing through ever-expanding circuits and the seduction of traps one encounters in this movement. Although surfers may go online with clear and limited intentions, who is not tempted to make the simple mouse clicks that lead one to follow a proffered link and soon send one hurtling down some channels carved out of cyberspace by the hypertext of website creators. Retrieving the original starting-point of this deviation can be difficult, but there is compensation in the unexpected encounters these detours have led to. In the case of the personal website it is not just anthropologists who are snared by the promise of insights into the intimacy of other people's sociality and revelations of the contradictions of the self.

The website as trap is always one point in a 'ring' or network that provides a potential flow of surfers to entrap. The more linked the site is, the more it provides a conduit for this flow of people, who can stop and enter into one's symbolic space and move on to spread one's name and fame. In the case of Trini websites, the ring that matters may be merely a circle of schoolfriends (Chapter 3) or a business community (Chapter 6); but it can also be the place of Trinidad itself on the Internet. In the latter case, one's own expanded fame is bound up with expanding the fame or presence of Trinidad itself on the Internet. More than this, however, as we noted in Chapter 3, the creation of networks objectified in hyperlinked websites takes on eminently practical functions in reproducing and expanding Trinidadian social structures, whether local or potentially global. School alumni lists and Patricia's Trinidad-Online webring are both conscious and practical attempts to link Trinidadians at a global level and to place them collectively on a global stage. The same can be said of portal sites such as TIDCO (see below) or the ISP portals, which attempt to organize the Trinidadian presence online by reducing the confusion (and obscurity) of Trini websites to one point of entry with clear information design that leads surfers efficiently on to the websites that they need to find. They are therefore traps that hope to capture an increased flow of surfers (and hopefully therefore some advertising revenue as well) and divert them into Trinidadian circuits. Hence, we are talking about more than symbolic seduction; these are practical projects of furthering social or even nationalistic prestige and interests (supported by government funding in the case of TIDCO). They can legitimately be thought of as strategies of positioning, even when they are less consciously formulated than in these cases.

Personal Nationalism

The most striking characteristic of post-teenage websites created by Trinidad-ians, both living in Trinidad and abroad, is the way this expansion of personal identity is subsumed within the sense of being Trinidadian. They use their resources to make a contribution to an overall sense of the fame or web-brilliance of Trinidad. The assumption is often that to understand the indiv-idual the viewer must first understand what it means to be Trinidadian. At its simplest this means the home-page is replete with various core symbols of that country, such as its flag, crest, a map and some basic statistics, while links lead to photographs and further information about Trinidad (Plate 4.6). This may even include the playing of the national anthem on the home page, or opening on to a Trinidad beach with the sound of waves crashing on the shore (Plate 4.7). Core symbols include those evocative of Carnival, calypso and soca music, Carib beer, or key Trinidadian personalities (e.g. Plate 4.8).

In some cases the process goes much further than this simple presentation of national culture and identity. Specifically Trinidadian idioms can be employed to explain the process by which strangers should become acquainted with the world of Trinis. For example Weslynne's Big Lime (see Plate 4.9) not only uses Trinbago symbols (she is from Tobago) but also demonstrates how the process of surfing can be translated into local terms. The surfer joins her on a lime, or is teased for being *macotious*, that is nosy about her private affairs, or is accused of being too *fass*, which implies that one is getting to know her more quickly than is considered civil in offline relation-ships. In a way this draws attention to the very lack of control the website constructor has over those who visit, and some ambivalence about the often very personal information that is included.

The sites often show a sense of space that ignores any hint of a real – virtual separation. There may be a map showing where the surfer has landed (i.e. in Trinidad), introduced in one case with, 'Well, for those of you who have no idea where you are.' Most sites have a separate page of links, which tend to include Trini-based ICQ, chat and information sites about Trinidad. A more evocative page starts with: 'Whoa! That was a big wave! Glad you surfed on in here . . . never mind the dents you put in the coral reef! Hi I'm Sharon, and I am thrilled to welcome you to my little piece of Paradise! I live on a tiny island (not much more than a blob covered with grass and trees, surrounded by water) called Trinidad, which is in the Caribbean.' What is striking is how many of these sites are actually run by Trinidadians currently at colleges in the US. Yet unless one is looking hard as a surfer one would assume one has landed on Trinidad, and not on a US college such as Cal-Tech (Plate 4.10).

The degree of Trinidadian content is often commented upon in its own right, for example: 'Welcome to yet another proud Trinidadian's homepage. Plenty Trini *ting* here. Browse around and enjoy it'. As well as links to statistics and photographs, key personalities may be represented, such as Ato Bolden, the world champion sprinter, and above all Wendy Fitzwilliam, the 1998 Miss Universe. Trini-style jokes are also common. The representation of Trinidad is often personalized through representations of the website author. Males, for example, now based as students at a US college, will often have images of themselves in a dinner jacket at their graduation party or with their family, females may be on their favourite beach and either may be seen in Carnival photographs (Plate 4.11).

The sites that have been described so far are still recognizably personal websites. There is, however, a further genre of sites that takes this much further. These are individuals who have taken upon themselves the role of producing national home-pages and have completely subsumed their own presence within the larger concern to present the nation. Many of these often large sites were constructed by college students or professionals living in North America who came relatively early to the Internet; they seem to have taken the responsibility for ensuring that their country had some representation in this new space, ensuring that despite the then lack of much Trinidadian presence online, the rest of the world should learn about it. In the most extreme cases the site will have a name such as the Unofficial Trinidad Home Pages, and the only sign of the individual concerned is at the base of the home-page, where it states who the site is maintained by. Some sites do this in a more particular style. For example a site called 'A Workbook on Trinidad and Tobago' (Plate 4.12) presents itself in the form of a traditional carnival figure, a crowing cock. It introduces itself in the following style, employing the classic banter of the traditional Carnival figure (Pearse 1988 [1956]):

For I am Chanticleer, cock-of-the-rock, master of this barnyard: your Tour Guide. I am the herald of the new and the old. My diversity, magnificent in the rising sun as I announce the new day, gives rise to the multitude of opportunities the day offers. My majestic silhouette as I put the day to rest, exemplifies the serenity of a job well done: I invite you now to follow my tracks. Click on the "Welcome" balloons for an enjoyable Virtual Tour of Trinidad & Tobago. To see and hear how we celebrate Christmas go to "Visit our Christmas Page" where there are recipes for preparing foods and drinks enjoyed in Trinidad & Tobago during the Christmas season.

In addition to a plethora of national symbols, these sites often include a list of local recipes, a small dictionary of common Creole terms, and in some cases instructions on how to compute the value of the Trinidadian dollar. There are two main concerns that dominate such sites. One set impress by the sheer number and scale of their links to other Trinidadian sites (sometimes over a hundred), leading to every ISP and many useful commercial sites, as well as news, weather, media and other information. They thereby make themselves into key portals to Trinidad as constituted on the net. Alternatively such sites attempt to be virtual guidebooks, with pages of photographs and accompanying texts that cover well-known tourist sites (for examples see Plate 4.13).

These two types of site – the virtual guidebook, and the links to Trinidad on the net – represent the core of the genre. Many other sites do not try to stand for Trinidad as a whole, but turn their personal websites into introductions to aspects of Trinidad. So we find one site representing traditional folklore, another an introduction to Trinidadian literature; another provides a guide to Gay surfers, another to stamp collectors and one is more pedagogic, trying to correct misconceptions about the origins of Trinidad. On occasion, as with the school age sites, they may use their guestlists as almost a newsgroup discussion of their favourite topic such as soca music. Surprisingly few of these sites are used for commercial purposes (Plate 4.14).

Those who created and maintained such sites tended to stress the low level of work involved, mainly in dealing with the emails they attracted. They were happy to take on this semi-official role as representatives of Trinidad. One noted that around half these emails were questions about Trinidad:

For example one recent e-mail asked me if we have facilities and food etc. for Jews in Trinidad. Just before Carnival I got an e-mail asking me if I knew the phone number of one of the bandleaders in Trinidad. Most of the people who email me for information I could help. About 20% of the e-mails are from companies trying to sell books or movies or some kind of related commercial activity connected with Trinidad. For example recently I got several emails from a group in New York asking if I could help promote a movie which was filmed in Trinidad. About 20% of the e-mails are from people saying how helpful my site has been to them.

This is especially gratifying for me. The other 10% of emails are from other Trinis who miss home and like to chat with other Trinis etc.

Another website that was not even attempting to be a portal to Trinidad attracted around 1,000 queries, of which about 45 per cent were Trinidadians. These included people looking for lost Trini friends, and people moving to the island wanting information, or coming for a vacation. There is some sensitivity to the way the country is represented. One web creator has received a complaint against a reference to 'Trinidad as a blob surrounded by water'. We also were roundly reprimanded for the 'aesthetic' map of Trinidad on our original project website, which was a nineteenth-century replica and thus hopelessly out of date and uninformative, according to the complainant. Most important was the way these website producers saw the positive representation of the country as a natural aspect of website production. As one put it: 'I think it fully represents me and my feelings about my home. I think this is a great place and I am very happy to live here and it shows.' If anything such speakers want to have more Trinidadian content on their websites, and are apologetic for the degree to which they might have emphasized themselves as individuals as against the country as a whole.

Websites are generally wrapped in yet another Trinidadian idiom: competitiveness. But any competition between website creators feeds into the large competition in which Trinidad itself is pitted against all other nations in a kind of global beauty contest (Wilk 1995). Comments left on website guestbooks reflect this combination of competitiveness and praise for showing Trinidad in the best light. The commentator is saying that this site is 'the best', not only in showing how great Trinidad is, but also how effectively Trinidadians can express their greatness, in this case through a really great website:

Thank God for you guys. Keep up the fantabulous work . . . my Trini people!!! One Love.

Great job! It really makes me happy to see that there are Trinidadians out there that are pushing themselves further by getting into computers and what it has to offer!

Allyuh kno de trini's and dem have de sweetness in we so leh meh see allyuh trini in unity. TOGETHER WE ASPIRE TOGETHER WE ACHIEVE

Let me begin by saying thank you for the exceptional work you have done in presenting our beautiful home to the world. . . . Your HomePage is very educational. Please allow me to share in your pride of our beautiful Islands. I looked forward to the day when I can retire back home.

Trini Hot Links

For a tiny country spanning 5128 sq. km with a population of only 1.3 million, T&T has an impressive online presence. Just look how many Trinis have their own homepages and all that.
Says something, doesn't it?
So to all them Trini netizens, keep the flag flying proud.
Just check out the number of sites, for Trinis, about Trinis, by Trinis!

Presenting Trinidadian Culture

In this section, we will argue against any attempt to generalize the way in which websites fit into the development and representation of cultural forms. Specifically, it will be shown that while in the case of mas' camp websites, the trend towards inauthenticity is accentuated, exactly the opposite process can be seen as the effect of steelband sites. If websites are concerned to spread the 'fame of Trinis' then Carnival should occupy a crucial position. As far as most Trinidadians are concerned the international reputation of Trinidadian culture is based above all on Carnival. Most Trinis assume that alongside Rio, Trinidad is THE internationally recognized Carnival, a view reinforced by the sheer scale of Carnivals in areas such as London, Toronto and Brooklyn that are largely based on the Trinidadian model. Although locally Carnival forms a triumvirate with steelband and calypso, the last two are more restricted to the Trinidadian Diaspora.

For the 1999 Carnival eleven mas' camps provided websites suggesting a core model (Plate 4.15). An overall theme will be established around the issue of pluralism. For example 'the true global village that is the circus has never concerned itself much with race, religion, or national origin' or 'we will explore many galaxies to meet their alien beings and sample their diverse cultures' (cf. Alleyne-Dettmers 1998). These themes then break into segments, which get down to the business of introducing the costumes around sub-themes such as 'Bring on the clowns' or 'It's magic.' Some, such as Peter Minshall, tend to elaborate on this model, while others, such as Children's Carnival, present more attenuated versions. Those directed to Jouvay tend to a more earthy flavour. For example, the `Mudders International' 1999 theme of 'ain't nothing but a mud thing' goes sequentially from 'foreplay' through 'commess' to 'ecstasy' and then 'sublime'.

The websites reveal that most costumes are sold out prior to Carnival, notwithstanding the fact that many charge around US$150 basically for a bikini with some ribbons attached. An article in the *Sunday Express* (14/2/

99) notes that the major mas' camp websites received around 13,000–18,000 'hits' that year, or 7,000 for a less well-known site, although Internet sales reached 10 per cent at the most. This reflects our finding: in the main people visited these sites to check out the costumes, making their final selection at the mas' camp. The government's site TIDCO (Plate 4.16) connects Carnival with the two other main representations of Trinidadian culture, that is Calypso and Pan (steelband). By comparison, specifically East Indian Trinidadian forms are largely absent from the web. In addition, many personal and portal websites contain considerable Carnival material such as photographs, and may also focus on Soca (Plate 4.17). A few individual Soca stars such as David Rudder and Machel Montano have their own sites (Plate 4.18).

Although these sites have only existed for a short time, this material is sufficient to contradict any simple analysis of the relationship between websites and prior cultural forms. At first glance these cultural sites seem to reflect merely the interests that lie behind them. So Minshall and Rudder have sites commensurate with their status as international stars. The mas' camps reflect the commercial imperative to sell costumes, while TIDCO reflects the government interest in selling Trinidad as a tourist destination. But behind this lie more subtle distinctions. Many Trinidadians see the 'pretty mas" of Carnival Monday and Tuesday as having lost something of its authenticity. It is seen as increasingly linked to both the elites within the country and the Diaspora, and also to foreign tourism. Stewart (1986) argues it has become a kind of hyper-enactment of Trinidadian culture sundered from its roots. This critique is exaggerated, however, and ignores the vitality of both the fêting that leads up to Carnival and the importance of Jouvay, both of which are as crucial to the mainsteam population today as they have ever been.

Nevertheless, this critique applies generally to those features that have come to dominate the websites themselves. There is a case for arguing that the websites exacerbate the separation of Carnival masquerade from its roots in Trinidadian popular history and culture. What the surfer tends to see is dominated by the largest bands, those directed most clearly to expatriate Trinidadians and Carnival tourists as well as to local elites, who can afford to pay large sums for 'bikinis with bits'. The sites in general depict white models, and strongly emphasize sponsorship. Activities locally associated with the mas' camps, such as costume creation and band launch fêtes, are hardly present on the web. Only the Jouvay sites mention fêtes and limes and link them back to the contexts that can deeply embed masquerades within the cultural life of the country. The governmental links are also intended mainly to service outside and particularly tourist interests. So an analysis of masquerade sites might well conclude that the internet has accentuated the trends in

Carnival that have been subject to trenchant critiques in recent years, and that threaten to alienate it from much of the population.

If, however, we compare the mas' camp sites to the sites devoted to steel-bands we see something altogether different. Within Trinidad, pan (the local term for steelband) is regarded as deeply rooted. Steelband was the music of the streets and the poor, and indeed famously likes to associate itself with the gang warfare that took place in its early days, when steelbands fiercely represented the geographical areas they were associated with. Today, however, much of this class distinction has gone, since pupils at the best schools are expected to learn pan and all social groups take pride in these instruments as a Trinidadian contribution to world music. While attracting increasing sponsorship, steelband has deep roots for Trinidadians, many of whom are involved in perfecting their technical abilities and engaging in competition.

The pan-related websites seek a closer connection to their popular base in Trinidadian life. Although there are some sophisticated sponsored sites such as Amoco Renegades, and a strong commercial interest based around the manufacturers of pan instruments, which sell in some quantity to international buyers, these are supplemented by a much more powerful amateur presence. Such sites reveal and cultivate a more devoted interest, often providing encyclopaedic information about all aspects of the instrument's history and performance (Plate 4.19). There is also a pan webring that links pan sites and exchanges information to keep the pan *aficionados* connected. Even the commercial sites have far more information than is really required for com-mercial purposes. For example, both Lincoln Enterprises and Trinidad and Tobago Instruments include extensive technical details, while Pan Pelau provides a kind of sequential exhibition about the making of a steelpan (Plate 4.20). Much of this is essentially educational. So commercial pan websites all relate back to their context of production and consumption. This is also true of the strong foreign presence in steelband websites. The fullest listing of the Trinidad bands is on a foreign site, which lovingly includes information on every band in the country as well as separate biographies for 52 individuals.

So with steelband, as with masquerade, the effect of the Internet has been to accentuate a previously existing trend in their relationship to the wider Trinidadian society. In the case of mas' camp sites this might be seen as a trajectory towards inauthenticity, while in the case of steelband it appears as a deepening of the local and international grounding of steelband in its history, the perfecting of its playing and the mutual respect that is generated amongst artists and manufacturers. To conclude: the same phenomenon of websites can deepen and entrench a cultural form or can separate and displace it. The calypso and soca sites fall into a position somewhere between these two extremes, where their commercial and tourist appeal are fairly seamlessly and unthreateningly wedded to their elaboration of amateur enthusiasms.

A Nationalist Industry

We have seen that in order to understand the way in which cultural websites represent Trinidad we need to understand their place within wider commercial and governmental projects, as when the TIDCO site integrates Carnival within what is effectively a government economic programme to promote tourism and other non-oil-based industry. In turn, government and commercial interests are grounded in national projects and values. Chapter 1 already introduced the ideal of the free market entrepreneur as not just a figure Trindadians felt they could realize through the Internet, but one experienced rather surprisingly as particularly Trinidadian. This is not because Trinidadians are especially given to neo-liberal economics *per se*. On the contrary, there is much resentment over the treatment of Caribbean banana exports and the powerlessness they feel against the structural adjustment that is being foisted upon them, and discussions about the degree to which telecommunications should be deregulated will be met in the next chapter.

The point we are making here is rather different. In many ways Trinidadians' sense of the economy is much closer to that in the United States than that in Europe. The independence movement led by Eric Williams that created modern Trinidadians' passionate nationalism refused the more socialist versions promulgated by figures such as C. L. R. James, and instead argued for a rapid industrialization based if need be on foreign capital. After 1973 it achieved this using the muscle of oil wealth. The intention was to be perceived as a First World nation rather than as a Third World dependant. Today what is celebrated in entrepreneurialism is an ideal of being able to compete, to 'hold one's head up', within the global free market. It is the analogy with freedom itself that counts. So what is espoused is not an economic ideology such as neo-liberalism, but an avenue for Trinidadian national aspirations. Being Trini here means being a successful Trini in the new free-flowing information age symbolically represented by the Internet.

So being Trini in chat and representing Trinidad in websites is complemented by the development of a Trinidadian internet industry. The industry sees itself as in the vanguard of attempts to develop Trinidad within and not outside the global business environment to which it is increasingly exposed. As in chat, both the smallness and the potential of Trinidad are experienced on a new and expanded stage. These points were made with such clarity and conviction in an interview with the head of the vanguard IT company in Trinidad that we will quote him at length:

We have a lot of nationals that are of a very high literacy level. That is in all aspects of literacy, going all the way through computer literacy. We believe that with the right exposure and the right experience, this is very exportable. Not in the physical sense, but in the intellectual sense for revenue. Maybe about five years ago I was chairman of the Free Zone Company. I was there because I presented to the then government that I believe that the future of this company was in going up the food chain in information processing. Going above Barbados in data processing into the higher levels. I believe it is the solution to a number of the unemployment problems. A way to really increase the wealth and decrease the poverty of this country. I believe that from a nationalistic standpoint and I believe it's also a great business opportunity. A lot of the studies that have been done when you look at Trinidad and our wage rates and so forth and you compare that against the quality of life that we enjoy, you realize that this is an ideal destination for developing that resource. When people say that you are educating people simply to lose them to the developed world–I totally disagree with that. What we do not yet have here is enough of an industry that attracts back not just our nationals that have left, but in fact foreigners who now desire to develop their careers here. Why? The perception of living on an island, sitting down on a beach and developing high-tech code for Microsoft, it's very appealing. So the attraction is the opposite direction. So we've got to get some big names in here, we've got to do some cutting edge stuff. Expats who have come to live here in Trinidad don't want to go home. Currently, we have been very successful. We are actually re-exporting training services to Cisco. My guys are currently doing Cisco training for GTE and Bell South. We plan to do the same thing for Oracle, we plan to do the same thing with networking technology. Some of the project team that worked on the internet site are right now doing Macromedia programming for the guy who does Miss Universe Inc., who is a contractor.

I think it's just fundamentally that we have a great education system. I hear many people, who should know better, say that they are going to the US to live. When you ask them why, they say for my kids. That could absolutely be the worst reason in the world. If you look at our education system compared to the public education in the United States, we're light years ahead of them. Just at the high school level, we're generating and putting out a fundamental kind of training in our teenagers that gives them the capacity to learn and absorb. I've got tons of people that work for me that don't have degrees, but just went through that simple high school system, from prestige school to junior and senior secondary, which is supposedly at the bottom of the education scale. These people worked for me and could hold their own in any IT organization doing programming. I think Trinidad is an industrialized country, has created an opportunity in its home market to cultivate these IT skills, unlike some of the other Caribbean destinations. So, with our energy sector and our oil dollars, and all the investment that government has made in the public sector in its own right, we have the opportunities in our companies to market ourselves and have our people at least pay the bills to develop the skills sets more and hone them. So because of the existing economy, which is the largest really in the English-speaking Caribbean, you have this base of IT skill sets that are being honed.

Much of this resonates with the original ambitions of Eric Williams (see 1942, 1969) in forging Trinidad and Tobago as a nation-state. Coming back to Trinidad with his Oxford Doctorate on the relationship between capitalism and slavery, he saw education and economic advancement as the key to the future for the descendants of slaves and indentured labourers. Neither we as authors nor you as readers need to be in sympathy with either the aspirations of nationalism nor those of entrepeneurialism. What this volume as a study of the Internet does require, however, is the act of empathy and analysis that allows us to understand why such aspirations arouse such passion and why in particular the Internet and IT technologies would seem to so many speakers in this chapter to be the form in which they might finally be realized.

Conclusion

One of the delights of ethnography is finding out just how wrong one can be. It seemed self-evident that the Internet would lead to a reduction in national identity and nationalism, since the Internet is so clearly a global rather than a national phenomenon. The substance of this chapter demonstrates how misguided our forecasts turned out to be. Of all the parameters of identity it is nationalism that is most fully strengthened and extended within what we termed in the first chapter the dynamics of positioning. This is not at all to say that nationalism or national identity is unchanged. Quite the contrary.

Nationalism was not bound to grow in this way. Only a few years previously, many Trinidadians were participating in an earlier Internet phase of Usenet newsgroups and flaming that produced a regional, Caribbean-wide internet community. This more or less disappeared once a specifically Trinidadian presence could reach a certain critical mass. Of course, it is quite possible that any generalization we make now about nationalism could turn out two years down the line to be just as misleading and short-term. But it is not just that what seemed to be a historical trend went into reverse. In investigating the commercial sector (Chapter 6) we were constantly told that for business purposes operating merely at the level of Trinidad was *passé* and that everybody was now trying to work at a Caribbean level. The content of this chapter is therefore a lesson in not merely reading off the consumption of Internet use from the pressing needs of its producers and commercial agents.

Why then are Trinidadian websites so nationalistic? This has to be understood from the stance of our theme of expansive realization. In the case of nationalism what we have is an as yet not fully realized aspiration. As Miller argued in 1994 (314–22), nationalism comes across as something of a triumphant resistance to forces such as slavery, colonialism, and imperialism. This was a people being transported, ruled, and mixed up by forces against which they had no power and yet somehow striving to create and perform a unity that transcends both history and difference. But this nationalism is still fragile. Indeed, the initial experience of Trinidadians going online is to make it appear still more fragile, given that they find people hardly know that Trinidad is a place, let alone where it is and what it is like.

So it would be quite wrong to assess this phenomenon of internet nationalism as though it was merely one more case of some general category of nationalisms. This is a most particular nationalism: it is not Bosnia or Ireland or Spain or Quebec. There are several parochial reasons why Trinidadians use the Internet to realize nationalism in a situation where it has been fragile and largely suppressed by more powerful forces. This particular internet nationalism is clearly not opposed to, but strengthened and refined by, the increasingly global context within which it is enacted. Not only that; but what here is addressed as national identity (which we recognize as extremely problematic) in other places could be manifest in some quite other form of cultural identity. The important point that we have demonstrated in this chapter is how by virtue of being global the Internet can gift people back their sense of themselves as special and particular.

5

The Political Economy
of the Internet

We recognize that the information technology area is the future . . . because we have been so dependent on our oil resources, and the government wants to diversify the economy and create employment. Information technology is one of the centres that they want to focus on . . . We can have many companies set up here online with the companies in the United States, doing work, processing and all these things, there's a lot of interest in doing it here because of the literacy level and the English and the external communication links, but because of this monopoly situation, it is holding back a lot of investments and job creation (Interview, Director of Telecommunications).

What this quotation makes clear is that whereas the preceding three chapters document developments that have occurred across many dispersed actors and interests both personal and technical, in this and the following chapter we will encounter already clear 'paradigms' about Internet provision and Internet business as the basis for future national economic development. This accounts for the structure of this chapter. The first half presents the major players in the Internet Political Economy, that is, the Internet Service Providers, the government and the principal Telecomms company. We shall explain why there is a dominant narrative according to which the telecomms company has become the bottleneck preventing further and faster Internet development. We will show how this simple tale ignores a much more complex and ambiguous situation in which both the telecomms company and the government have to face in several directions at once. To understand the discrepancies between what we can observe and the ways this is presented in this narrative, we then investigate the paradigm – that is the ideals that are held about how such developments ought to be proceeding. We also have to appreciate that these are not simply paradigms about technological change, but have deep resonances in Trinidad's constructions of its values and its self-conception.

This is why the second half of this chapter is about the nature of the paradigm itself. It provides the background and context for the main 'story' that has been told. The paradigm draws attention to how the players are not just jockeying for position, but are struggling over the way their strategies are represented and legitimized. Throughout there is a powerful sense of the impending: of trying to be in the right place with respect to what appears to be a series of inevitable developments where the pitfalls are as frightening as the rewards seem enchanting. It is in this area of political economy that we find the themes of freedom and normativity in the context of prior colonialism and dependency rendered particularly explicit.

The manner in which these paradigms and practices are embedded in larger struggles over basic values links this and the previous chapter. There we saw how the use of the Internet was driven by national concerns and indeed nationalism – the dynamics of position by which Trinidadians seek to be 'at home' in the Internet world. The chapter ended with an examination of how this applied as much to the Internet business as to Internet use. This chapter starts from where the last chapter left off – that is the political economy of Internet provision. Many of the same themes will emerge, with huge institutional bodies such as the telecomms company being judged by very similar criteria. Indeed it will be striking how factors that we would expect to become dominant when it comes to political economy, such as profitability, seem almost secondary – they emerge as a future struggle over telecomms markets, but for now they are displaced by the current struggle over who is to blame for any delays in the development of Internet provision.

Introduction: Developing Trinidad

'. . . this is not a tourist island: not even Tobago . . . In every other island in the Caribbean all the roads go to the beach. In Trinidad all the roads go to the interior, because that's where the oil fields are, that's where the cane grows, the cocoa grows. Trinidad has had an industrial base since Churchill made the British ocean-going battle fleet burn oil instead of coal in 1938 . . .' (a Trinidadian advertising director).

Trinidadians ideally place themselves in the First World and do not see themselves as an underdeveloped or Third World nation. This positioning is fraught with worry, self-doubt and self-criticism (though very quick to rise to any external criticism or doubt). Nonetheless, the Internet washed Trinidad up on to global shores at an opportune moment of both economic buoyancy and strategic planning in the direction of both deregulation and diversification: both features seemed capable of bringing Trinidad even closer to the unqualified place on the global stage that it always felt it merited. The Internet appeared, then, as a vehicle of what we have called an expansive realization of Trinidad's self-identity.

Trinidad has followed an industrial path to development based on petro-chemicals and allied industries that distinguishes it from most of the other Caribbean islands, and puts it closer to neighbouring Venezuela: agriculture and tourism (except in Tobago) are minor in terms of output, trade and employment. At the time of fieldwork in 1999, there was a general sense of economic optimism and buoyancy amongst both the general population and the business community. Following a long period of decline throughout the 1980s, after the hugely prosperous oil years, by 1999 Trinidad was into its sixth successive year of economic growth (3.2 per cent in 1998) under conditions of consistently low inflation (around 4 per cent) and stable exchange rates. Although 1998 had slumped slightly (largely as a result of shocks such as world financial crisis, bad weather, and another oil price decline) this was interpreted as a blip in a generally healthy pattern. Even energy price slumps were largely offset by massive foreign direct investment (largely American) in new petrochemical and shipping plant (e.g. the Port Lisas Development Corporation) and major new liquefied natural gas plants were about to come on-stream. Forecasts all suggested that growth rates for 1999 and beyond would be high, and in line with the best in the region. Even if it were not justified (or were qualified by high unemployment, between 14 and 16 per cent), Trinidadians encountered the Internet through a popular sense of confidence and optimism.

Present and future development as a modern industrial economy was seen as bound up with two issues in which the Internet was deeply implicated: liberalization and diversification. Firstly, Trinidad obtained high marks from the international agencies like the World Bank, the IMF and the Inter-American Development Bank for its economic management. Following econ-omic policy restructuring in 1995, the government has maintained a tight fiscal and monetary policy with low budget deficits, despite revenue problems (associated with slowing oil production and declining oil prices); it maintained exchange rate stability through market mechanisms (which involved relatively high interest rates); and was pursuing open-market policies both in terms of external relations (removal of tariff and other barriers in line with WTO agreements) and internal restructuring or privatization of remaining public enterprises such as gasoline distribution and the sugar monopoly Caroni. If the oil price bounces back as it has done in the autumn of 1999 Trinidad may yet (*pace* the predictions of Miller 1997: 35–57) escape the worst consequences of structural adjustment seen elsewhere in the Caribbean.

As with many other countries and international agencies (and indeed under their encouragement or pressure through treaties such as WTO), Trinidadian institutions understood the Internet very much in relation to liberalization policies. The Internet, firstly, was a means to further free trade, not only as the major free trade zone of the new millennium but also as a symbolic and strategic wedge in prising government and business apart: the second part of this chapter examines how the association of Internet with liberalization focused all attention on the deregulation of telecommunications. Secondly, and conversely, it was felt that the Internet could only work and be properly exploited if seen in terms of deregulation and free trade. This generates the paradigm we return to later on.

In addition to liberalization, Trinidad encountered the Internet in the context of enormous pressure to diversify its economy away from dependence on petrochemicals. Access to the oil fields shared with Venezuela produced a development pattern in Trinidad unlike those of most other Caribbean islands (wealthier, more industrial, urban and educated) with the exceptions of Barbados, Bermuda and the Bahamas. However, the centrality of petro-chemicals opened Trinidad to the twin perils of declining output from maturing fields and oscillations in energy prices, which could have an overwhelming impact on a broad range of economic indicators and government revenues. In fact, oil dependence had already diminished to the extent that 'since oil now accounts for about 15 per cent of value added in the domestic economy, growth in other sectors can moderate its negative effects if those sectors could be energized to be the engine of growth and employment generation' (Haque 1999). The Internet could seem a godsend in this context. Significantly, the first Trinidadian website was actually TIDCO, the government-supported agency whose brief is to foster non-oil enterprise: at the very beginning, the Internet was both an area of economic activity in its own right and also a means of marshalling resources for diversification. The site included informa-tion on Trinidad (history, culture, economy, politics) , help in doing business with the country and sites for a huge range of local businesses. TIDCO has since developed this in ever more sophisticated ways, its business- and trade-related websites matching its coverage of culture discussed in the last chapter.

A range of diversification strategies have been pursued since Independence (Ryan 1988). Firstly, investment in developments outwards from oil-based production such as methanol, iron and steel, shipping facilities (as with Port Lisas) and liquid fuels. Secondly, a major drive to develop tourism, in which the Miss Universe competition (see Chapter 6) was a major symbolic move. The tourist route met with some scepticism on two counts. Firstly, Trinis don't believe that they are cut out for service industries (an oft-repeated comment: Jamaicans and Trinidadians hate serving customers; but Trinis, unlike the Jamaicans, are unable to hide this fact). Secondly, whereas Tobago fits the postcard picture of the tropical island paradise, urban and industrial Trinidad simply does not.

On the other hand, information technology in general, and the Internet in particular, opened up a range of diversification strategies that were constantly mooted by informants (not just governmental ones), many of whom assumed both that these options were well suited to Trinidadian character and 'human resource assets' and that they were inevitably part of the country's future. The extended quotation that ended the last chapter exemplified the way this was manifested as concrete strategies of positioning for many of our informants. In essence it was clear to them that the future of Trinidad depended upon seizing a moment in which Trinidad has finally realized its competitive advantage in its capacity to provide high-value technological services to the world.

Networks and Bottlenecks

The scale of these high hopes for the future can be measured by the intense frustration, which currently dominates all discussion, at what is seen as the slow pace of Internet development in the country. This frustration is almost obsessively focused on what is known as the 'bottleneck' represented by the local telecommunications monopoly, TSTT. It practically and symbolically focused articulations of both the golden opportunity to be grasped and the forces holding the country back. Above all, if the 'level playing-field' metaphor dominated a sense of how the Internet might allow Trinidad to realize its potential on a global stage by being freed to do so, the story of 'the bottleneck' was particularly bitter: the very telecommunications infrastructure that should deliver them to this playing-field was itself far from level: it was a monopoly part-owned by a British multinational, which seemed literally to be keeping them from the world and from their destiny, from an expansive realization of their rightful global position, accomplished through free exploitation of the technical and entrepreneurial potentials of the new media in the form of ecommerce (discussed in the next chapter).

The term 'bottleneck' could refer confusingly to many things, but all of them revolved around the way in which TSTT, the local telecommunications monopoly, occupied a strategic economic, political and technical position, which it used – according to popular belief – to hold the country back through inefficiency, irrationality or abuse of power. The primary point here is not to determine the extent to which these charges are true. In this particular case, the implication of Trinidadians' understanding the barriers to Internet (hence national) development almost exclusively in terms of the TSTT bottleneck was to reduce political-economic debate almost entirely to pressure for deregulation.

TSTT was jointly owned by the Trinidadian government (51 per cent) and the British-based multinational Cable and Wireless (from now on C&W) (49 per cent), which was in a similar, sometimes stronger, position in several other Caribbean islands (see below). This partnership arose from a restructuring and partial privatization of a traditional public utility in 1989, one result of which was 'the agreement' between C&W and the government, which was to run until 2009. Its contents were secret and hotly disputed, but were presumed to establish TSTT's legal monopoly over voice transmission in Trinidad, and therefore to rule out any access to the Internet other than through TSTT (companies using satellite links would be considered as potential alternative phone systems).

We will expand on all of these issues below; but here we will briefly summarize the huge shadow this situation cast over all infrastructural provision. Firstly, TSTT controlled the *external* pipeline, the connection between Trinidad and the Internet backbone, through one (or later two) cables that carried all voice and data: Americas 1 and 2. The alleged dearth of bandwidth in Trinidad (hence slow connections, and brakes on expansion of access and viable Internet media) were popularly blamed on the inadequacy of TSTT's investment in this connection, and on its monopolistic obstruction of alternative provision (wireless and satellite). Secondly, TSTT controlled the Internet 'gateway' as well as 'the local loop': through its monopoly over phone lines, switching and the equipment at the end of the incoming cables, TSTT controlled everything from the backbone to 'the last mile' (the wires going into individual houses). In this gateway capacity TSTT was charged with failure to make adequate investment and properly to supply cabling and phone lines (so that, for example, ISPs found themselves waiting 18 months to establish a new point of presence, or went without an adequate number of dial-up lines). Quality of connection is the subject of endless complaint and a little debate. It is generally experienced as extremely slow, especially during business hours: patterns of usage are skewed by this traffic, so that many people say they go online largely at night, some only after midnight. This was blamed on the inefficiency and irrationality of a monopoly and bureaucratic enterprise; but it was also blamed on something far more malicious, which links to the third problem with TSTT: it was an Internet Service Provider itself, as well as the monopolistic supplier of all telecommunications facilities on which competing ISPs depended. Indeed, it was by far the largest ISP in the country. Therefore it could easily be charged with unfair market power: it could use its position to offer rates or facilities that other ISPs could not hope to match, and it could use its position to kill (or threaten to kill) competitors by failing to provide necessary infrastructure or by simply cutting off their phone lines.

'The bottleneck' was therefore a very precise and apt visual image: TSTT sat astride the Internet pipeline coming to this island, old, leaky, squeezing its way through a half-open tap in the TSTT offices, beyond which the company could cause either desperate drought or the flowering of a Caribbean oasis. The pipeline metaphor is additionally resonant because of Trinidad's intimate connection with oil: as one ISP owner put it, TSTT has effectively turned off the gas on the telecomms revolution and information economy, or reduced to a trickle the flow needed to sustain either private profit or national development. Hence, 'the bottleneck' emerges from our ethnographic engagement in several forms: as a set of practical, everyday problems in getting online and doing business there; as an ideological issue about national development; as a political task posed to the industry and country; and as a part of the uncertainty of the business environment in the region, including knowing what was and was not legal.

The External Feed

TSTT's monopoly on the external link was widely blamed for an inadequacy of bandwidth in Trinidad. It was actually unclear whether any inadequacy existed. Figures about bandwidth supply into the country were tossed about with great abandon by all parties, most with very little understanding of how data is transmitted and what bandwidth actually meant. More technical people tended to argue that the external link was not the crux, and in any case, Americas 2 was being laid even as we spoke, evidence of considerable C&W regional investment. As the Director of Telecommunications put it:

I really don't know where the problem lies, because as far as I know we have Americas 1 fibre-optic cable coming to the country, we have satellite links out of the country, we have the eastern microwave system going out of the country. Americas 1 is being upgraded to Americas 2 right now. They are going ahead with the work, because the cable is coming in. So when one looks at it, you would want to think that there shouldn't be a problem. External circuit: what I have been told is that the bottleneck is really not the external circuit, the bottleneck is really an internal telephone company problem.

Whether or not bandwidth was adequate, there was a massive demand for alternative technologies and there were several waiting in the wings, intensifying a sense that irresistible pressures were being built up against TSTT's position. Partly, there was the claim that opening the external link to competition would reduce both prices and the power of TSTT. However, there was a broader pressure that arose from other entrepreneurial projects that sought to take advantage of opportunities opening up in the new technological spaces of telecommunications and felt unfairly hindered during a very narrow temporal window of opportunity. Hence, despite TSTT's official monopoly, most ISPs have satellite feeds that could at a moment's notice bypass TSTT completely. They are simply waiting for the green light to link their ISP operations into such broader telecommunications strategies (see below).

Moreover, alternative external feeds may hook more effectively into other technologies, allowing more effective use of convergences that may take an enterprise well beyond simply being a better or bigger ISP: e.g. Rave (an ISP) aimed to establish regional, satellite-based corporate communications services; several other companies sought to exploit convergences between cellular, Internet and pager technologies; and the most ambitious operator (Computers & Communications) were upgrading their entire cable TV network for two-way cable modem delivery of Internet, which would also allow them to bypass the phone system, feeding it through either satellite or TSTT's link.

Gateways and Local Loops

Whether or not the external cable was adequate, there were the issues of the 'gateway' (TSTT controlled the interface between the incoming cable and the ISPs, including itself) and 'interconnectivity' to 'the local loop' (the connection to and quality of the phone system itself, through which the Internet is actually delivered to individual PCs). This was where most technical people located the problems. The general opinion is that TSTT, a self-serving but short-sighted dinosaur from an earlier techno-political age, was pushed into making any Internet provision at all in 1995: it responded to mounting and frustrated public demand for the Internet in Trinidad, and to government pressure to bring Trinidad into the late modern world. As one ISP manager put it: 'Rumour has it that the then Minister of Finance in 1995 told TSTT to get off their arses and put in a gateway, something TSTT was ambivalent about, not much revenue, hassle, etc.' It was popularly believed that TSTT moved into the business without enthusiasm or understanding of the scale of the phenomenon. Alternatively, it is argued they understood it all too well, but that they, and some would add the government as major shareholder, saw a huge threat to their profits as a phone company. Either way, TSTT was primarily a telecomms company: 'The infrastructure, the telephone company infrastructure, really wasn't set up to provide a high-speed-data kind of communication, it's really a voice network. They have been trying to increase the capacity and then there is the poor quality because it's sort of integrated with their voice network.' There have been subsequent criticisms of all the stages in provision: the gateway was inadequate to the traffic levels, as were the provision of numbers of phone lines, the cost of interconnectivity, the provision of equipment to establish new points of presence and so on. Moreover, they were seen as short-sighted and petty: 'TSTT says if you are making a buck using our phone lines, then we should get a piece of that,' said a competing ISP owner.

TSTT's position was no different from any other national telecomms provider. It is ultimately a public-service provider of a national utility that requires massive investment and is engaged in a highly detailed and fiddly operation. This includes costly relations with a huge number of individual customers – virtually the entire population. As an ISP manager told us, 'Our main problem is really dial up lines, the local loop, the last mile – nobody really wants to do that, who wants to lay all that cable?' At the same time, the biggest and most profitable revenue comes from long-distance traffic, where the costs are minimal compared to that of 'the last mile', a zone filled with hassles and costs. The Internet has the double disadvantage for TSTT of requiring a whole new layer of service provision at the local level while at the same time threatening their long-distance revenues: as another ISP manager put it: 'Every time anyone sends an email to their brother or sister in Brooklyn or London or Toronto, it's a phone call that wasn't made.' Moreover, 'voice over IP' (Internet telephony) potentially reduces *all* long-distance calls to local ones.

Our research was carried out at the end of a two-month period of monumental disruption of TSTT's Internet service during which time they were rectifying the gateway problem by installing entirely new equipment, as well as a new cable. Ironically, although TSTT was basically doing the 'right' thing finally and making provision for the titanic growth in Internet traffic, which they had not foreseen, the disruption coincided with a heightened period of attack on their monopoly position. The disruption was not interpreted in terms of investment in the future but as further evidence of TSTT's inability to provide the services that people wanted. TSTT had long passed the point at which it could ever be construed to be doing anything right.

The ISP Business: The Players

TSTT not only sells bandwidth and facilities to independent ISPs; it also itself runs the largest ISP by far. This is widely felt to be anomalous, giving rise to unfair competition, conflicts of interest and abuse of power. 'We buy our Internet connection from them, and they also sell dialup access . . . so we compete with our provider. There are no laws governing their operations or provision or cross-subsidization of services.' It also meant that TSTT could be publicly held responsible for virtually anything that went wrong with the Internet, from the backbone to one's modem. TSTT managed to appear both domineering and reluctant: although the company claim that they carried out extensive market research and planning exercises throughout 1994–5, the public perception is that they did nothing until pushed by a government and public opinion that understood the deep perils of not getting on to the net and that when they did kick into gear they did so in a confused way. Their decision to go into the ISP business themselves was taken as evidence of their confusion. Their subsequent use of their technical position to offer numerous points of presence, free phone access numbers and the hefty bribe of free connection hours per month was taken as evidence of unfair competition: 'Sell the service at $150 and give away $600 of toll charges . . . I don't know if it was a purely defensive move but I know they are losing money on it.'

Of the ISP rivals to TSTT, Opus, the company through which Trinidad entered the Internet age in 1995, was anomalous in having its roots in pre-Internet BBS (Bulletin Board) services and computer subcultures, going commercial mainly to fund expansion of what was really a hobbyist enthusiasm. This has carried through into a relatively small (600) but loyal user base with a techie image and user profile, and competition on service rather than price. Yet even for Opus the connectivity business is not profitable: their money comes from corporate installations of network security (antivirus) and network management. And its owner conceptualizes its future in terms of embedding the ISP within a larger media/telecomms operation, in this case a kind of national intranet. Wow.net was another early entrant, associated with all manner of big money, including financial capital that later moved on into the computer retailing business. Just after the end of research, it was sold out to an earlier ISP owner.

InterServe was also a very early player, launched in September 1995 with extravagant promises of investment returns; as one informant put it, 'The only industries that I know that give you that you tend to go to jail for.' Of course, it just didn't happen: hence the take-over by C&C, for whom it now serves mainly residential accounts. CaribLink was founded by a refugee from InterServe and took the route of higher prices and slower, more stable growth, often through corporate defectors from InterServe. It too was purchased by C&C, for whom it now serves corporate accounts. C&C itself entered the market as potentially the biggest player in Trinidadian, if not Caribbean, telecommunications, and was the source of the quotation that ended the last chapter and the website that begins the next. Its third ISP, CableNet, was actually formed by C&C in late 1996, opening early 1997, to build on their already dominant cable TV business. Most subscriptions came with computers bought from C&C. Altogether C&C had about 7,500 accounts, and a history of 100 per cent growth per year. At this stage its main aim was to introduce cable modems to Trinidad, a promise almost but not quite yet delivered owing to the huge cost of upgrading their network and the TSTT bottleneck on satellite feeds.

Satellite feed was critical to the final and the newest ISP entrant RaveTT (online February 1999). It was funded by revenues from the lucrative Trinidadian pager market. It is looking to synergies between pagers, email and the Internet business. It was relying on getting a green light to run lines that could carry voice and an ISP based on satellite downlinks. In the future they hoped to set up total communications solutions for regional companies. So far they were tiny, stymied, they claimed, by TSTT's failure to set up POPs for them, which was the subject of a court case.

The current tally of seven ISPs is rather more than the one or two found on some other small islands. Each has its own website (see Plate 5.1), and these exhibit a range of styles. Some emphasize services, such as web directories and rates charged; others include extras such as games and things for kids. While this plethora might be beneficial for consumers (who nonetheless complained all the time), it meant intense competition on both price and service under the adverse commercial conditions of very low margins, technical limits on growth (most ISPs claimed to be 'maxed out' already on number of lines) and high rates of 'churn' (movement of customers between ISPs). Above all – it was claimed – there was TSTT's anomalous position as an ISP and as the telecomms provider to ISPs.

This history of ISP development suggests three main phases. The first was based on creating business models and jockeying to establish working relations with TSTT. The second involved extremely intense competition starting from late 1996 and lasting till late 1998, in which every offer made by any ISP was bettered by TSTT. This was almost entirely price competition, and focused on the two central features of connect time and call charges. TSTT kicked off both with the introduction of a toll-free and non-metered line: customers could call an 800 number and connect for free up to an hourly limit per month, after which connect time was quite expensive. ISPs scrambled to meet this challenge by both moving over to non-metered services and trying to expand their POPs (which all claim was significantly frustrated by TSTT, acting in its capacity as interconnect monopolist). The generally agreed upshot of this was a huge increase in the market and huge decline in service, as well as profitability, as all lines became swamped and the technical limits of the system were exposed.

Hence Phase Three: alongside all the other forces of deregulation (such as WTO agreements) was the simple fact that the price war had to give way to a return to metered services, competition on service quality, and the desperate need to increase bandwidth not only to improve service (speed and connection time) but also to expand business. All fingers pointed back to TSTT. At the same time, technological alternatives to various aspects of Internet provision, such as satellite, cellular and cable, were now immediately available both to get round the TSTT blockage and – perhaps more important but less acknowledged – to move the potentially bigger players into more profitable synergies (for example, with cable TV or the bandwidth resale business).

Clearly some of the blame that landed on TSTT reflects intensified dynamics that are present throughout the ISP world. In some respects TSTT is little different from the other ISPs (with the exception of Opus) in supporting its ISP business through its general telecomms strengths. Rave, the C&C companies and Wow are all backed by much bigger money, and WOW had just sold out to even bigger money. Even Opus is part of a larger business. The representative of one ISP said that the history of the Internet in Trinidad has involved: 'huge amounts of money being poured into it. InterServe went bust twice, it did huge marketing campaigns, we sat back and looked at these guys and said well, we don't have those pockets but we also can't see how they're making money out of it. We don't think they ever did.' What all this means, in fact, is that the ISP business as a stand-alone enterprise is not viable in Trinidad: Opus is exploring the idea of online communities and a return to BBS-style services, and is in any case seeking most of its revenue from anti-virus and security software. Wow.net's founder was desperate to go where the real money now is: buying and selling bandwidth (see below). In the case of Computers and Controls and RaveTT, the ISPs are part of much larger computer/telecomms empires, and significantly involve ambitions to derive revenues from corporate rather than domestic Internet use.

The simple story was that there was no money in the business. In fact, while the public story played out as an attack on TSTT as a bottleneck and distortion on the specific market for ISPs, in fact something rather different was taking shape: it was much more like a proxy war in which the ISPs were part of a broader initiative against TSTT as a telecomms monopoly, not on behalf of the ISP business (which was not viable) but on behalf of major regional players who wanted a slice of a deregulated telecomms cake. The real issue is a jockeying for position to get at the revenues that arise from deregulation of telecomms and media. This explains something of the profiles of the seven ISPs, several of which are in effect markers put down for something bigger.

The 'Agreement'

We are arguing, then, that the battle over the ISP business – while it looks very important as a battle over access to the Internet – was ultimately seen by most players as a small part of a war over telecommunications strategies:

the issue is that TSTT stands directly in the way of major money in telecomms. Or rather its owners – C&W and the Trinidadian government – stand in the way on the basis of 'the agreement'.

'The agreement', signed in 1989, and due to run for 20 years, was a 'shareholders' agreement' between C&W (49 per cent) and the government (51 per cent). It was negotiated in advance of the Internet, and at a point during which Trinidad politics was focused on privatization but not competition or deregulation: that is to say, it was part of a typically 1980s divestment of a national utility company that simply transferred a monopoly into private hands.

The agreement was at the centre of a very surreal situation. It was this document that established the entire structure of telecommunications provision in Trinidad, and was universally regarded as wielding veto power. And yet it was a confidential document that very few people had seen; it had not been tested in the courts; and everyone we talked to had a different account of what it contained. There was much talk of loopholes and grey areas; yet in point of fact even the main lines of the contract were shrouded in mystery. Finally, while some parties took a legalistic approach to the telecomms situation – one that focused on what could be done within the legal agreements, or how they could be legally set aside – others recognized that the situation was actually held together by power: TSTT could enforce its own version of the agreement, up to a point, because of its operational control over the phone service (in short, it could cut off recalcitrant parties). The government could choose whether or not to use its own power (both as majority shareholder and as elected authority) to enforce more or less open interpretations of the agreement. And C&W seemed ready to wage in Trinidad the same kind of rearguard battle royal they were waging on other islands where they were similarly ensconced (above all, Barbados, Jamaica and Dominica) in order to keep their authority and profits.

In most accounts the crux of the agreement was that TSTT was granted a monopoly over voice transmission within Trinidad and between Trinidad and the rest of the world: hence their control over external cables. When this agreement was reached – in advance of the Internet – data transmission was not only easily accommodated by existing lines and posed no special problems, but had also not significantly converged with telecomms (for instance, its most advanced form in 1989, EDI, was accommodated by leased lines clearly separate from voice). The Internet obviously changed all that, not only in terms of the exponentially increasing demand for raw bandwidth, but also in terms of fudging the distinction between data and voice transmission. Internet telephony, or 'voice over IP', means that voice transmission could and no doubt would be embedded, undetectably, in any data flow.

Any strict interpretation of the agreement therefore would require all tele-comms to be routed through the TSTT monopoly.

The voice/data distinction was buttressed by two other legal-governmental concerns. Firstly, the Director of Telecommunications was concerned that ISPs remained completely unregulated and required no licence (anyone could set up as an ISP) and – despite one isolated speech by the Prime Minister expressing concern about children's access to pornography, and some concern about unlicensed gambling – there was no apparent worry as to what they did with it. The basis for this was that 'We view [an Internet service] as an information service, not as a telecomm service.' Should the ISPs start acting as or being perceived as telecomms providers (or indeed as television or radio broadcasters) they would then be subject to regulation simply because tele-communications historically has always been regulated (and always taxed through VAT and licence fees). The Director of Telecommunications' concern seemed to be entirely political: he opposed all regulation; if ISPs were con-strued as telecomms companies he would be faced with the inconvenient political problem of deregulating all telecommunications in order to keep these new markets open: 'It's difficult for the government to simply just give up these things' – especially the revenue. This was precisely the kind of head-on confrontation that all governments had avoided over the years.

Secondly, the voice/data distinction seemed to dovetail with the separating out of value-added services from primary provision, a distinction that was central to WTO commitments. If ISPs were information services operating on top of telecomms infrastructures then their freedom was required under international treaties. In point of fact, TSTT's monopoly over voice, as Rave and others pointed out, was conceptually anomalous, leaky and ill-enforced. For example, various corporate voice networks such as leased lines or wireless trunk and radio systems had been allowed to carry on; and in fact wireless itself, in the form of cellphones, was a direct abrogation of the monopoly. Indeed, in the event, the licensing of cellular phone services (rather than permission for satellite feeds into the Internet) was the wooden stake that the government planned to drive into the heart of the monopoly. Moreover, the provision of cellular licences could be legitimated in terms of explicit commitments undertaken by the nation under WTO. All of this was taken as further evidence that the TSTT monopoly was simply a corrupt and inefficient vested interest, a licence to print money in opposition to the public interest, and legitimated on grounds that were patently absurd. Nonetheless, TSTT rested its position on the voice/data distinction.

Publicly, the entire battle was brewing up around satellite feeds. If ISPs could get their connection to the Internet backbone via satellite, they could bypass TSTT completely, creating a competitive market. The case for allowing satellite delivery was partly made on the basis of bandwidth scarcity: the pipeline into the country was said to be technologically too narrow. As has already been noted, there was much confusion over this, and in any case the pipeline was being upgraded. In fact, what satellite would do was to open up price competition, reduce ISPs dependency on TSTT for external feed, though not for interconnectivity, and, perhaps most importantly of all, completely undermine the conceptual basis of TSTT's legal and commercial position, for then any ISP would effectively and indeed inevitably become another telecommunications provider carrying voice traffic and data traffic. In immediate terms – already experienced on the balance sheet of TSTT, as on that of every other telecomms operator in the world – who would make a long-distance call, the highest-profit sector in the business, when you can reach anywhere in the world over the Internet for the price of a local call?

For the moment, however, everyone stuck to the distinction between the voice transmission business of a telecomms company and the data trans-mission business of an ISP. It took the following practical form: all the ISPs had satellite connections, but officially they used them for download only: data came down the connection to supplement the TSTT feed; data went out of the country only through TSTT. This preserved the notion that ISP provision was not about people talking to each other, but only about trans-ferring data. Of course, even this cumbersome fiction did not stop anyone from using Internet telephony, though the speeds still made for stilted con-versations. However, it maintained the status quo for the moment while nonetheless allowing the ISPs to ready themselves in terms of both skills and equipment for the inevitable day when that status quo finally disintegrated. For the moment, the letter of the (actually unknown) law was observed: even the satellite downlinks were treated as supplemental only; it emerged as a high-profile issue mainly when TSTT was down or overwhelmed (as it was around the time of our research). The irony was that if TSTT was down everyone looked around to see who was still up and running, which told them who in truth was using satellite to bypass TSTT. But this had not yet reached the point of open confrontation: we were in a phoney war as yet.

External feeds were only one part of the picture. The other was inter-connectivity into the local phone system. This broke down into two easily conflated issues: firstly, the ISPs ran dial-up services, so they were reliant on TSTT's actual phone systems to allow people to dial up and download information; above all, this meant they needed provision of lots of POPs (points of presence), phone numbers with lots of lines into their banks of modems. The quality of their service, in a highly competitive market, thus depended on TSTT's phone provision. Secondly, in order to do business (in most cases more lucrative other business) they obviously needed phones. Quite simply, TSTT could turn these off. Stories were rife both about TSTT's flexing its muscles by switching off the lines for an hour or two; and about its failures to provide essential services, arising from either inefficiency or unfair competition or both. But here too TSTT was about to face serious competition. CableNet was at last nearly ready to provide a cable modem service that could do the last mile by cable rather than TSTT phone lines; also, there was an emerging cellular market of both pagers and third-generation cell phones that could deliver email and eventually Internet direct to handsets, albeit still at slow speeds.

In other words, there were technologies and eager institutions ready, able and indeed frothing at the mouth with both frustration and greed to break the TSTT monopoly and open up the market. This readiness made a mockery of the distinctions and rights upon which the agreement was based. It also built up a pervasive feeling that destruction of the monopoly was only a matter of time: it was both inevitable and imminent. This inevitability was construed technologically (alternatives to TSTT were both efficient and convergent); economically (force of demand, of international competition); and politically (no government or law could resist these forces).

The Government

'The agreement' was murky and secretive, and produced a murky, confused market. Who was TSTT? Was it a front for C&W, a front for the Government or was it another autonomous body? Indeed, who was the government? The murkiness was increased by the government's lack of position. Indeed, because the situation was viewed as ludicrous and untenable, it was also viewed as predominantly an issue of political will: in the end, the question was, why hasn't the government acted? Why could it not enforce a loose interpretation? Why could it not pressure TSTT into better service provision even within the terms of the agreement? Moreover, this was a government that portrayed itself as modernizing both through free-market policies and through diversification of the economy, partly into hi-tech sectors.

Firstly, there was a widespread view that the government's lack of political will had self-interested if not corrupt motives. Why was it, people constantly asked, that despite a being majority shareholder with a 51 per cent stake, the government seemed unable to overrule the minority shareholder, C&W? Why was it that C&W had more control over TSTT here than in, say, Jamaica, where it had a majority holding (a 70 per cent stake)? Cronyism was one clear suggestion. Revenues were another: the government received from TSTT 3 per cent of gross receipts from international traffic. Although government officials argued that this did not amount to much after collection costs, it loomed large in the public's mind, and it is hard to believe that it did not loom large in the mind of a government committed to reduction of public debt under conditions in which its other main revenue sources depended on the highly unstable price of oil.

A second issue, discussed above, was the fact that the Internet had no clear departmental home. The Director of Telecommunications, reporting to the Minister of Information, was very explicit that the Internet is the concern of his office 'only . . . when there is a telecomms problem', which he largely defined as 'linkage to the outside world'. This was not bureaucratic hair-splitting: it was central to his position, outlined above, that information services should not be regulated or licensed at all, which they would have to be if as telecomms companies they were covered by his office. He acknowledged that, 'The fact that we are not licensing, the fact that we have no regulations or so, in itself, probably presents people with problems. That they don't know who to go to, because a lot of them think that the people in this business should be licensed, they should be regulated. But I don't want to get involved in that.'

Finally, the suspicion of political weakness was confirmed by the refusal of any direct confrontation with TSTT or C&W, and a constant resort to what were seen as legal fictions or verbal circumlocutions. Two examples were very typical. Rave reported an interesting legalism whereby one could apply for satellite or wireless licences, but the government would not actually give you one. Instead, they gave you a copy of a letter sent from the Director of Telecomms to the Minister of Information supporting the application and requesting ministerial approval of it. People set up operations on this basis in such a way that they could not be shut down, but the government none-theless avoided confrontation with C&W or TSTT.

The other example was a newspaper story about TSTT that was being discussed by everyone during our research trip. In it, a government spokesman from the Ministry of Information was quoted as saying that 'there is no monopoly in Internet services in Trinidad'. The government and some others (including Rave) interpreted this statement positively as the government clearly acknowledging that there is no *legal* monopoly on data that the government considers to be value-added service and therefore open to com-petition under WTO commitments. (They are also committed under WTO to open up satellite.) But everyone else interpreted it as *legalism*, as cynical legalistic word-play: of course anyone can set up an ISP, but they can only access the Internet legally through TSTT, which therefore has them all over a barrel; and this therefore constitutes a monopoly situation in any meaningful sense of the word. As an ISP noted, how can you deal with a government that resorts to these empty word games?

This focus on the government's supposed lack of political will has to be set within the broader geo-political picture, yet few people did this: we constantly found ourselves reminding them that TSTT was jointly owned by C&W; everyday speech tended to refer only to TSTT and the government. C&W of course have huge clout, and were fighting ferociously throughout their Caribbean holdings: they had engaged in high-profile court cases again ISPs, for example in Dominica, and there were stories of major confrontations both in and out of court in Jamaica. 'They have a substantial investment in the Caribbean area and they control all over the country, and they are fighting anywhere they can to hold on to their monopolies. But they have been losing, they've lost in Bermuda, they lost in Jamaica, Dominica, and here they have to renegotiate. So they are fighting it.'

Nonetheless, by the time of our research visit, public impatience, industry fury and government concern had reached a decisive point:

> We have passed the stage of trying to get the telephone company to respond to problems and provide the country with the necessary infrastructure, and so it's not just Internet. We have telephone service and other areas. The business community is very dissatisfied with the provision of data circuits to link their offices, computer-to-computer communication. So there is a lot of complaints about the telephone service. Well, the government has taken the decision to break the monopoly and we expect to start renegotiating the agreement very soon. We have already decided to license cellular – additional cellular users. All value-added service are open [under WTO], but of course, you still depend on the telephone company to lease circuit. And the basic service is what we're after now to break up and will be renegotiated. The agreement has to be renegotiated. . . . Because the country can't afford to continue with this poor infrastructure.

Evidently the balance had shifted in government. The Director of Communications could not have been more unequivocal: 'The policy right now is to break up the monopoly, licence cellular, open it up, have an open market. Let the market decide. So there is no opposition in government any more – whatever opposition there was, they are being pushed aside. So I think they have accepted that we have no choice but to go this route.'

How was this to be achieved? There was still far from a clear answer to that. There was talk, but no evidence of re-negotiation of the agreement itself. Instead, soon after the end of our fieldwork the government announced the completely unexpected step of divesting itself of its majority shareholding, transferring it to a holding company, and opening the shares up for sale without any restructuring. Most surprisingly, this seemed to open up an option for C&W to buy a controlling share from the new holding company. The rumours going round were that the government was simply trying to raise funds by selling off assets (it was simultaneously divesting itself of two other major holdings). Implausible this may be; but it testifies to the cynicism with which the government position was viewed: this would imply a concern only for short-term gain rather than attention to a situation it should be dis-interestedly adjudicating. It then appeared to bar C&W from such a bid, leading C&W to threaten to walk out of the agreement immediately, without any chance of their position being properly transferred.

In the meantime the government seemed to have turned a blind eye to loopholes such as satellite downloads that eat away at TSTT's monopoly. Further attrition would be caused by the decision to open up the market for wireless and cellular licences. In addition, the government was moving cellular in to areas where TSTT was showing its inadequacy: for example, the provision through cellular of a wireless solution to gaining quick Internet access for all the country's six hundred schools. Cellular and cable were finally being almost encouraged to subvert the prior voice/data distinctions to create a communication field with several competing players, more or less as the major companies had hoped. Not surprisingly, TSTT no longer knew if it represented C&W against the government or vice versa.

The Paradigm

Trinidad and Tobago, according to the World Bank, has the potential to become one of the most accessible and efficient regional business, financial and manu-facturing centres of the Caribbean. The country is also well placed to increase its information service exports. English and Computer Literacy rates are amongst the highest in the Caribbean. (from Ministry of Public Administration and Informa-tion Report, 1998)

Internet-based businesses as well as businesses that re-organize themselves around Internet facilities seemed to play directly to a host of Trinidadian competitive advantages that were constantly enumerated by informants. The main advantages that informants consistently stressed lay in superlative 'human resources' that could be purchased by foreign companies at relatively low rates. Trinidad could provide an English-speaking labour force that was highly educated and had already developed an impressive skills base not only in technical matters but also in design, marketing and project management. This pool of high-tech workers was within easy physical reach of the US, and of course instant electronic reach. It was avid for and responsive to technology transfers, was cosmopolitan and comfortable working in and with foreign contexts. At the same time, because of exchange rates, lower overheads and generally lower wage levels, it undercut Northern wages by large amounts. Trinidadians could already point this out in a small way in terms of the cost of web design in Trinidad versus US.

> Trinidad is located near to their shores where people can get to Trinidad and back to the United States in one day. If these potential customers come to our shores for a few days they are guaranteed communication, 'eating curry', sun, sand and 'sin'. We are looking at some of these as major incentives, if they can offer this and still charge you less than what a programmer will charge you in US, maybe half or a third.

This combination of advantages, clearly expressed in the extended quotation that ended the last chapter, added up to one major new model of development: Trinidad would do high-value-added offshore work for foreign companies. The Internet would provide much of the content of the work – webdesign, database and other programming, intranet and extranet projects and project management – as well as the means for accomplishing it: with the Internet, this kind of work can literally be done anywhere. Trinidadian companies could enter into contracts and more long-term relationships with large American companies that would also be recompensed in skill and technology transfers. The exemplification of this model will be the Miss Universe web site (see Chapter 6), which produced work at the cutting edge of Internet technology for North American firms, simultaneously effecting important technology and skills transfers for future work, as well as garnering more business. In the process the company (Computers and Control) that produced the site and its charismatic entrepreneurial leadership (who provided the extended quote in Chapter 4) managed to realize on an expansive world stage an ideal of Trinidad's place in global modernity.

In fact, as we shall see in the next chapter, this mapped out a far from easy road. Miss Universe was an exciting test case, but done for free, on spec. Webdesign, portals and other businesses that focused on Internet products (as opposed to simply selling goods over the Internet, as in ecommerce) had not yet found a business model that made money. Several people quoted to us a current business guru, Michael Porter (1998) whose book, *The Competitive Advantage of Nations*, argued that when barriers to entry are low, nobody makes money. Barriers to entering the Internet business are low. The same issues were replicated at a national level: Trinidad is of course not the only country of the periphery aiming at this relationship to the metropolis, and informants were clear that their own way of competing with these countries had to be compatible with their sense of who they were as a country, both practically and symbolically. Trinidad, as we have said, is not a low-wage, unskilled and largely service or agriculture economy. It is highly educated, entrepreneurial and industrial. They felt a clear need to distinguish their development path from two alternatives with which they would none-theless have to compete: these were symbolized by Barbados and India. Barbados represents a proletarian path, arising from an earlier moment of post-industrialization, which there and elsewhere in the Caribbean (Pearson 1993; Freeman 1998) comprises low-skilled and low-waged data-entry for US firms. Trinidadian entrepreneurs would rather see themselves as subsuming Bajan (the local term for Barbadian) labour within their own more global schemes. For example, a Trinidadian conglomerate (Neal and Massy) operates a software company currently sited in Barbados; however, they argue that Barbados does not offer a sufficiently skilled workforce (partly because of the size of the university there) and they have therefore been advertising for Trinidadians. (Elsewhere in the region, Bermuda also offers an offshore centre for insurance and other financial services, based on high-level IT, open markets and stable government.)

The other developmental model is India, which a Trinidadian might con-sider a *lumpen* path, paradoxically, in that it comprises very high-level software design and coding expertise, working in close conjunction with US companies. However, it does so at very low wages. One informant, himself ethnically Indian, argued that they could never compete with India, 'dollar for dollar', because Indian fees are 'give away' and because Trinidadian want to ensure facilities for staff that 'makes sure of their self-worth and proper working environment. We do not want Neal and Massy to be like a sweatshop or a contract race.'

Competitive advantages pushed to their limits would make nonsense of Trinidadian identity – Trinis feel themselves to be educated, modern First World citizens, not key-pressing Bajans or desperate Indians. Moreover, most local entrepreneurs present themselves as part of a national project: they are not just capitalists, they are always Trini capitalists. And in this context they operate with a much more complex version of competitive advantage than simply wage-labour rates. Factors such as 'sun, sand and sin' – an almost proverbial notion these days – have a tricksterish quality to them that fits the Trini self-image neatly. Tobago is destined for general tourism, but Trinidad will accept expatriate businesspeople, seeing itself rather as a hi-tech player on the global stage that also entertains its clients. Businesspeople talk as though an ability to design websites and to create cultural contexts for living can be seamlessly connected through style and cool, which is perhaps felt to be one of their really major competitive advantages. Local executives relish tales of foreign expatriates breaking into tears at the thought of leaving Trinidad when their posting is finished.

The model of high-value-added high-tech/high-skilled offshore subcontracting is only one model of positioning opened up by the Internet. Two more models stood out. Firstly, Internet facilities enable new levels of internal corporate integration (often operationalized as intranets), whereby a Trinidadian firm can have offices (or partners) in Seattle, Caracas, Jamaica, etc, all integrated on a real-time basis. This was not only important on the North–South axis, but was possibly already more advanced on a regional basis: the Internet certainly helped integrate multi-island operations in the Caribbean through systems that had been set up by Trinidadian companies.

The second model is the obvious one of market integration: 'the market' is drawn from a universe that comprises 'anyone with Internet access', or even 'anyone who has a friend or relative with Internet access', and that 'anyone' could feasibly be 'anywhere' at any time. We will discuss this in the next chapter under the concept of ecommerce. Here we might note, in relation to global positioning, that this new economic geography could include integration across language communities: in addition to breaking through barriers of organization, time and space, barriers of linguistic communication are potentially minimized; quite simply, there is little extra expense involved in running parallel English, Spanish and Portuguese websites. Whether or not this will come to anything, there was a great deal of talk about the historically undeveloped trade links between Trinidad and Latin America despite the huge size of the market as well as the wealth of its geographically and historically closest neighbour, Venezuela.

The adoption of new paradigms that we have been discussing at the level of business strategies is also apparent at the national and governmental level. For example, a 1998 government report explicitly characterizes the country's new environment in terms of 'a networked society', which it defines almost entirely in terms of global economic competition: 'The timely exchange of information is critical to competitive viability given the rapid integration of global markets.' Government's role is to enhance competitiveness in this new context, and to modernize its own ICT provision both to facilitate the development of national infrastructure and to 'become a model . . . for emulation by the other sectors'. The report notes that the IT-based success of some Asian countries was partly due to the pro-active role of governments in information policy and infrastructures. However, 'as the information age evolves, marked by a world of increasing globalization and liberalization', governance is seen in generally non-interventionist terms that are seen as almost inherent in the technologies themselves, or at least appropriate to the world they increasingly dominate; hence, 'government's role is seen essentially as that of a socio-economic facilitator'.

Opportunity and Danger

The Internet appeared – in a context of optimism, liberalization and diversification – as an opportunity that played to Trinidad's sense of its competitive advantages as well as an expansive realization of its 'true' identity as an upscale world player. But as an external pressure the Internet was simultaneously an inevitable and dangerous challenge. It was part of the same inexorable opening-up of the country as WTO-style deregulation. And behind WTO was the United States and international agencies: the US ambassador had made several public (in addition, it was rumoured, to countless private) pronouncements about the centrality of telecomms deregulation and free trade, including the first speech he made as ambassador. The destructive capacity of structural adjustment was well known to Trinidadians from its effects on countries such as Jamaica (Miller 1997: 35–57), and from recent strife over Caribbean banana exports. Local deregulation was not matched by an ending of US protectionism against Trinidad products. Ultimately, the level playing-field was an illusion if power remained asymmetrically with the US government and US companies. 'Opening-up' could leave open the way to equally monopolistic companies that in effect closed down any freedoms or alternatives. But from the perspective of Trinidad there seemed to be no choice about whether or not to move towards these new opportunities and dangers. The scenario for the future looked inevitable, and the main question that faced Trinidadians was whether they would enthusiastically jump into the new technological wave or be pushed and pulled, in which case they would end up swamped and washed up by tides running way ahead of them.

There was generally a denial that they were being pushed, and yet there was also constant anxiety about the lack of speed in the Trinidadian response. This focused on both the slow response of the business community and the government and particularly the backwardness of various key infrastructures: online credit-card authentication and security; and above all the interlinked upgrading and deregulation of telecomms infrastructure. Two key business conferences during our visit (a meeting of the Southern chamber of commerce and a breakfast symposium on ecommerce, detailed in the next chapter) involved the delivery of a uniform message from advanced local and international business figures, such as IBM and KPMG. Both seemed designed to make the Trinidad vision as scary as it was promising, through talk about the head-start of US companies and about competitors that were already taking their business away. Just as the Internet brought the local Trini enterprise cheaply to global markets it also brought huge international operators (Amazon, Cisco, etc.) on to the local highstreet. At such moments people would forget that in fact the Trinidadian Central Bank was involved in a regional consortium that was piloting systems for international financial settlements in an electronic business environment that was to be extended throughout the hemisphere; or that there were plenty of local entrepreneurs with vision. It all seemed too little, too late.

These worries link up with the kinds of scenarios mapped out in Castells (1996, 1997, 1998) or Lash and Urry (1994) or others writing about problems of the information poor, the un-networked, the information ghettos. However, there the concern is with populations being left out of the loop and therefore deprived of the knowledge and contacts that will save them from post-industrial pauperization. The issues for Trinidad are instructively different: they are already in the loop, and therefore have a clear view of the opportunities they would like to grasp. Their fear is, if anything, not pauperization but a proletarianization that is incompatible with the kind of realization of a world position that the Internet seems to hold out to them.

What emerges from this material is an articulation between actual contradictions that beset the process of deregulation and liberalization, contradictions that if anything seem exacerbated by the entry of IT and the Internet on the one hand, and a contradictory discourse that simultaneously expresses desperate fear and enthusiastic opportunism. So the self-confident speech reported in the last chapter coincides with a quite different sense of what a US company such as AT&T might represent: a kind of imperialist monster that would gobble up Trinidad, which had only a short window of opportunity to develop a Caribbean-wide infrastructure that was big and powerful enough to resist. This is the dynamics of positioning at its most practical and opportunistic: how can a small country with big ambitions find its place?

Finally, an important distinction that was only beginning to emerge into public discourse during our research visit had huge implications for strategic thinking about the dynamics of positioning: many informants pointed out (and this was borne out in our interviews) that too many business and policy actors were slow to respond to the Internet because they were looking only at the local online consumer markets, which they deemed to be extremely small as yet (though we found that it was rather larger than they reckoned), while failing to take up the opportunity to reach online consumers abroad (many felt they did not have sufficient products for international consumption). What this ignored was business-to-business commerce. This is reckoned by many to make up the lion's share of ecommerce throughout the Internet; at the same time it was extremely promising for Trinidad, with its petrochemical base and its major trade connections with North America.

Conclusion

The first thing everyone mentions is TSTT as the bottleneck. This is what all the major players are fighting over at present, castigated as a dinosaur, the unholy child of an old national utility monopoly and a neo-imperialist multinational, abetted by a cronyist government. The fact that the phone service in Trinidad was actually rather good, that TSTT was actually in the process of completing a major upgrade of precisely the facilities demanded, and especially the fact – as everyone acknowledged – that C&W was more than likely to be simply replaced by AT&T or MCI within a short span of time – none of this counted for much as against the profound connections that Trinidadians inevitably drew between free-market entrepreneurialism and Internet technologies. It was the ideal of freedom as much as any actual profits to be made that seemed to dominate discussion.

Moreover, this discussion took the form of 'reframing' (Callon 1998) the Internet market in terms of the more global and hugely lucrative market in deregulated telecommunications, a market that would embrace an almost endless series of submarkets in means of communications, computer hardware and software, and information infrastructures. The local Internet market – ISPs operating under the shadow of a monopolistic telecomms supplier – was believed to be framed in archaic terms that restrained players from participating in this wider market, or from getting there in time to be the actors they thought they could be. Moreover, the current restrictive construction of the market was seen as untenable, not only because it was restrictive but because it was out of tune with the unavoidable realities of the global context. The actual Internet market was believed to be sustained merely by legalistic fictions, illegitimate power and vested interests, whose demise was surely imminent. It was, at it were, the merely 'official' market, increasingly held in contempt as a façade, and it was a 'false' market because it was trying to hold back inevitable changes. On the other hand, the 'real' market, as people saw it, the global deregulated telecomms market, was already prefigured and emerging in everyday business practices (for example, the use of satellite, the quasi-legal introduction of cellular, etc.) as much as in the more overt lobbying and pressure that filled public discourse. On this basis, the battle over TSTT and the ISPs, indeed over the Internet as one technology, were both symbolic struggles over freedom as deregulation and proxy wars in a much larger battle.

Hence, in Trinidad the dominant narratives of political economy in regard to the Internet were expressed in terms of a deregulation that would literally free them to realize their participation in a more global context, one understood as the reality of contemporary economy. These narratives included liberalism, diversification, deregulation and the technology of information flow. Freedom is on the lips of all the players. Government waxes lyrical about the fact that ISPs are unlicensed as much as an ISP condemns the TSTT bottleneck as a monopolistic suppression of freedom. Yet at the same time everyone is trying to construct the normative, which here is not just cultural and moral conformity about how something should be expressed, but often simultaneously the possession of the technological means by which it will be expressed and the struggle over which technology that should be, satellite, cable modem, cellular phone, conventional phone, etc. They are all hoping to command and control the channels through which this supposed freedom will be delivered. Contradiction is facilitated by the multiplicity of representation. TSTT as a front for neo-imperialist C&W, TSTT as a primary source of government revenue and expression of government interest, TSTT as a separate telecomms company with its particular telecomm interests, and TSTT as a leading ISP. These are all the same company, but seen from particular angles.

So the political economy of Internet provision no more reduces to simple equations of profit and efficiency than the consumption of the Internet reduces to cost and time. The Internet is already a powerful force that acts as the idiom through which core values are expressed and challenged and their contradictions are made manifest. If the topic of relationships in Chapter 3 seemed to be an expression of a profound struggle between the desire for freedom and the struggle over what would be accepted as normative, then how much more so has this been true of the material presented here. Similarly, even the most hard-bitten commercial players understand their interests in terms of a larger collective identity of national interest, and the dynamics of position are here (as in Chapter 4) the position of Trinidad, terrified and yet in thrall to the prospect of this arranged marriage to a new technological bride. The issue is not one of choice – the Internet is regarded as fate; it is about strategies of positioning between freedom and control that will allow Trinidad to realize itself.

The reason these values can dominate such powerful institutions as huge media companies and the government itself is because they are not mere creatures of the political economy. This chapter is properly set within the larger surrounds of the chapters before and aft. The deepest concerns of Internet provision overlap considerably with values such as national sentiment and freedom that we have met in quite different contexts. One reason for this is that it is of course the same individuals that here are met as speakers in struggles over Internet provision that are also online helping their children with their homework or chatting to their relatives abroad. The interdependency between these aspects of provision and consumption will become still clearer in the next chapter, where the Internet emerges as itself the critical medium (and as in this chapter, also the critical discourse) that promises a new form of integration both forwards in integrating firms into the desires and concerns of consumers and backwards in integrating the businesses themselves and their systems of provision.

6

Doing Business Online

Business Ideals: Miss and Mr Universe

The Internet presents Trinidadian business with a transformed environment, and there is today a real urgency to the drive for rethinking business organizations and practices in this context: how to 'adapt' in order to compete and prosper. In the last chapter we have seen that, along with its dangers, the Internet seems to hold out the promise of a kind of ideal positioning of Trinidad *vis-à-vis* global competition; but this was coupled with tremendous frustration over the slow pace of getting there. In this chapter we will find a similar dynamic working out at the level of individual firms: the macro picture drawn in Chapter 5 is here found realized in the hopes and frustrations of the many individuals involved. There is an emerging model of what 'ecommerce' should be; but while many in business feel this must be quickly realized if the country is not to lose out, they feel constrained by a larger business environment that seems to them conservative, lacking in vision, and, most important, simply not prepared to pay the money and develop the professionalization and infrastructure needed by the nascent Internet industries. Indeed, one of the conclusions of this chapter will be that the discrepancies between ideals and practice, which in the case of users seem to have been a spur to further development, in the case of business may have acted to delay business development.

A number of those who saw themselves as progressive said that what was really needed was a 'test case', one really big and high-profile Internet enterprise or website that would clearly demonstrate to the business community the value of being online. During our research visit a site was launched that came very close not only to the ideal of high-value-added offshore work for North American companies enunciated in the last two chapters, but also the concepts of leading-edge ecommerce that we will explore in this one. Appropriately enough, it was the Miss Universe website (Plate 6.1).

The forty-eighth Miss Universe competition was held in Chaguaramas, Trinidad, in May 1999. This was a huge event in both resources and significance, and one that was experienced as placing Trinidad in a global spotlight.

It was a major national preoccupation for weeks, partly because such contests have an important place in Trinidadian culture (and Trinidad has won Miss Universe and Miss World a disproportionate number of times), but probably more because it was a very public test of Trinidad's ability to manage an international event. Miss Universe was generally framed as a party that Trinidad would be throwing for the world, an event that would demonstrate to an international audience simultaneously the country's exuberance and its ability to organize at a world-class level. The event was locally deemed a success – they put on a good show – though it was often pointed out to us that a people capable of that astonishing annual feat of bacchanal and bureaucracy known as Carnival, entailing months of co-ordination across thousands of dispersed people, hardly needed to prove this to themselves.

The Miss Universe website was part of this show, and was also by and large deemed a success. The site was certainly the largest and most sophisticated web-enterprise ever attempted locally (the only thing comparable was TIDCO); and it was by far the most globally public: as far as Trinidadians were concerned, the whole world was watching them for that week, and the 9,000,000 hits scored by the website could be construed as an objectification of that attention. The show put on by the website was good on several counts. Its appearance was hugely polished and professional: it had a world-class 'look' to it. It was an organizational feat, in that it was a very large site that 'worked' well: links and facilities all functioned. It also employed all the latest web-technology to produce a real multi-media feel: streamed audio and video through RealAudio; a spectacular chat facility (provided by Palace Chat) that allowed people to talk to the contestants, located in a special telecomms set-up in their hotel; and an ecommerce site – described as Caribbean Things. As the lead designer put it: 'We try to use the whole range of Internet technologies, the ecommerce side of it, the online shopping, the chat side of it, visual chat; we had the information side of it of presenting the information on the delegates.'

The level of enthusiasm was not limited to the site's producers. Wherever we went people told us about their visiting the site. They avidly looked up the details of each contestant, drawing up their list of favourites before the show and integrating the website information with that coming from television and the newspapers. The chat site was seen as particularly exciting, in that it enacted a kind of mass public participation in popular culture via the Internet: using the latest chat software, Trinidadians could chat both with people abroad and with contestants. There was plenty of discussion and dispute amongst users as to whether it was actual contestants they had been talking to or other visitors 'trying it on'.

The Miss Universe site embodied a leading edge concept of what could be done on the net through ecommerce and design interactivity. It used a wide range of sophisticated technologies in a commercially disciplined way to create a space of absorbing interactivity; and it integrated a range of business functions (advertising, information and databases, ordering and customer relations) both technologically and conceptually into one ecommerce operation. It therefore looked like the major test case that Internet promoters had been waiting for: a big project that would demonstrate what could be done on the web both technically and commercially and would make the net a fact of business life. It was entirely fitting that this had been accomplished by the local Mr Universe of the ICT economy, Computers and Control, which – as we have seen in the last chapter – generally represented the leading edge in new media and information enterprise in Trinidad, if not the region. They produced the site for no fee, taking their recompense in other invaluable currencies: the site put them in front of all local competitors in terms of its size, international audience, and international links. At the same time, it projected Computers and Control on to the international stage, not only because the site gained an international audience, but because the company and its site were seen alongside such sponsors as Microsoft, Real, Palace and Oracle (including ads displayed on their sites). Concretely, C&C gained experience of contacts and competition at the top levels of global Internet enterprise. This included working with Donald Trump, a central player in the Miss Universe operation. It had actually achieved in the most public way the ideal of Trinidadian business: C&C's Miss Universe site represented a Trinidadian firm providing cutting-edge high-value-added information services to Northern multinationals on a cut-price basis, using skill-based competitive advantages (high education, technical proficiency) as a lure for both technology transfer and revenue. Moreover this was effected and solidified (C&C were awarded the subsequent year's Miss Universe contract, and were bidding for Trump's online casino) by a company that was making a plausible bid to become a major regional media and telecommunications conglomerate.

The realization of this business ideal was clearly experienced at the level of the webdesign team itself. Internally, the website involved the company in a multi-levelled skills transfer from US companies, and within a crushingly short time-span. Firstly, their staff worked closely with teams from Microsoft, Oracle, Palace and Real, who brought them up to speed on the most up-to-date web technologies. This included not just bells and whistles like chat rooms, but core ecommerce functions such as back-end integration via Oracle, i.e., software that extended the website (and its users) into the business, and the business out on to the web. Secondly, the team learned these technologies in the larger context of a commercially defined operation in which design and technology were integrated within a complex business concept. They gained a conceptual understanding of how these technologies could converge into the most advanced available model of ecommerce, in which, far from merely 'selling things', the website became the centre-piece of processes that integrated consumers/audiences, suppliers and the Miss Universe operation itself. Finally, the team carrying out the project took Trinidadian webdesign to a new conceptual and organizational stage. The size and complexity of the Miss Universe project allowed them to experience webdesign in terms of large-scale 'project management', including a large core team: 'There were a lot more people involved in creating the web site. They had 13 or 14 people here, 5 or 6 people involved from the pageant side, or 2 or 3 from the TIDCO side, 5 or 6 people involved from McCann [Ericksen] and all the different ad agencies. Photographers hired, there were a lot of other people. It was a big project.' This produced a complex division of labour and a split between strategic and technical thinking. Hence the team leader – whose background was largely in graphics and webdesign – focused on 'the initial structure, the integration of the information. How the pages are re-connected together. The interactivity, the user friendliness, and the basic look and feel of the web site. That is basically my job.' He could then draw on a range of programmers from within the company – plus visiting teams from various software companies – specializing in, for example, Java Scripting, Visual Basic or Oracle. Part of this experience of large-scale project management was organizational experience of constant liaison with Miss Universe and with the Pageant company on all level of detail, client relations, and so on. Dealing with hugely organized and experienced clients not only meant learning but also 'it makes us see that you kinda have to hint to our new clients to try and get that organised, to organise their information before coming to us. You can't bring ten brochures to us and say, build us a web site.'

Through this kind of involvement the design team came to formulate the huge qualitative and quantitative leap from what had gone before to what was possible now. Most Trinidadian websites, they argued, were patched together:

> they don't understand the amount of technology that can go into it, the amount of information. A lot of people come in and say that they want a web site: 'Put our annual report up.' That is not what you want to put on a web site. You want info that is useful, people can draw from, that they could use as a reference. That has kind of hindered a lot of the web sites that have been built before . . . I think what has happened since I've come here is the clientele has become a lot broader, a lot more information-sensitive, they want to get their information out there, they want people to be able to interact with it easily. Such as Miss Universe Web site, Royal Bank's web site.

Whether a beauty pageant was an effective way to establish Trinidad's relationship to global modernity via Internet technology is open to question (local doubts related far more to its expense than to issues of modernity or, as in our case, feminist critique). Idealizations of feminine beauty aside, the site certainly objectified three other ideals. Firstly, through the Internet it successfully projected Trinidadian culture and business into a global space, an idealized Trinidad of beauty, tropical exoticism and at the same time of professionalism, acumen and entrepreneurialism. Secondly, it accomplished an international level of technological achievement that was also integrated within leading-edge business models of ecommerce. Finally, it embodied the notions of high-value-added offshore enterprise wedded to high-level technology transfer that, as we saw in the last chapter, would exemplify Trinidad's leap, ahead of anyone else in the region, into the new economy.

The Stages of Website Evolution

To describe the Miss Universe project as 'ideal' or 'highly evolved' implies some model of commercial evolution. What are the stages that lead up to Miss Universe as the ideal achieved? What might 'Internet sophistication' mean either to us or to local business? There is obviously no uniform answer to this; we need to observe emerging criteria and at the same time note the continued disagreements over what constitutes good practice. Nonetheless, we were not surprised to find some clear outlines emerging, particularly from those engaged in Internet promotion and leading-edge use. We were even less surprised to find these outlines conforming to emerging international assumptions about what ecommerce should be. Overall good ecommerce is the coming together of two broad dimensions. The first emerges from the problems of webdesign – with media and aesthetic concerns to the fore. The second is concerned with selling goods and services – with marketing and organizational concerns to the fore. In practice, however, the two were intensely interrelated and terminologically confused (either ecommerce or webdesign could be used as the all-inclusive term subsuming the other).

To return to the theory of the aesthetic trap (Gell 1998) introduced in Chapter 4, the first aim of a website is to draw in the surfer to that site as opposed to others. The aesthetics of the site should make the surfer want to engage in exchange with this site in particular. The lesson that was quickly learnt, however, is that surfers do not treat the Internet like television, willing to be passive spectators. They must be persuaded to undertake actions such as obtaining information, buying things, having engrossing media experience: it is activity that keeps them on the site. So the key distinction is whether the surfer encounters a static page declaring the existence of a home furnishing company and its fax number, or whether they enter a space in which they can do things such as look at samples, obtain advice about design or try out a Java applet that allows them to paint fabric textures on to 3D models of furniture.

For the designers this implies a wide range of both design skills, such as good graphics and conceptual interconnections, and software skills, such as using the latest shockwave for animation or Java to create interactivity, which comes down to the basic questions of, 'What can we make a click do?' This has to be harmonized with the issue of ecommerce, which can mean no more than the ability to take orders and verify credit card payments online. Increasingly, however, it means a much more complex system of integration, relating organizational entities such as suppliers, departments, consumers and financial facilities into what appears to the surfer as a seamless whole. This then in turn implies increasingly sophisticated marketing skills for getting consumers to products and products to consumers and organizational skills concerned with issues such as efficiency gains.

In practice these various dimensions and skills are relatively independent and can develop very unevenly. Later on, we will meet young web designers who have high technical skills in producing dramatic online animations but little knowledge of ecommerce in either a marketing or an organizational sense. Animation does not help a client wanting to integrate a website with their inventory database. Conversely, highly sophisticated ecommerce (for example, online banking) could be coupled with boring or confusing information design. Nonetheless, it is possible to create a model of three stages of progress in which Miss Universe becomes the third ideal stage, and which does come pretty close to the types of business use of the Internet most commonly mentioned to us in the course of research, as well as to the models put forward by consultants (see below):

1. *the 'flyer' or 'advertisement'*: this is a simple 'presence' on the net, usually a static website, stating what the business is and how to contact it, with little interactivity beyond a hyperlink or two and an email address. The designer is often a student or hobbyist with limited software and design knowledge. There may be little or no integration between this and the rest of the client's marketing. What the client gets (which is often all they ask for) is a presence on the web.

2. *the 'catalogue' website*: this often mirrors a traditional offline catalogue, which includes advertising functions but also involves the consumer in shopping, selecting, ordering, and feedback. It involves a higher level of information design skills (organizing the site, layout, coherent visual styling), though not necessarily much higher software skills. More

sophisticated sites include online ordering and selling. So the site is part of marketing, but does not imply a reorganization of the other departments.

3. *the 'interface'*: the firm makes a large investment in establishing a website that allows high levels of consumer involvement, such as interactivity and freebies. Through 'lots of back-office integration', the consumer gains direct access to databases, ordering and corporate communications, for example, allowing them to track goods once they are ordered. The function of the site is to involve the consumer in the organization itself, but also for the organization to treat the Internet as a mode of increasing efficiency in all aspects of its operations through integration, cost savings and speeding up transactions.

Table 5.1 Three stages of progress in the commercial application of web-design

| | Webdesign | | Ecommerce | |
	Design skills	Software skills	Marketing	Organisational
Flyer	Page layout	Basic HTML	Presence	Advertising only
Catalogue	Information design	Frames and tables	Transactions and Feedback	Marketing
Interface	Event design	Interactivity	Incorporation	Corporate Integration

The ideal types summarized in Table 5.1 are similar to those proposed in models of ecommerce that are found internationally in business communities. For example, they come close to what was presented at a breakfast seminar held at the Trinidad Hilton by the local branches of IBM and KPMG for the highest echelon of Trinidadian businesses in June 1999. The seminar collectively worried about the slow pace at which local enterprises were adopting ecommerce models and creating infrastructure appropriate to the emerging digital economy. The first speaker emphasized that they needed to shift from seeing the Internet merely in terms of advertising or a presence to a means of restructuring one's business in its entirety and to make use of – 'to leverage' – possible cost savings and marketing opportunities. Speakers from Canada delivered multi-stage models of business evolution in the information age, including stages such as first passing the 'security chasm' (secure online handling of payments and confidential information such as credit card numbers), leading to online transactions. After breaking through a second barrier – access to the business's core systems, such as inventory and order tracking – consumers are enabled to check prices and availability directly, track their orders and contact all service departments directly. What emerged was an insistence that sophisticated ecommerce is defined by integration at 'front end' and 'back office'. The point is that the net is not just a communications medium.

The seminar was there to suggest not just that this evolution was inevitable (consumer demand as well as competitive gains would ensure that), but also that those who got there slowest would lose out or fail. One speaker argued that in the transition 'from postindustrial economy to information/network/ digital economy', 1998 was the critical year. Anyone getting into ecommerce after that point was already getting less advantage, as the curve had already started to level out. The message was: move faster because it's already too late. More crudely, as the concluding remarks of the breakfast put it: 'There are already businesses that you may or may not know about, operating in a cyber context, who are already taking business away from you.'

Business Realities

If we can accept for the moment that a model of more and less advanced ecommerce was emerging, and being imposed, then we can look at the difficulties encountered at various levels of Internet business. In what follows we will try to replicate our three stages of website development by fleshing out not only the kinds of involvement with the net that are represented by each stage but also the kinds of players (web designers and businesses) involved at each level.

Flyers? Getting Advertising Off the Ground

Most of the initial websites created in Trinidad were flyers, that is static, one- or two-page websites, representing the initial impulse simply to have 'an online presence' rather than any particular concept of what to do with it. For example, TIDCO provided an early standard form for companies wishing to have a presence (Plates 6.2). Others look like single-page printed flyers (Plate 6.3), or a little more elaborate (Plate 6.4, for instance). Craft enterprises often come closer to a catalogue style, and generally include an email contact, but no other facilities for ordering goods (e.g. Plate 6.5).

We cannot assume every such site represents merely a stage, rather than an intentional design strategy. As is argued in Miller (2000), the design of some sites, such as food wholesalers (Plates 6.6), may be intended to suggest that the products are dirt cheap. With little clearly spent on website aesthetics, the effect is actually to put off the individual consumers, who would just be a nuisance, while attracting the attention of the large retailers that the sites want to attract. Nevertheless, by the time of our research, there was a pervasive sense that the flyer phase was largely over. As in North America and Europe, many of these were created by one-person shops with little or no training, experience or capital. Webdesign had very low entry costs (a computer, an Internet account and rudimentary HTML), and was therefore more exciting as a major career opportunity for the webdesigners than as a business opportunity for their clients, who saw it mainly as a rather mystifying necessity: you had to have a 'presence' on the net. In all these respects, early webdesign resembled the 1980s 'desktop publishing revolution': a low threshold of software skills promised to translate into business opportunity until design, marketing and organizational capital asserted themselves as the marks of distinction. In the meantime, as an advertising executive put it:

> The technology began to arrive in Trinidad largely on the level of very young people in their teens, as it was all over the world, where for example my eldest son, who went on to become an accountant, began to create his own HTML language. . . . It was his generation, his friends, literally, [xxx]'s son and a couple of other guys whose names I can't remember, it was they who began to build web sites as a joke among themselves.

One of our most curious findings was that advertising agencies in Trinidad had not developed ecommerce any further than the one-person shops we have just been discussing. We had predicted on the basis of previous research (Miller 1997) that the lead role in ecommerce development would come from the advertising agencies, who had an impressive history in developing local advertising to a level where it could compete with and usually replace internationally sourced advertising. Furthermore, they tended to handle the entire marketing and public profile of companies, not restricting themselves to just creating and placing adverts. In fact, we were consistently told that advertising agencies were taking virtually no part in the development of the Internet in Trinidad; it formed no part of their media buying considerations. Few had their own websites (though see Plate 6.7). They had no in-house web-design capabilities, usually passing on this kind of work to young freelancers such as the ones just described; and they could not really conceptualize the Internet as part of an overall marketing programme.

Given their history one would have expected them to cast at least a proprietorial eye over the Internet as a new medium to throw into the mix, and on ecommerce as a new mode of integrating marketing services, rather than dismissing the Internet on the grounds that, as one executive noted:

'You can't do everything.' Their lack of initiative here was the more surprising (and frustrating to many agents) because the largest Trinidad agencies are all linked to (in one case owned by) foreign agencies that are pushing the net as the future. One agency had just received a memo from their New York head office 'saying that the future of above the line advertising has been flat ... And where growth is going to come from ... is certainly from non-traditional media, things like the Internet and direct marketing.' Indeed, direct marketing had just taken off in Trinidad, and was likely to be one route by which ecommerce would be integrated into advertising. The agencies themselves admitted that they didn't understand the Internet, and couldn't advise clients as to what it could do for them:

> To be honest I think it's just something that they know it's out there, they know a lot of big clients internationally are doing it, maybe we should get in on this. . . . Clients are only now beginning to look to the agency in any case. Previously I would guess that about 95% of them were developed by the clients on their own. It certainly did not go through any of the agencies.

The exceptional dearth of advertising revenues flowing through the Internet in Trinidad is revealed in the fact that almost no Trinidadian companies were spending on banner advertising on websites, nor were foreign companies putting advertisements on Trinidadian sites (the exceptions being sponsorship of Carnival sites, and of course Miss Universe). It was believed that levels of traffic would not justify any reasonable level of expenditure; and that the size of the local market would always hold this back. Various people, including an ex-advertising agent, were therefore looking at establishing Caribbean-wide portal sites. At that level, it was felt, one could generate the right dynamic between traffic levels and advertising flow. Trinidad without the Caribbean just wasn't worth the cost and effort.

The upshot of all this was that websites appeared more as an exotic form of advertising whose cost could not be justified, rather than as the visible tip of the emerging iceberg of ecommerce. Agencies were therefore seemingly content to leave this work to small designers of static advertisement-style sites, rather than looking to develop the broader potential. They did not even attempt to co-ordinate with the freelance designers who were handling their clients' websites. In one fairly extreme case, the young independent designer who had nabbed the commission for one of the few truly and obviously international Trinidadian consumer brands found that the company had little idea what they wanted, and made no effort to integrate it with their advertising at any level. In fact the designer did use graphics that were employed in the current advertising campaign, but that was his own decision rather the advice of either the client or their advertising agency.

Those in the agencies who were more orientated to the Internet saw the same attitudes in their clients. Businesses saw no value in the Internet, and therefore tended neither to demand these services nor to be willing to pay for them. The local Internet-using market was viewed as too small. There was no sense at all that the Internet was being used in Trinidad on the scale that we believe exists. So apart from giving themselves a presence, i.e. being seen to be there, there seemed no justification for a site that would need constant maintenance. The massive export-orientated companies in Trinidad were in the Petro-Chemical industry, which did not sell consumer goods. A few companies with international consumer brands, such as Angostura bitters and Carib beer, or local conglomerates such as Neil and Massy, had fairly evolved websites (though still not involving their advertising agencies to any great extent). But these were the exceptions.

Even where there was a perception that one should be moving to more sophisticated use of the Internet, companies baulked at the costs involved:

> For a local manufacturer or for local sales distribution set up to get people to shop them on the net, they will have to run an advertising campaign that will cost them tens of thousands of dollars to get people to look at their website. They will have to begin to build websites for viewing as an adjunct to their advertising, and they will have to make it interactive in a beneficial way. And that penny has not dropped.

We will discuss this move from advertising to interactive websites below. The point here is that for this advertising man, as for all the other people we talked with, the issue is that the Internet only works as serious business if conceptualized on a far wider scale than as an advertisement. But this would require an investment that a hardheaded business person could not yet justify, particularly costs such as suddenly having to support the website through offline advertising campaigns, not to mention maintenance. How does one justify a particular Internet expenditure? 'They send us stuff with rates and there's no point of reference, "It'll cost $10,000", well what does that mean?', said an advertising agent. The clients were demanding some kind of cost – benefit analysis to justify Internet expenditures. This seems reasonable until one reflects how far traditional advertising has escaped any such auditing, because it is extremely difficult to calculate the benefits of particular forms of advertising. Indeed, the irony is that it is much easier to obtain an extremely accurate measure of the number of hits on websites and where surfers are located. Moreover, websites are becoming vehicles for collecting customer information, including their response to the website itself. The webdesigners knew of and carried out such monitoring of guestbooks, feedback forms and so forth, in one case informing the company of which countries are showing an interest in their product.

What these demands for costed benefits demonstrate is that the Internet was seen by most advertising people and their clients as an ineffective means of advertising rather than as an effective means of commerce. This may be part of an answer to the conservatism we encountered. It was already becoming evident that the model of advertising was exactly what was preventing websites becoming part of interactive ecommerce. For all subsequent stages of development the websites would have to become involved in economic activities, within which advertising agencies traditionally play no part. So while in the abstract we might have expected these agencies to be in the vanguard of website development, there are structural reasons why they have swiftly become one of the most conservative forces, bogged down already in some inappropriate measures of efficiency: while it is quite possible to measure hits on websites as though they were advertisements, they shed little light on the complex interactions of ecommerce that transform the relationship of consumers to companies.

The issues involved are much closer to the hearts of the commercial webdesigners. They are already involved in more sophisticated concepts of feedback, as one noted:

> since they have upgraded their site certainly the amount of information coming in . . . has more or less doubled. There is a lot more people writing in asking questions, sending bits of information to them. But they are not using the site commercially at all. And it's hard to say whether or not putting information, say about promotions that they are having, on their site has affected sales at all.

It is the website designers who have a keen interest in showing to companies who have invested in such sites that there is a great deal more that they could do with them and learn from them. It is not surprising, therefore, that when we turn to the next stage our primary interest is no longer in advertising agencies but in website designers.

The Mid-range, 'Catalogue' Websites

To move from the simple flyer and rudimentary catalogue to something more sophisticated involves at least two things: much greater technical sophistication and a much more productive relationship between the webdesigner and the client. In our first example we can find plenty of the former, but not yet the latter. You would not know from Millennium web design's own very professional, corporate and international-looking website (Plate 6.8) that it comprises an 18-year-old schoolboy and friends operating out of his family's office (through which they get most of their commissions). The boys have a good design sense (they all have art training and are heading for either graphics or architecture degrees in North America) and they have a clear facility with the latest in software technologies. However, in both areas their expertise and enthusiasm clearly lie in the multi-media aspects (for example, heavy use of shockwave) rather than marketing, database and back-end integration. They would probably rather be doing something more 'creative' (e.g. Plate 6.9) than websites for local household furnishings companies. At the same time, they were commercially very disciplined and professional: they had a clear understanding that this was indeed commercial work; they simply did not extend this very far. The reasons seemed less to do with them than their clients: '[The clients] are never clear about what they want, they just say, we want a web site, you take it from there. They hardly give you any direction. They just don't have the time, as far as they're concerned, they just want a presence on the network.' For example the only thing a client in the music business knew 'for sure that he wanted was "ecommerce," "ecommerce". He knew what that meant, because apparently someone else was doing it selling his CDs, where they would go on and order the CD and he would send it to them in New York. He said that he wanted that done down here, as well as away. So it very well could be an international market.'

The boys complained that clients won't even have meetings to discuss sites:

> 'You can't speak to them at all, when you want an interview, when you want to discuss how the site is going to be laid out, you can't. They don't know what they want, they just want you to do it. . . . NO one that we've encountered so far, have even known what they don't want. They loved it when we delivered it. Their eyes lit up, because of all the colours and lights and sounds.'

The reverse side of this situation is the low or no pay, which in turn precludes building up a greater skills and organizational basis for evolving ecommerce. On the one hand, this is not a valued service, because no one has a clear sense of what it is worth, what it accomplishes, what one is doing it for: 'Clients don't understand, they figure the Internet is supposed to be free, la la la. When you run down the cost of them, they have this confused look on their face.' On the other hand, there are plenty of webdesigners, either young ones like this or those in the initial stages of setting up more serious businesses, who are willing to work for very little or nothing, for experience, for a foot in the door, as some kind of investment. Hence payment for these basic (and even not so basic) sites is driven well below what is required for a viable business, both because clients don't value it, and because at this level 'anyone' can do it. This obviously applies largely to the middle or lower range of businesses that a firm like Millennium would encounter; but similar issues arise at much higher levels, with advertising agencies and bigger clients.

So the professionalism of Millennium and their skills may not prove sufficient in themselves. In the next two examples we find it is those with a more integrated involvement in commerce itself who may be in a better position to move the clients forward or to exploit new niches. Our first example shows the push factor of advancing technologies and the second the push from advancing commercial acumen.

One of the cybercafés studied which had always done bits and pieces of local advertising and webdesign, at the same time – by dint of gleeful opportunism and techno-enthusiasm – was building up leading-edge Internet software skills; there were also people there with long-term interests in graphics (including a former US graffiti artist) and music. At the time of our research Internet animation produced through Shockwave Flash was the latest development, transforming the look of many websites, as well as upping the technological ante, or entrance fee, on doing web-design. The café uniquely seized on the idea that they could produce 30-second advertising spots using shockwave (at almost no cost whatsoever) and transfer these to video (for the price of a video capture card), both undercutting any other mode of TV advertising production and making more money than they'd ever imagined. Their first TV ad was for a medium-sized music retailer. They could equally produce radio spots. With their combination of design skills, software skills and entrepreneurial organizational knowledge (particularly well adapted to small businesses), one could easily imagine them moving up the value chain to both media production and marketing for particular business sectors.

In the second example, a freelance webdesigner recognized that the marketing of websites (publicizing and advertising them, getting them listed on portals and on the websites of businesses in complementary markets) was as important as the website itself: indeed, this marketing involved a wide range of media (ensuring that web addresses were on letterheads and cards, hyperlinking to relevant sites and portals, getting into webrings, publicizing sites through on- and offline media such as press ads, mail shots, email, etc.). That is to say, marketing a web site involves both publicizing it and making it integral to all corporate publicity. The designer was just about to take on a marketing partner specifically to carry out these functions, at which point one can again see a move on to the patch of the full-service advertising agency.

[The agencies] don't see that as a threat to them as yet. They will. Ok! And a lot of the companies will go through their agencies basically asking them to, you know about web design and hopefully by then, with my marketing fella, I would arrange a relationship with the advertising agencies . . . because, this is, as far as I could see, is the future of marketing as such.

So the central issues for the small band of webdesign firms and freelancers that were establishing themselves as serious businesses centred around professionalization: how to differentiate themselves from all the young whizz-kids and how to present themselves and the Internet to real paying clients of a reasonable size as sellers of a professional service. The main defining feature of professionalization was in the relationship between webdesign and ecommerce: they could not only produce good-quality graphics backed by skilled use of software, but they could subordinate this to a clear understanding of the marketing and organizational needs of their clients. In the context of the Internet, this might well mean educating their clients in both webdesign and ecommerce. It also meant establishing a clear contractual and payment basis: handling the relationships between firms. In other words, professionalization already implied pushing beyond the bounds of website as advertisement to a rethinking of both medium and business in relation to each other.

One of the more established designers we spent time with was a net-enthusiast, but felt his main task was to keep his clients both realistic and yet excited about what the net could do for their businesses. A difficult balancing act. He was offering commercial solidity: professionalism; clear briefs and execution; a design process driven by business needs rather than the technical or graphics potentials of the net. The results were neat, solid design with an emphasis on information presentation. Jones (as we shall call him) adamantly stuck to low-tech solutions: no Java, no frames, no plug-ins, no database integration, and so on, so that they could be quickly downloaded by surfers with low-level computers and web browsers. Nevertheless, unlike that of earlier local webdesigners working at a similar technical level, his work exuded both commercial professionalism and very good information design, such as clearly presented information with detailed attention to navigation and lack of clutter. Interactivity, however, was very limited: there was not a lot to do on the sites besides filling in feedback forms. Jones also paid great attention to those aspects of website marketing that could be dealt with within the site, such as meta-tags and descriptions. Jones's catchphrase was, 'use technology because it is applicable, not because it is available.'

We can see some of the tensions operating at this level of the business at a consultation meeting Jones held with a prospective client. They were developing a business involving music production, song-writing, artist development, studio rental and more. The two men were well connected, with an international client base and international experience, and had lived along the usual axes of London, Toronto and Trinidad, but were now basing themselves in Trinidad. Jones focused on thinking through their complex business in terms of a website: how could it be presented clearly so that an anonymous international audience would know what it was and what they could get from it?

The clients had come to Jones for precisely this kind of conceptual rigour: his sites 'worked'. They also agreed with his basic design philosophy. This comprised the use of high-quality visuals (spend at least as much on photos and graphics as on web design) and not too much text; and very little information at the top level of the site, with more information presented as you dig deeper into it. At the same time they were worried about being slotted into a standard format (they said that Jones's sites each had different 'flavours', but essentially the same structure) and while they wanted professionalism, they adamantly did not want to look corporate or cold (like coming into a 'steel room'). The two had done a lot of homework, looking at a range of sites to see what they wanted, and they had their own sense of what a website was, certainly for their kind of business. For them, a website was not a place to present a business, but a space in which an audience could interact with it. This took the form of 'offering something interesting, things for people to come to the site for': lots of MP3s and music-related software to download, lots of 'free stuff', loads of information about music and the music business (e.g., how to become a star), tips and tricks on how to mix music, a mixing competition (people could download a sample and offer remixes for a prize). They also wanted to launch a major new female artist with an online launch party involving 24 hours of streamed audio and the artist chatting on ICQ. 'Very interactive.' They also had a clear look in mind: low-tech in imagery, but hi-tech in webdesign and web technologies. This was clearly geared to a younger audience who expect an all-singing site, but have to feel at home in it, feel ownership of it (they discussed going for 'ghastly graphics' – crude, punky, primitive – that would offend older people).

The clients described all this as ecommerce; Jones tended to reserve that term for the incorporation of things like order forms or feedback forms. They were very clear about why the term applied: doing business with their audiences went beyond presentation of their business (advertising) and beyond enabling online transaction; it involved a complex of exchanges (information, free stuff, commodities), ostensibly within a culture. It involved a space of pleasurable activity: the 'aesthetic trap' went far beyond representation to embrace forms of interaction. Finally, we need to put this in a specifically Trinidadian context. The clients were very explicit that this approach was essential to the global reach and feel of a website. They wanted a Caribbean feel in order to 'maximize their selling point', but they wanted a site that was in synch with global online music culture. All three talked specifically and for a long time about that 'old postcolonial attitude that things outside Trinidad are always better', and the perennial issue that Trinidadians are capable of world-class accomplishments, yet always expect the worst of Trinidad (they claimed that companies export goods to Venezuela for assembly just so that they can be reimported into Trinidad as foreign). This kind of discussion was not external to the business at hand, but part of doing business.

Jones clearly recognized that this was where the web was going, but he and Trinidad were both going to get there slowly and cautiously, following the route of neat design and professional business relationships. For Jones this realism stemmed from the limitation of the Internet in Trinidad (including his own business): he could not do some of the high-tech stuff himself (though he was confident he could source it locally); there were issues of bandwidth (and hence of speed and the quality of people's experience of the site); and technical and software constraints. In many respects Jones represents the fullest development of the catalogue-style website. This genre of sites dominates current Trinidadian website production across a wide variety of commercial sectors, such as catalogues for clothing but also in selling Steelband and cosmetics and in the tourist industry, which we did not cover, since this is geared more to Tobago (Plate 6.10). The range of websites which represent the website designers themselves are also instructive (Plate 6.11). They are obviously more professional and dedicated to the particular task. Others tend to offer website design as part of a package of possible IT work, though often including a portfolio or a list of prior clients. They may also include other products on sale, such as CD roms and gimmicks such as a virtual pan site (Plate 6.12).

Case Study: Exporting Clothing and Fabrics

Each of the three medium-sized clothing and textile firms we visited had a catalogue-style site that displayed their wares with some clear relation to their specific identity, market and consumers. Their websites allowed each at least a rudimentary means of taking orders online, if only through email, and all of them had indeed found themselves making direct contact through the Internet with customers whom it would otherwise have involved too many intermediaries or been too expensive to reach. This was particularly significant in that all three firms were attempting to develop their export market and would wish this to become the mainstay of their business, and all three are looking to the more expensive up-market niches. All three benefited from some funding obtained for them from the World Bank ETAP scheme through TIDCO, which also helped them in their export drives, including attending trade shows abroad and creating their websites. Hence all three were moving outwards from website as advertisement to a broader sense of ecommerce that was also providing a fulcrum around which they could rethink (to quite varying degrees) what kind of business they could be running. In addition, the Internet and ecommerce were already playing a clear role in other aspects of organizing their business such as sourcing, relations with retail outlets and gathering market intelligence.

The oldest firm is also perhaps the most up-market. The director retains many of the ideals of her original London training, in creating what she describes as a 'minimalist' or 'clean' image. She tends to black, white and the natural colour of linen, except for a new range of youth-orientated clothing. Although she describes herself as computer-illiterate, she quickly seized upon the ways the Internet made previous tasks easier. She comes to work at 6.00 a.m. and goes on line: 'I would read the front-page of the trade journals every morning on the net, just to keep me abreast. And I would put up collections like Armani's home page to look at, because they change all the time. I read everything coming out of every major city every month, but this is instant.'

She has one retail outlet in Trinidad and one in Tobago; otherwise she sells through what she regards as the most upmarket and stylish shop to be found on each of the other Caribbean islands. Although she has made tentative inroads in Sweden and the US, she clearly relishes the custom of Italian and German tourists in the Caribbean, who 'appreciate' her attempts to create this minimalist style, which goes against what she describes as the Trinidadian desire to sell itself only as tropical colour: 'they think me boring here'. Although she started working on a website even before she was using email, she was dissatisfied with the first effort. While it is her business partner who runs the marketing side, she is clearly in the process of formulating her own ideals. She is excited by the prospects of the website, and even more by the potential of ecommerce for selling directly to Europeans, and she has made some early enquiries about those possibilities. But she is already cautious about how the new media might impact on her image. Quite clearly the multi-media and glitzy potential of the Internet does not appeal; somehow she has to keep the cool clear simple line that will retain her image of her main line as 'very, very sophisticated'.

The director of the second firm also trained in London as a designer, though in this case because she is English by origin. Here (Plate 6.13) the range is batiks, with various furnishing such as curtains and cushion covers as well as swimwear and accessories. Both she and the previous firm gained a recent local boost by being featured during the fashion show that formed part of the Miss Universe competition. In this case the motifs and style are more evidently 'tropical', which also fits one of her main markets, the furnishings of hotels in the region. About 90 per cent of her sales are outside Trinidad (but not Tobago). The two firms are similar in size, employing between 16 and 20 people for their main production. This second firm had the advantage of more direct access to relevant computer knowledge. Having a 17-year-old son was handy in this regard, as was the fact that a leading web designer had already used her products for another commercial venture of his own. She was therefore able with the help of ETAP money to produce a full website, and was much happier with the content, which gives the colour, context, range and vibrancy she would want to communicate. She assumes the relationship to the web designer is long-term, and that he can handle both maintaining the website and also the logistics of ecommerce if this expands, which is helpful since she is not herself computer-literate.

The third firm is less than a decade old, and has expanded very rapidly to become a major presence in clothing retail within Trinidad; it also has its own shops in many of the other Caribbean Islands. 'We concentrate on the very trendy fashion forward-type apparel.' In some ways the website (Plate 6.14) treads a path between the two previous cases. It provides a quite dramatic sense of styling, which befits its own up-market and internationally focused designs (again with a strong linen presence), but also in form is closer to the catalogue that is found in the second firm's website. In this case the Internet became a much more natural part of the commercial project, since the formal training of one of the directors is in electronic engineering. His emphasis is on the constraints of the current Internet, with enthusiasm for the kinds of graphics, downloading and multimedia that new bandwidth promises to make possible. The only thing preventing full ecommerce is that the banks do not provide all that he needs (real-time, online authorization of credit card payments). While consolidating at present, the intention is to follow up their first recent foray into the US at a Las Vegas show.

Already the Internet is an integral part of how the firm works. Many items are purchased by them on the net, such as software, packaging and labelling. They are close to having an instant inventory of all outlets online, so that the director can check it from a computer, wherever he happens to be. They are geared up to changing the website from a form of advertising to a form of commerce to the extent of working out the insurance implications of home-delivery/credit card purchase systems. They had even done a survey of local ISPs and their market base. By the same token the technology is an integral part of their image. While the earlier-mentioned firms sell a more 'classic' image of modernity or tropicality, this firm sells its sense of the present. For this reason the drive towards ecommerce comes from much more than just its potential for reorganization and logistics, or even advertising. It has to do with the self-conscious modernity of the firm. When developing their style they tend not to investigate the competition; rather they look for influences, in movies, music and architecture. As with the bulk of Trinidadians surfing, it is the MTV site they look to first. Not surprisingly, then, the website is an upfront part of their image creation, and they intend to have computers in their shops so that customers can browse the website and use its planned ecommerce facilities while shopping. 'The generation we appeal to is very much in touch with what's happening. It's well-educated. So like Nike, you must be on the web.' In this case, then, we have a firm that comes close to the situation we described in Chapter 1 as the 'expansive potential'. It is not just that they see the Internet as realizing that which they wanted to be; here they look to the Internet to tell them what they could be in the future, and they recognize that the Internet is becoming absolutely central to the sense of style in contemporary Trinidad and beyond. The duality we have pointed out throughout this chapter between the problem of webdesign and commercial skills here becomes a triad, when the connection between them is actually incorporated into the aesthetics of the company: its goods and its website construct their modern image.

Towards the Interface – Activity Centres and Modes of Involvement

We can discern a movement from the catalogue site to the fully functioning interface and ecommerce site both in the cautious but steady progress being made by webdesigners such as Jones and in the third clothing firm, appropriately named 'Radical'. Once again the key was to move the pieces of the puzzle, that is website aesthetics, software skills and commercial and organizational acumen, in step with each other. This was by no means straightforward. The issue for designers like Jones and their clients operating at this level was to keep technological gadgetry subordinate to efficient but attractive information design. This placed limits on the exploration of new, more elaborate and more web-specific forms of engagement with their sites. Indeed, Jones foregrounded disciplined information presentation even against his clients' desire to push all the medium's potentials for interactivity. By contrast, the designer responsible for the Carnival sites featured in Chapter 4 argued that people needed to feel they were getting more from a site; in that case he meant large amounts of background information, streamed audio or video clips of the bands and competitions or trivia quizzes: basically, lots of things to do or get. In the case of one of his export-orientated brands he placed great stress on offering free screen-savers.

As one advertising agent argued, the Internet had to be seen as very 'niche marketing' in that, unlike the conventional media situation, where a mass of consumers 'happens' by a billboard or TV advertisement, people actually have to go to a website in order to see it. Hence, he said, reaching for an appropriate metaphor, smaller clients don't understand that the Internet is 'publishing' not advertising, because you have to offer information to people so that they will be interested in visiting and returning: 'So you want to sell your cosmetics, then you have to publish a book, a magazine, on the net, on beauty care to sell your stuff there. So you have people come and look at your page because what your page tells you is how to take care of your . . . hair and your miserable toes and all that sort of stuff, as well as sell their junk.'

Information is not the only way of attracting people into a generalized involvement in a site whose primary function is really to sell. A designer on the Miss Universe site put it very clearly:

> Besides visually selling the site, I mean the girls are what sold the site. That is what generated the hits. Other sites could generate hits in other ways from online chat to making notice boards, creating memberships and so that people almost feel like they have become part of something. And are given information. . . . Especially, people like products, have sales and online purchasing, a lot of different things. It depends on the products, really. What it is you want and how much your budget is to market that product.

The point is how to use the arsenal of media-specific technical and aesthetic possibilities to generate a kind of involvement that is specific to the dynamics of mediation on the Internet (or at least different from what companies and agencies had previously felt they had dealt with in the marketing mix). Buying online is itself a form of interactivity, it is doing something, being engaged sensuously and actively by the website. It is this aesthetic – the website seen in terms of modes of involvement – that seems to characterize ideals of Internet use in relation to business. When seen in terms of Gell's (1998) theory of aesthetic traps, which must involve agency as much as art, the point may be extended to religious and social uses of the Internet as well as to many visual forms that preceded the Internet.

But the paradigm of interactivity and involvement goes still further, integrating the website into consumer activities that transcend the specific commercial context. For example:

> I was talking to the account executive who handles Drince [we shall call it]. She's telling me that Drince wants to develop a website, locally. Now even though Drince is an international brand, we, the team that manages it, which is the client and this agency, we look at it as a Trinidadian thing: this is how we promote the product. They wanted to have a website, so I said to Linda, 'Linda what do they want to do with this site, why do they want to put a site on'? Because an 11-year-old kid who is going on to the net, if they even go on to a site that's about milk [laughs], they are not interested in grams of fat and the amount of calcium. What are you going to do with this site? Her response was, we don't know, we'd just want to

put a site on so we can put information on. What kind of information? And the point of that story is, and I think it typifies the understanding with clients now, they know [the Internet] is something they should be in but they don't know what to do with it. And again, the agency can't advise them. What I said to her, what they have is a kids' club, which – they have something like 18,000 members: Drince Milk Kids' Club, and what they do with that kids' club is they offer discounts because this group also owns [several key resaurant franchises] in Trinidad, so you can get coupons through that, on your birthday; you can get information if you want to get their team to come to your school; they offer help in buying computers. I said to Linda, basically think of what you do with the kids' club, that is something that you can do on the Internet.'

However, to see Internet design and ecommerce at this level of sophistication also involves a massive commitment of resources: programming and database design and input, email and other responses, co-ordination of a programme that goes beyond simply selling things online to an entire educational operation and youth club, and an equally large commitment of funds to advertising both the website and the programme through offline conventional media.

In our original typology the 'interface' denoted Internet use that was well-developed in terms of both user engagement and corporate integration. This second criterion – corporate integration – requires more than just better web-designers. It means looking at all levels of the firm and its relationships to both customers and suppliers in terms of IT. It depended, for example, on whether and how a firm computerized its inventory and potentially integrated it with online query techniques. Or using email both to enhance customer relations procedures and for intra-firm communication.

The picture was very uneven. For example, large petrochemical companies might have long been set up with EDI data transmission, but no IP-based intranet; hence the day-to-day business of the firm and their Internet presence might bear no relation to each other. Even larger regional companies might use intranets to achieve corporate integration across the islands, but without opening this up at all to consumers for ecommerce. At the same time, we found quite large firms, doing international business (for instance, an industrial goods company and some advertising agencies) in which computers were not internally networked, or only within different departments and not communicating with each other. In similarly large firms there might be only a single machine that was on the Internet, through a single ISP account, which was operated by a single hard-pressed secretary or an all-purpose techie through whom all email, web-searches and maintenance were routed. Indeed, the government itself could be included here: there was no co-ordinated IT policy; each department procured software and hardware autonomously, with no overseeing of interdepartmental compatibility or communication.

That is to say, the kinds of leading-edge ecommerce advocated at the breakfast seminar by IBM and KPMG made no sense at all if there was no 'back-office' with which even the most interactive website could feasibly integrate. The Miss Universe site in this context appears as a truly utopian moment: it points to an exemplary practice that presumes the complete rewiring of enterprises in terms of the perceived potentialities of the new media technologies. And this is indeed where future planning, if not present realities, were being directed. For example, one of the clothing companies discussed above saw numerous possibilities for transferring important organizational elements and processes online: they were opening up leased lines connecting their main retail outlets to head office, allowing real-time information about sales and inventory; this could be made Intranet- and Internet-accessible, front-ended in online kiosks in each outlet, where customers could look up their styles, prices and availability, and order goods; finally they were making available on the Internet the line drawings and possibly textile samples on the basis of which retailers on other islands could order stock. This is of course far more of an ecommerce approach to the Internet than that pursued by some of the larger companies, whose websites, however extensive, had very little to do with the rest of the firm, and as was suggested above it had a great deal to do with this company's understanding of what it means to be 'hot' in contemporary Trinidad.

Nonetheless, with the exception of Miss Universe the interface model was always part of a discussion about the future. This was most conspicuously true of the banking sector. They presented a paradox, in that on the one hand the banks were seen as being the most conservative force – second only to TSTT – in slowing down Trinidad's ICT future, largely because they had not yet enabled online, real-time verification of credit card purchases and hence seemed to make ecommerce impossible (if one defined it narrowly as simply online purchasing). And yet on the other hand not only did the banks seem to have the most advanced and coherent ecommerce plans for their own businesses, but they were in fact responsible for the last major consumer technology revolution – ATM machines – which seemed to have transformed people's relationship to money: it now flows from numerous sources, at any time of day, in response to need or whim. Indeed, the banks' general strategy seems to have been to build on the increasing abstraction of money as material culture first by moving people on to telephone banking, and then to online banking, in relation to which online shopping would make self-evident sense. Rather like TSTT, it seemed that however intelligently and inexorably they were moving towards the Internet, with considerable investment and planning, they were still seen, impatiently, as conservative, as another bottleneck. They had many excuses for delay, such as the huge cost, effort and possible dangers involved not only in the installation of security systems and credit card verification arrangements, but also in the establishment of international systems of electronic financial settlement, which were actually waiting on co-ordination between national banks and the World Bank. These seemed eminently plausible concerns to us, but could not assuage the impatience of their critics.

For the moment all this is at planning stage: most banks are currently restricted to advertisement-style websites and some telephone banking services and online form filling. One bank does attribute the low level of implementation to banking 'conservatism', particularly on security matters (which has included the Y2K obsession). Concern over credit card security seems to run together in the public's mind with concern over the safety of Internet transactions generally, such as popular paranoia about viruses. The other important brake on ecommerce cited by banks was the same as within many consumer sectors. They blamed the low levels of ecommerce on the limits of the domestic Trinidadian online market. At the same time, however, banks were far more sensitive than most to the fact that the Internet itself breaks down market boundaries in ways that turn financial institutions into *de facto* international players for whom the domestic market occupies an entirely new conceptual space. With Internet facilities, and in the context of worldwide financial deregulation, money can flow anywhere, easily and cheaply. Even the smallest savers can move their money to wherever in the world they can take advantage of a fractional percentage point interest-rate advantage. The Trinidadian banks could see huge potential earnings by being able to offer marginally advantageous rates with low withholding taxes for North American investors and being able to benefit from repatriated money from Trinidadians living away. Conversely, the combination of Internet and deregulation can render the very concept of a local market meaningless. The introduction of ATMs has detached the idea of 'accessing money' from any sense of brand loyalty: you stick your card into a machine on the basis of nothing more than convenience. The Internet simply extends this to one's own desktop. Trinidadian savers and investors could also move their money anywhere, or access other online financial services such as day trading, which would cut out the Trinidadian banks.

Hence, online banking was seen as both inevitable and to some extent both an ideal and a threat, along with financial deregulation. It is perhaps the embodiment of the Internet dream that Bill Gates evocatively pictured as a 'frictionless economy' or the IBM and KPMG speakers talked of as 'disintermediation': a free flow of money, goods and desires, as smooth as electrons flowing through a superconductor, and with just as few regulatory hurdles to jump. Ultimately the trap is also an aesthetic ideal, Trinidad within Miss and Mr Universe.

The Consumers

Almost everything in this chapter on the development of ecommerce has of necessity had a provisional air to it. At present there is considerable debate as to how far along an ecommerce line particular companies should go, and the chapter began with the remarkable disparity between the speed of integration found at Computers and Control and the sheer conservatism of the advertising agencies. But even in the case of the former no money had as yet been made out of the web. Almost all the debates revolve around an assumed close future where for many people money will only be made if one is on the net, (and as the breakfast seminar warned darkly, money will be lost if one is not on the net); but this is still almost entirely speculative. To understand why money-making has taken so long, and why indeed much of this speculation should probably be tentative and uncertain, we need briefly to examine the other side of the coin, that is the evidence for shopping and consumption. In effect most of this book is about consumption, since most consumption of the Internet is concerned with topics such as family relationships and chat. Here, however, we have to narrow down consumption to that which is of interest to the development of ecommerce.

If under 'shopping' we consider only direct payment for goods and services obtained through the net, then the evidence so far is that this is relatively slight. Trinidadians had for some time been involved in buying goods cheaply through direct purchase in the US. This was facilitated by the development of the SkyBox, which preceded the Internet. The Internet, however, fitted well into this strategy, and the technologies were combined to make direct US purchase still more common. Amongst the wealthiest groups there was knowledge of foreign ecommerce sites, and some people reported with pleasure the tracking online of a spare part for a Japanese car from Japan to Trinidad. Particular interests such as English football team kit could also be more easily traced and purchased thanks to the Internet. Book purchasing on Amazon.com was probably the most commonly mentioned use of a site abroad for actual purchasing, and at least researching, if not purchasing, Carnival costumes the most common use of local sites. Nevertheless, such direct purchasing was relatively slight. In no case did it seem to be proportionately important to people's shopping as yet; and in any case, most people do not have international credit cards.

Obviously purchasing is likely to grow as ecommerce facilities grow, but it is important also to think about this from the point of the view of the consumer. Although goods that are paid for are not very important, obtaining goods and services was already of considerable significance to many Trinidadians. As part of the background to this, it is worth noting that the ability to obtain things for free is seen as a national trait that is mentioned with pride in any of the joke lists that relate to the specific character of 'being Trini'. In a systematic analysis of a 'Spot the Trini' competition (Miller 1993) the desire for what is locally called *freeness* came across clearly as one of the top three self-defining traits. In those jokes the examples included were of how a Trini could break into a fête (party) without paying. But with the Internet the possibilities have grown immensely. It was no surprise that one of the cybercafés where we worked had a prominent wall-chart of everything that could be obtained on line for free.

As we write, the most popular keyword for most search engines is MP3. For Trinidadians it is not just that these allow people to obtain music quickly and turn individual tracks into their own self-made sequences of music as opposed to a conventional CDs. Most importantly, it means that they simply don't have to pay for the music. Apart from the costs of downloading, MP3s are free. Indeed MP3s are the tip of an iceberg. The same obviously applies to pornography. Even though we do not believe the high figure given by many informants for usage, whatever pornography was consumed was found almost entirely through free sites and largely replaced materials that would have had to be paid for. The same story could be told of using the net as an effective stock of online magazines instead of ordering and paying for offline magazines, of obtaining academic materials instead of paying for books, of sending e-greetings in some cases instead of purchased cards, and so on. In addition there is the by no means insignificant factor that no one outside a very formal business environment ever even thought of paying for commercial software and games. In financial terms perhaps the biggest saving of all was an end to an 'addiction' to expensive overseas phone calls. Hence, in considering those Trinidadians who had become regular users of the Internet, if one considers both those goods that are now free and would previously have been paid for, and the goods, services and information that are now consumed partly because they have become free, then the amount of Internet-related consumption and shopping was in some cases rather impressive (though admittedly less impressive when the costs of computers and monthly charges by ISPs are thrown into the account).

This raises a crucial issue. We have come to understand the history of this century as one of increasing commodification. Commerce and capitalism have grown largely on the ability to commodify goods and services – that is, turn them into things that we pay for. The involvement of commerce on the Internet is based on the assumption that this will further ratchet up this process. This is obviously reflected in the huge and overblown stockmarket value of Internet companies. Most of the players in the industry have confidence that what we see now is just a stage. Indeed, the more the Internet can give away for free the more speedily it can be transmuted into the nub of future commerce and sales. So MP3s might lead to an increase in music sales, just as videos were not the death of cinema. We have to be careful here. It is quite possible that this is just the harbinger of its opposite. But it is more likely that the future will see some genres and services undergoing genuine long-term decommodification, as people will no longer need to pay for them: that is to say consumers will become richer without firms gaining profits. In other areas the predictions of commerce will be fulfilled, and there will be an expansion of commodity trade not only on the Internet, but with a positive spill-over into expanded trade in general. The problem is that the industry really has no idea which genres of goods will go which way, as must be evident to anyone writing in a week when the *Encyclopaedia Britannica* has just announced that it is giving up on selling itself in the form of CDs and is instead going on line for free (though one assumes with the expectation of attracting considerable advertising revenue). There will be plenty of debate as to whether this is a commercial masterstroke or a commercial disaster. But commodification and decommodification should not be seen either as mutually exclusive futures or as independent processes. Right now the Internet has created more decommodification than anything since early socialism, and more commodification than anything since late capitalism. What the Internet makes clear is that each can be a tool of the other.

Conclusion: Internet Enterprises

In the cases of political economy and ecommerce we have clear models but messy businesses. For every other chapter, it is we as the academics that have to supply the models; but within the ethnography there are some fairly clear lines of development to model. People seem to know what the Internet is and what they can do with it. In most respects, this clear grip is very pragmatically based: they can see, in quite practical terms, how the Internet can help them do things they always did, or wanted to do: communicate with family, lime, or even obtain religious guidance. On the other hand, in the case of political economy and ecommerce, there were clear paradigms for Internet development: it was the practice that was seen as problematic.

The advertising industry and many of their major clients could see the Internet as a new space in which to place a flyer, an advert, or an announcement, but they themselves saw this as of dubious value. As a result they would not really pay for it, and this attracted low-paid but keen amateur designers who had little insight into the commercial side of things. This situation is no different from international structures of employment in the net sector (self-exploitation by young people), and indeed can be generalized to a great range of emergent culture industries such as fashion (see Ross 1997, 1998; McRobbie 1998, 1999). The discrepancy between promise and practice sets up the structure for the Internet industry in Trinidad: it is regarded as the inevitable economic future, yet it seems impossible to make a living out of it. Or to put it another way: no more in Trinidad than elsewhere have people found the business models that will work on the Internet. In any case, the failure of advertising agencies was in some ways appropriate, since the latest model of ecommerce started from the premise that advertising was the most primitive model for ecommerce, and one they should evolve out of as soon as possible.

When facing outwards to both local and foreign business people who were judging them by what were seen to be leading-edge models of webdesign and ecommerce, Trini business was backward, unable to see the potential, using the media incorrectly and – far more importantly – falling behind. By not reaching for real ecommerce, they were actually imperilling themselves and the country as a whole. This critique was allied to that which in the last chapter was launched against the government and TSTT, who appeared to have stymied the ideal of the new value-added, offshore IT company. These models of an ecommerce future might be partly hype: IBM and KPMG after all are the kinds of international consultants and virtualists (in the sense of Miller 1998b – where formal models of development come to dominate actual processes of development) whose own livelihoods depend on claiming to see a future that they could both sell as a model and then be paid for helping to implement in countries like Trinidad. On the other hand whether or not these ideals are in touch with actual consumption and the complex processes of decommodification and commodification that are already under way, they certainly made sense to people. They were not simply imposed from afar; and, as we have tried to show, they were not far from the internal stages of website development that we could trace on the ground.

As we have argued, in personal and cultural life, the Internet allowed ideals of social relations to be realized on an expanded communicative terrain. By contrast, in the case of political economy and business, the Internet itself expressed the ideals of free market relations, competitive advantage, and so on, in relation to which actual social relations and practices were judged to be primitive. Perhaps ironically, if the Internet is not generally virtual when it comes to personal life (which is where most of the Internet literature presumes that it will be), it really *is* virtual in the political economy (which is where the same literature would argue that hardheaded commercialism undermines virtuality).

7

Religion

Ending this book with a chapter on religion may not seem intuitively obvious, and yet it represents one of the few predictions in our research that we ultimately feel we got right. We believed that there would be a number of structural properties of religion that would make it an arena in which Trinidadians themselves would express with clarity and considerable reflexivity the general issues and dilemmas that arise from internet use. This allows us to return to the themes we put forward in the 'concluding' first chapter of this book, but more through the ways in which many Trinidadians expressed them.

A recent issue of the Internet journal *Cybersociology* is devoted to the topic of 'Religion Online and Techno-Spiritualism' (Bauwens 1999). The title suggests the coming together of a widespread interest in the spiritual implications of the technology, found in some of the cyberutopian literature, together with an interest in the use of the Internet on the part of established religions. The concern of this chapter is largely with the latter. Our prediction that this would be a revealing area of enquiry rested on three premises. Firstly, religions tend to be relatively self-conscious about new developments, often agonizing about whether something is or is not appropriate for them to use. As a result they may have to explore the intricate details of changes and the new possibilities offered, which can thereby help draw our attention to nuances we might otherwise miss. Secondly, religions may feel the need to use creative analogies with what they take to be precedents in order to apply religious laws that were formulated under older technological regimes. Thirdly, previous studies have shown how richly religions have used even technologies as basic as language to explore issues of agency, performance, context, form and transcendence (Keane 1997).

Fourthly, we would draw attention to a point made by Gell (1988) based on Malinowski's (1935) book, *Coral Gardens and their Magic*: religion itself is most commonly practised as a form of technology. The contemporary academic world, where most people are secular, focuses on the spiritual nature of religion. But in most regions where religion remains largely taken for granted the issue is not one of belief or spirituality but of practice, and therefore a problem largely of how a ritual or law should most appropriately be carried out (see also see Hakken 1999: 65; Kirshenblatt-Gimblett 1996; Pfaffenberger 1990, 1992).

The practice of religion as technology is brought out well in a study of the early use of the Internet by ultra-orthodox Jews, with their concerns for the precise techniques by which religious law can be applied (Kirshenblatt-Gimblett 1996). What at first looks like a rather archaic community tends to be involved in the vanguard of new technologies, such as using new chemical analyses to determine whether a pharmaceutical product is kosher, or a new means of shutting off light on the Sabbath in a manner that does not contravene the law against working on that day. So the Internet was quickly exploited, for example, to allow Jews on five continents to recite simultaneously a particular prayer, or to give the grave of a Rabbi an email address for sending petitions, or to discuss the rather evident point that the sacred books of the Talmud seem to be structured more like a hypertext than a simple narrative.

The Dynamics of Positioning as an Expansive Realization

The Internet has been used by Trinidadian religions to help foster identity within what may be seen as a series of concentric circles. First, the Hindu community will be considered in relation to its sense of a global Hinduism. Then the Catholic websites will be related to the Diaspora, the Caribbean, and finally to local communities within Trinidad. What emerges from these cases is the manner in which the dynamics of positioning work through what we have called an expansive realization.

The Hindu community in Trinidad, which represents around a quarter of the population, is dominated by the organization of the Sanathan Dharma Maha Sabha. Historically, there were powerful forces for internal homogenization represented by this organization (Vertovec 1992: 117–27), though with some internal diversity reflecting higher-status (Klass 1991) and lower-status groups (Vertovec 1992: 213–22). Its outspoken leader Satnarine Maharaj has long recognized the highly political nature of working for the interests of the Hindu community, which he sees as constantly under threat from Christian and especially Pentecostal groups, who still promote the idea of Hinduism as primitive and devil-worshipping. This concern is clear in their website (Plate 7.1), which consists of a home page with decorated columns and motifs such as a conch shell linked to 16 sub-sections, including 'Hindus prepare to strike back', 'Jesus lived in India' and 'What is Ramayana'? A more extreme and outspoken version of Hindu interests, but one without official foundation, was noted in Chapter 2.

Given this sense of being under constant siege locally, the sudden immediacy of the Internet as a global medium was viewed as something of a 'godsend'. For example, an international evangelical preacher, Benny Hinn, had recently come on a crusade to Trinidad and talked of the country's being half-full of demons and of the Hindus as devil-worshippers. Information from the net was used to make counter-claims that this preacher was under investigation in various countries; that his 'miracles' had been exposed as shams; and that he had suggested he was an actual incarnation of Christ.

The contemporary Internet represents a second phase of much more extensive contacts. It replaces the more limited possibilities presented to the Hindu Diaspora by electronic bulletin boards (see Rai 1995; Mitra 1997). Trinidadian Hindus soon discovered that the net was being used by nationalist political organizations such as the BJP (currently the governing party in India) and the more extreme RSS (in this case a branch based in the US). These groups have been trying to mobilize the Diaspora Indian population. Trinidadian Hindu organizations were happy to gain from the wider exposure this gave them. As one of those most involved noted: 'due to the efforts that we're making down here, what is happening right now in Trinidad in the Hindu world here, is known globally because of the outreach that we have been doing. we are known to the BJP right now.' This speaker emails material on the Trinidad situation to over 50 sites, of which around 60 per cent are in South Asia, most of the rest in the USA and the UK, and some in Caribbean regions with similar problems. He regularly publishes material about the Trinidad situation in magazines such as *The BJP Today* and *India Abroad*.

The public exposure of the local situation is closely tied to the pervasive defensiveness about the Hindu population of Trinidad. The same speaker stated: 'In case we should ever degenerate into a Guyanese situation with the Blacks taking this kind of militant role, at least our position in Trinidad would be out there. For if there is an international review, we have something out there existing already and they would not be dependent on information coming out of Trinidad at that particular point in time.' There was particular sensitivity over such eventualities because Trinidad has an Indian-led government for the first time, and there was a feeling that the press was therefore looking out for anti-Indian stories. So a recent newspaper report about a nun who was raped in India was countered by information taken from the net suggesting that this story had been disproved. Use was made of an RSS facility in which news about Hindus from the press in fifty countries was collated and circulated on a daily basis. This meant the Trinidad community was forewarned about problems. For example, in an episode of the television show 'Xena', the god Krishna appears in a manner they considered unsuitable.

Knowing this in advance, they could try to ensure the programme would never get airtime in Trinidad (or anywhere else).

The situation is not entirely straightforward. It was suggested that many within this Diaspora Internet presence wanted to view themselves merely as what are called NRIs, that is, 'Non-Resident Indians'. The Trinidadians, however, wanted to be seen as PIOs, or 'People of Indian Origin'. They saw the difference in these terms:

> NRIs – they still have this direct link [to India], but basically since they are in the majority living in American or European society they can never dream to really control any aspect of that society other than their own particular sphere. But PIOs, whether in Trinidad, Guyana, in Fiji, and Mauritius – we have control of the state's resources, we have access to that, we are more than what the NRIs are in terms of political influence.

This reconceptualization of the Diaspora has been facilitated by Trinidadian Indians finding out, partly via the Internet, that many of the other Indian Diaspora populations differ from South Asian Hinduism in similar ways, as a result of common factors such as the decline of caste, changes in family structure and the influence of Christianity (Vertovec 1992: 1–65). For Trinidadian Hindus, although they have not been isolated for quite some time, connection to the Diaspora community through the Internet, with its daily reinforcement, goes well beyond any prior form of international contact.

By comparison the Catholic Church, which accounts for more than a third of the population and accounts for much religious website construction in Trinidad, does not need to create a global Church. It already has the Papacy. The first of its three major websites is the Internet edition of the weekly *Catholic News*, which has a fairly straightforward newspaper style, with sections such as editorial, parish news, 'ask-me-another' (which is directed to the Archbishop), gospel meditation and Caribbean news and features (see Plate 7.2). It comes over as a well-established newspaper that integrates religious concerns with a general moral stance on contemporary issues.

In practice the website is of limited interest to Trinidadians living in Trinidad, since they can easily obtain the paper version. Nor would it be of very much interest to non-Trinidadians. The clear 'market' for the website is the extensive population of Diaspora Trinidadians. These are the people who tend to give email feedback and dominate the website guestbook. Here, as in relationships more generally (Chapters 3 and 4), the Diaspora is thereby able to evolve into a Diaspora community. This is also true of the next website, the Living Waters Community, although its aims had originally been more parochial (Plate 7.3). This is the most 'glossy' of the Catholic sites, as seen in its opening page, with its animations. Living Waters is a fairly recent charismatic community, which is in part a response to the growth of Pentecostalism. Indeed, one of its leaders is said to have 'passed through' a Pentecostal experience. With around 500 members, it includes a lively coffee shop in the capital Port of Spain, and a smaller community in the second city of San Fernando. Their professional-looking website emphasis aspects of prayer and sacrament, but also the active ministry to the poor and oppressed.

At first the website producers tended to be focused merely on having a presence on the web, and only then considered its relationship to their consumers. They admit that it was difficult to have much of a sense of its usage: 'Initially when we started, it was really directed to anybody at that time who was interested. Because you really don't know who is really interested in what. It feels like you're putting something out there and it's just blowing in the wind.' That it was the Diaspora population that responded through email and guestbooks was entirely congenial to the organization, both in terms of such people visiting their community when they travel to Trinidad and because of the importance of fund-raising to the community, though this was not what they had in mind in establishing the site.

At a more parochial level there had been a long-term desire for a regional Caribbean theology based on the common historical experiences of many of the islands of the region. This had been constrained by the travel costs and the delay in relaying messages. Now for first time they find it is possible to build up routine communication between like-minded theologians from different Caribbean islands, even when they may be currently on courses in the UK or the US. The prospects for a larger Caribbean theology were therefore much more upbeat as a result of internet use.

The final Catholic website – the Sacred Heart Cathedral in Port of Spain (Plate 7.4) – has the potential for a still more parochial appeal in both senses of the term. The site is both an introduction to the Cathedral itself, its history and its facilities, and also to the local parishes of Trinidad. So there is a fairly detailed calendar, information on youth groups, and a newsletter that deals with topics such as a 'special' elderly parishioner being honoured. So although its initial use may have been related to the Diaspora, or giving times of the mass to visiting tourists, the content clearly anticipates a largely local consumption, which was also clear when talking to its creators.

Finally, it should be noted that the Hindu community also has plans directed to its local adherents. One of the new initiatives planned by the Maha Sabha, apart from having computers in every Hindu School, is the desire to have online computers in the local temples. This is in part a response to the success of the Christian churches in turning themselves into youth centres with sports and similar recreational activities. The Hindu leadership feels that computer games and online communication could help keep their congregations congregating.

What is noticeable about the way that these religious groups talk about and use the Internet is that the intentions and aims are not at all novel constructions that can only now be envisaged because of the Internet. Quite the contrary: in every case the religious bodies are faced with what they see as dangerous or destructive forces that they associate with modernity, and that are seen to have prevented the religious communities from being what they always should have been. So the Hindus see themselves as part of the global Hindu population, and it is a catastrophe of history and political economy (viz, their arrival as indentured labourers) that has cut them off from their proper place in this community. Similarly, the Catholics found that the rise of migration over the last few decades has meant that many of their flock are part of an extensive Diaspora and no longer present in Trinidad.

Overall, then, the Internet is used as a form of communication that allows one to expand back into the realm that one was supposed already to occupy. There ought to have been a Caribbean theology, it was lack of technology that was preventing its emergence. Trinidad ought to have been part of a global Hinduism, and it is likely that most Hindus and indeed Muslims thought they were much more attached to global religion than had previously been the case. Similarly, with the Cathedral site, its creator noted, 'In other parishes the geography defines the community. And here the geography doesn't define the community. But this is still where you feel the fellowship. They can't interact the way of neighbours who live in the same street. So the Internet confirms our independence from Geography.' In all these cases, the intention is that a community that people already aspired to but was difficult to achieve may in the future become realized thanks to the Internet.

In these examples, then, we can see that the aspect of objectification that we have called the 'expansive realization' works through 'the dynamics of positioning'. One expression of modernity is used to resolve contradictions and forms of alienation that had arisen through prior practices and experiences of modernity more generally. The Internet allows for an expansion of communication, but in this case it is used to repair a discrepancy, thereby helping communities and people come closer to a realization of who they already feel they 'really' are. The mechanics involved require a sense of geography that defies the usual separation of the local and the global. In these cases the increasingly global use of the Internet across the Diaspora is a function of the re-establishment of local communications that had become sundered.

Dynamics of Normative Freedom

Established religions, just as much as the other institutions already discussed, are faced with an Internet that seems to represent a new potential for freedom. In most religions the authority of their establishment is closely bound to arguments about authorship. Ultimately, religious text is either directly or in some mediated form an expression of the authorship of God or Gods. The religious establishment becomes the mediator of divinely-inspired law or precept. Institutionalized religion thereby insinuates itself as part of the production of text, putting the lay person in the role of the consumer. But the authors of material on the Internet are often not those officially ordained. Ordinary Trinidadian internet users constantly talk of downloading medical advice, sections of public-domain school essays and religious instruction. Much of this could be to the despair of authorities. Just as teachers worried about whose essays are being copied, and medics worried about cranks telling their patients about the 'facts' of cancer, so also religious authorities fear they will lose control over which version of religious interpretation is emerging.

The consequences become clear when we look at the consumers of religious materials on the net. For example, a born-again secretary working in a cybercafé did not look at any Trinidadian religious websites, but surfed American-based evangelical sites. She focused on one particular ministry, which she felt had material that related well to her day-to-day problems and issues, and she relayed the information she obtained to her boyfriend, who was not online. She visited this site two or three times a week, and also received its monthly online newsletter. Overall she found this 'inspiring'. Although we found no Trinidadian-produced Muslim material on the net, the owner of another cybercafé used Islamic sites. As a result of wider contacts through previous media, Trinidadian Muslims were becoming increasingly aware of the ways in which their local version of the religion had developed features that were not shared by Muslims elsewhere in the world. As a young Muslim with considerable web access, she was starting to use it to try to sort out in her own mind which aspects of her practice were orthodox and which were local. Trinidadian Muslims would not generally be as aware of the existence of similar tensions between pluralism and authority, even in Islamic heartlands, which are themselves reflected in the already extensive Islamic websites (Azzi 1999); but they could employ these sites for their individual concerns. For example, she was very concerned about a possible religious prohibition on the use of music at her wedding, and had already located Koranic material on the net that she was using to question this prohibition. So for this user the web represented not access to a simple or single religious orthodoxy, but a set of sites with interpretations and arguments that allowed her to participate directly in theological disputes.

The consequences of this micro – macro relationship can be seen in a certain ambivalence within the perspective of Living Waters, the Catholic Charismatic. On the one hand the group wishes to remain orthodox, and often cites the Pope's encouragement:

> The holy spirit has raised up these [Charismatic] organisations when the hierarchy in the church really didn't have any place for us at all. And he is saying to these organisations, do not be afraid, this is the holy spirit doing something and just stay close to the church and the teachings of the church and let the holy spirit do its work. It's a whole new way of thinking, new technology, everything. . . . This Pope has seen himself as the Parish Priest of the world, which is very different from how Popes have constructed their role before. Technology has allowed it in terms of the television appearances but also travel and the ease of travel has allowed it. But the Internet has carried that project one step further. He puts himself into the Catholic faithful home before the Priest has the text. He by-passes Bishop and Priest and goes straight to the faithful. And there is a faithful group of the faithful who love it. Note, it undermines all your cultural Christianity and it is a very different agenda. But it is a very interesting use of the technology.

Here, then, one level of hierarchy is seen to have the potential to grow in authority at the expense of the intermediary institutional levels. But the same informant does not see the Internet as simply a one-way link to Rome. There were other possibilities for 'cultural Christianity'. Talking about Living Waters, a priest noted that:

> The fact that women led it is a Trinidadian phenomena. You will not find that elsewhere in the world. The other Catholic Charismatic wing internationally has been Sword in the Spirit and their thing is male headship. In fact, they have come to Trinidad several times and there has been very little meeting point in terms of communities because of their thinking. But then if you look in Trinidad the female in religion is very prominent. The Baptist tradition. The Baptist mother has always had that space on being the wise person in the community to whom you go when you really need something. And for the early years that's how the leaders operated. Now it's not just Living Waters that is led by two women. But there is one in Arima, there is one in Tunapuna, there is us and there's another in Port-of-Spain, so there are four and there were two others. All founded and led by women.

Furthermore he argued: 'It is far more democratic. People respond if they want. And if they don't want they just don't. So it is not a power tool in the way television and radio is. You have to be good in imaging or imagination to get people to respond.' The same priest wants to see internet cafés as part of religious organization and local access: 'You see the Parishes can be the levelling ground. So if you are Parishing a rural area there is no reason why you can't have machines that you beg somebody for with modems on them giving your Parish internet access.'

So even in such a deeply historical and established organization as the Catholic Church the Internet problematizes and to a degree dissipates earlier dichotomies between the local and the global Church and between who is a producer and who a consumer of religious materials. When we turn to other religions, which have no unambiguous global form as a precedent, the issue raises even more profound implications for religious organization and practice. The designers of the website for an Apostolic Church called the Elijah Ministries (see below) constantly wavered between two concerns. Their ideal was that users of the site would soon also become the creators of the site, as the site's next expansion was to be into interactive domains such as chat and bulletin-board-style discussions. Yet at the same time they were conscious of the presence of the 'elders', who are much publicized on the net and who are responsible for making sure that the material on the net reflects the 'truth' of the Church. The Internet might be a manifestation of God's current purpose, but people must be led from its depraved content to its true potential. The same tension was evident to its lay community. This can be seen by juxtaposing these two statements, which directly followed each other in a conversation with a Church member:

No longer can a church be held back by merely a leader. No, the believers can directly access the information, now anybody who could read, and has semi-permanent access to a computer can check and ask questions about doctrine.

The information that is put on the web sites is controlled because you want to strongly emphasise the doctrine of the church not just somebody's opinion, so therefore what is put there, is read by the elders.

As such the Internet extended a tension that is already evident in the previous use made by the same Church of the free market and free trade as an idiom for its religious life. The net extends the previous analogy because it is said by the Church to provide for a kind of level playing-field of pure competition where it can bid directly over the heads of traditional established religions for the souls of the globe, and it has a heady confidence in its ability to succeed in this pure market for religion. To some degree a more horizontal ordering of authority challenges the traditional vertical structure of authority. These tensions mimic those of freedom and normative order described for business itself in Chapters 5 and 6.

Just as in Jamaican Pentecostalism (Austin-Broos 1997), where the route from sinner to saint is both individual but is also subject to clear religious conventions, so the Elijah Ministries are explicit that they hold the true blueprint for the very individual process of being saved. In short, the more a religious establishment gives rein to the Internet as its idiom of self-conception and organization, the more it confronts the contradictions of new possibilities of both anarchy and control. Of course, these merely extend pre-internet tensions, and, as Simmel noted with respect to the Catholic Church, the ambiguities of a fixed place that is also a global space allowed religious culture to develop (Frisby and Featherstone 1997: 150–1). The Internet both extends and clarifies such contradictions and resolutions.

The Dynamics of Mediation

The Internet is not a simple new communicative device. It is a related series of evolving technologies, each with its own specific potentials and constraints. After an initial interest in website construction and email contacts religious usage often moves on to more developed forms of interactive media. Living Waters perhaps realistically saw a more complex multi-media usage emerging from its youth website, which they hoped would employ chat, ICQ, video clips, music and questions and answers. It could also be the springboard for distance-learning programmes, an idea being promoted by the government for secular purposes.

In discussing the implications of the net the most profound debates turned on these more precise details of the various technologies involved, and the way they mediate communication. Because it could be used much more frequently than letters and so much cheaply than the phone, email could take the form of a more constant relationship. The consequences can be seen in the use being made by Catholic Priests for the purpose of what was called 'spiritual journeying', in which a person is helped through dialogue to deal with 'the conflicts within this person's existence that do not allow a proper integration of body, spirit, mind, matter'. In using the Internet as a medium for spiritual journeying, it became apparent that:

> Part of the distinction is that in a face to face dialogue you have one set of benefits. I can interpret your words in the context of body language, in the context of clarifications that can be asked immediately, the context of a general sense that I have of tones of all sort of things that will give me ways of reading, of decoding your message. That's the benefit of face to face communication. The downside of face to face communication is, I'm expected to take all of this in, assimilate it and

process it and find the strands and feed it back. Which is a taxing thing at the best of times, and the more complex the journey becomes the more taxing it is. What I found with email journeying is that you can actually receive a message, read it and put it down. Not think about it too much and by the time you come back to it you have assimilated certain aspects of the message that you actually thought about from time to time during the day and so the response you would give out would normally be at a different level from the information that you have received. I find the time difference allows me to give a qualitative difference to the response.

Another potential advantage of the net was its anonymity. A member of the Elijah Ministries noted that 'you can transfer more intimate things across a modem, like when I sit here, there is a mask I put on and there is a response I put on, to your frowns, your smile and whatever, which in some ways resists the bond. On the Internet there can be a real free flow of information, sort of deep down things.' The point was developed further by a Catholic father:

I actually found that when you've done an email journey and you reach back now and you actually meet the person face to face it is very difficult. It is nearly as if you set norms for the relationship that allow a transparency that is not possible in a face-to-face dialogue. I have done it with several people and the first time I noticed, I did not think about it, and other times it became more conscious that you rupture something in this relationship if you shift it from email to face-to-face without understanding the difference . . . in fact I will go so far to say that some of the things expressed could not have been expressed in another media. I would even push it and say that my experience would be that people are trying to express and not even come close before this mode of communication. So like every mode of communication it opens for you new levels of interpersonal relationships as it closes off others.

One of the old traditions of spiritual direction prayer has been journal keeping. The journal has been a personal thing between the person and God. The reason we know so much about the saints. So writing has been a very old spiritual discipline. What the Internet allows you to do is to share that writing with someone who you are not seeing. It would be highly embarrassing for anyone to hand their journal over to another person if they were going to bump into them every day. But if they weren't going to bump into them every day, it is easier; hand it over and let them read it and send it back if they trust that the information being received would never be misused. And if they trust that this level of sharing would in fact enhance their journey and give them a sense of objectivity. One of the things you will never know is whether you are locked in your own head or whether you are actually seeing what you are seeing.

Overall the sense of those using the net for such purposes was that it provided new choices: face-to-face might work better for some, anonymity for others. It may be relevant that the next speaker was a woman:

> To me it's a whole process where you could really learn a lot about yourself and in a very sort of free way. In a sense, when you one and one talking to someone you are intimidated by the person's body language, by facial expressions and that, in a way can make you change what you are saying or not say certain things. Whereas using the Internet and using that medium, you really just go at it, then you pause.

But the same person also recognized along with other users that there was a balance to be struck and that online communication must be grounded in offline relations:

> but the Catholic Spirituality certainly is grounded in the flesh, in what was made real. The sense that the computer, that this is of God and it is a channel of God's grace that, that's how we see it, but it is never without losing sight of the human person, so that even if you embark on a journey as such where you are using this particular medium, at some point you must have that one-on-one encounter.

A key issue often raised by discussants was trust, which along with other similar issues was raised equally in secular uses (Slater 1998). But the religious contexts generated a high level of explicit consideration of the uses and limitations of each innovation. They may also subsume some of the issues raised in the earlier discussion of global communication. This was brought out by another member of the Church, talking about a practice called 'breaking the word':

> We would take a section of the scripture, read it, and you would sit here among five people and someone would say, this line struck me, and I get this out of the passage, and I relate it to the hangings next door, or I relate it to a poor man I gave a piece of bread to, and we get it in this context. When you get on to the net, you get this same thing, somebody in Europe, somebody in Australia, somebody in Africa, somebody in Latin America, somebody in the Caribbean and the five of you take the same passage and do the exact same thing and what comes out of breaking that word is much, much bigger. Certainly in an understanding and an appreciation of the scripture. Seeing it lived out in different places in the world and the different meaning. I've seen that happened already. It's only once with a group of people on the net that did that, and I saw the results. I wasn't in it, but I saw their results of doing it. Yes, they had the information on it, and it was very, very interesting. Where we would see it in the context of Trinidad and Tobago, where we would break the word and relate it to our own culture and our own life

here. When you're on the Internet, it's done for the whole world and it's a much bigger understanding and broadens your horizons and your theology in that way.

Not surprisingly, given the sudden arrival of this technology, there were also disagreements and uncertainties about its appropriateness as analogous with prior religious rituals and practices. An example was the issue of confession. For one priest the confession is itself an example of mediated communication that could be viewed as a precedent for the net:

But the point of the grid [as used in confessionals] is to make the person anonymous. If that is the point of the rite, then I have pushed, the grid could be the web and the grace could be mediated and there is another form that is tactile where you need to touch the penitent. In that form the Internet cannot do anything. But because there is a form that is non-tactile that is mediated through a grid, that is ensuring the anonymity of a person, I would push that this is a medium that needs to be considered.

By contrast another Church leader commented on confession that:

The rites of the Church are very definite and there's nothing in the rites that would allow that. It is a totally different thing, It's like when you go to communion, you have to be there to receive it, and there must be a priest present for confession. Sacrament is a one-on-one or community of things, or an expression of the presence of Christ between two people. It has to be done like that, you may not see the person in confession, but the person was present there and on the part of the rite, the priest can also place his hand on the head of the person to ask for absolution.

Two further examples demonstrate the variety of issues that are brought out when the consequences of the use of each technical aspect of the Internet are considered. The first is the impact on the sense of time, as in the following quotes:

I mean it was very nice to be able on New Years' Day to have a copy of the Pope's message for New Year and to be able to use it or to have stuff ahead of the newspapers and to be able to talk about it.

The time to construct a letter is different from the time to construct an email. The expectations to constructing a letter are different from the expectations of constructing an email. If I'm going to answer a letter there is no way I am sending less than a full page. And if you know a person well at all that is an insult. You have to give at least two pages. So mentally you have to set aside some time where you can think about something worthy of two pages of communication. With an email, if what I want to send is one line I send a line. If it is two or ten pages I send two or ten pages, but the difference is the expectation.

As in many secular discussions, the suggestion was that the month that an exchange of letters might take was something particularly inappropriate to Trinidadians, who simply work on a shorter time-scale:

> On the Internet too, you could use your own time, you can decide, for some people it may be 2 in the morning and they want to get on the Internet and spend . . . I know someone that wrote me that they get up every morning at 2 o'clock or 3 o'clock and they spend an hour and a half on the net reaching people and praying with people. That is kind of their ministry, and that is what they're doing. It could be very difficult for someone else to do that, yet still that's a special time available to them that they can use.

The final example builds on a new point, which is that the Internet enters into a history of media and their differential appropriation by these religious groups in the past. Similar issues had arisen in relation to those media. The most insightful comments arose in discussions about why particular religious movements may have focused on particular media. For example, while the Pentecostal Church had been in the vanguard of television broadcasting the Catholic Church seemed to be pressing ahead with internet use. As one Catholic informant put it:

> There is an immediacy about the image of a television or the voice of a radio that is closer to the structure of a Pentecostal mind in terms of the relationship they have got. God is immediate. . . . so the intrusion into the living room is a way of getting the message across. . . . But if you look at Catholic use of television, good Catholic television is much more image-driven. . . . If you want to convey a message I could stand in front of the television and give you a fifteen-minute discourse. The Catholic way as I understand it would be more sacramental. I would start by showing images of people eating. And I would focus it around the most human context that I can find of the different ways social interchange takes place around the table, and the image used in a way to show that there is something human that is very profound that takes place around this table. And that would be the foundation of my Eucharistic theology. It's a whole other way of appropriating the media. The Internet is not immediate, in a sense you don't intrude. It is far more democratic. People respond if they want. And if they don't want they just don't. So it is not a power tool in the way television or radio is. You have to be good in imaging or imagination to get people to respond.

To conclude, it is apparent to religious users that many aspects of the Internet – its nature as a spatial medium, its inherent temporality, its anonymity and its use of images – emerge as specific technological developments that can be exploited for the purposes of religious practice, which go well beyond the bland concept of 'communication' and enter into a dialogue about the nature of relationships both personal and theological. Furthermore, contrary to Boden and Molotch (1995), there are grounds for challenging the presumed superiority of face-to-face communication in contexts where that communication is particularly profound. Similar points were made in secular discussion about relationships in Chapter 3. But, as suggested at the beginning of this chapter, the topic of religion brings out the extraordinary degree of self-awareness that religious figures develop, because it is so important to them to establish whether these innovations are precedented and acceptable.

The Expansive Potential

Another religious website that had a commanding presence on the Trinidadian web belonged to the already mentioned Elijah Centre Ministries (Plate 7.5). This was a highly professional-looking site with many clear motifs and logos, such as a menorah, slogans and spinning globes. The ministry was founded by a lecturer at the University of the West Indies in 1990, and holds services at a credit union centre near to the University; but almost every other aspect of its activities is available online. As one of their website operators noted: 'Email is a very big part of our communication. We don't have a newsletter, everything is done online mainly. I believe that we're the first Church to mainly communicate through the net.'

They created the first Trinidadian church website in 1995, and this appears to be symptomatic of a Church that exists in a profound dialectic of objectification with the Internet. It describes itself as follows:

> Elijah Center is the church of an organisation called the World Breakthrough Network. We are the head church of this network, it's an international network of ministries, organisations, individuals, ministers and what we call Kingdom Businesses. Our site was conceived to service both the local and internationally. The doctrine of the church, if you want to call it that, did have an international appeal and so the site was always focused on getting the word out, not just in Trinidad, but across the entire earth. And we understood that the net was the most effective way to do that, of course.

It is the Internet that tells the members of the Church what it means when it claims to be an Apostolic Church. This is defined against the Pentecostal Church which, it views as the prior evolutionary stage of church development. Despite its global pretensions the Pentecostal movement is regarded as too grounded in its US origins and influences, and thereby too parochial. It did not have the right tools to imagine itself as truly global. It thus served as a John the Baptist to the Apostolic Christ. But the Internet gives one the first real experiences of what it means to be global, and therefore provides a means for the Church to imagine itself into existence as the global church mission. This is evident in the following quotations:

> As we try to remain on the cutting edge, both in technology, but also in terms of what we believe God is doing, we are progressive in that sense. . . . I think the Internet is the new. I think it's important to understand how, it serves to highlight how sovereignly God can bring people, groups, organisation and individuals together, without preconceived ideas. . . . I always try and contemplate new ways to get the word out to more people, so there's a scripture in Isaiah that says that your gate shall be continually open. The way I interpret that is that the Internet is that always open gate. You don't have to have service starting at 7, you just go on any time you want, anywhere in the world, any time of the day and you get access to what would be a service. So our gates are indeed continually open. So that is scripturally linked. One of the things we are increasingly trying to do is to sense a greater sense of community by our web site, where we are actually encouraging people to interact with each other. So our Caribbean contact section seeks to be the forum that cultivates that type of an interaction.

At the same time that the website was developed, a separate company called Telio systems was created. This primarily develops websites for companies and engages in new software development, while maintaining the Church sites as part of what its Directors see as their 'tithe' of labour. It also recently helped a Nigerian Church to go online. As such it exemplifies what the Church sees as 'Kingdom Business'. As with the Catholic Church, there are discussions about the changes in time and image construction that come with internet use; but here it becomes an integral part of the foundational self-conception of the Church.

> We have something called governmental prayer, which is every morning we have what is called battle lines, where we have specific things to pray about. And because these battle lines are sent out to the network, via e-mail and via the web site and that has proven to be THE most effective way of quickly getting out prayer focus. Well, every week, we replace the prayers and the battle lines. If there happens to be an emergency situation or issue to pray about, again via e-mail, it gets sent out, in a way that simply was just not possible five years ago. . . . We understand that as it was with Paul, he went along the Roman trade routes, he didn't cut a path through the hills, he went along the trade routes instituted by the Romans.

The relationship is also discussed on the website itself. For example one commentary is called 'Bill Gates and God, What's the Connection?'; the central section reads (Plate 7.6):

> This control of a fundamental aspect of the communications technology is evidence of the globalization momentum of our time. And it presents a useful paradigm from which we can evaluate the ultimate purpose of this globalization phenomenon. Bill Gates' success is unparalleled in his industry at this time. But his thrust and momentum stem from an internal human mechanism predating him. Throughout the ages, man has been driven by a desire to control the earth. Globalization in all its dimensions provides a mechanism or platform for the establishment of God's plan and purpose for the whole earth. However, there are always attempts to oppose or distort divine plans. Hence the adverse effects of globalization must be expected. For just as the Internet makes the current and accurate speaking of God available world-wide, it also disseminates elements of depraved, defiled and degenerate lifestyles.

This use of the Internet develops from a core aspect of the Church itself. This is the contemporary and most literal version of Weber's (1958) characterization of Protestant Churches as looking to the World itself for evidence that they are saved. So the Church looks to the most contemporary idiom for its routes to salvation. It is clear from their materials that they were already using the language of commerce and the free market in a similar fashion, as something that could express their potential as a global Church. The Internet was quickly seen to push still further the possibilities of this self-understanding of what the Church or (as it would see it) the message of God must be, and the net was therefore appropriated as the imagination of the Church.

This integration of web consciousness and salvation is found also in the everyday practice and thinking of the users of this site. One such user was describing the experience of a friend of his in making extensive use of chat-lines. He felt that in being an African based in Trinidad talking theology with an East Asian helped them both to sense a transcendence of space. This in turn fuelled the feeling, expressed by the user, that in the profundity of the global conversation he had had a direct experience of God. The user was himself quite clear that in fact the Internet actually exists for this very purpose. It was necessary in the progression from Pentecostal to Apostolic Church that God should give humanity the Internet so they would finally be able to envisage the coming future of global salvation:

> the Internet came right back slap into the whole philosophy of the church in that, since the net was so global it immediately allows the church to feel global . . . You go on from Trinidad and you meet someone the other side of the globe that has

the same kind of thinking, the same mentality that you have. What it does is make you feel that God is doing something consistent through the world and that you are part of a masterplan. The purpose of your community is alignment with a larger plan that God is doing ... All technology comes from God, and so the Internet is something God created using men to actually articulate this particular idea that God wanted to do right now. This particular move, the Apostolic move, what we call the reformation of the church, has been radically changed, to become one that is more relevant. So therefore, in order for this to happen, the Internet came right bang into this move.

One can therefore see why even when only a proportion of the congregation can use the Internet the Church has poured itself into becoming an increasingly online experience. It requires its congregation to have experience of the Internet in order that it gains the consciousness of the Church mission itself as expressed through the Internet as the gift of God to humanity to show them the path to salvation.

Other religious bodies with their histories and establishment could not enter into such a full-fledged dialectic of objectification with the Internet, but they too could see a correspondence between the Internet as material culture/medium and wider theological goals. Here the sense is not of a new consciousness, but rather that using the net shows an aspiration towards consciousness of the divine. As one of the leaders of Living Waters noted:

> Something that's within them, whether it's God, or whatever, or some higher power and when you get on to that net, you're looking for something like that. You're not going to look for something that you see everyday or you interact everyday. You're looking for something that is going to be meaningful in your life and eventually you come to God. ... The sense of the transcendent, that's almost what it's like, I feel that, what else could it be? That something so huge, that can take over the world: what else could it be? Although it's a distant thing, it's about communication, it's could be very deeply about God. I think almost 90% of the people who come in, boot up, and go into that Internet, deep within them they're seeking something deeper than themselves. Ultimately they will come to that. I think the Internet is a tremendous avenue for that.

It is, however, significant that in religion as in the previous chapters the process of objectification can work through practice as well as working through consciousness. In contrast to Elijah Ministries, there is another Church that has also transformed its self-understanding of its mission as a result of the Internet, but almost entirely through changes in practice. They do not seem to frame this as a theological process, or even of theological significance. The Caribbean Union College is probably the largest Seventh

Day Adventist college in the Caribbean (Plate 7.7). Set well up a valley on an isolated campus, it has over 1,000 students, more than half of which are recruited from outside Trinidad. Forty-eight countries are represented, and that year students had come from Iceland and Poland who had discovered and applied to the college entirely through the Internet. Just as with the Elijah centre, the new technology seemed to be about to replace commerce as the dominant idiom through which in practice the college reconstitutes itself as the sign of modernity. In this case, however, everything was mediated through concepts of educational advancement rather than theology.

They thereby exemplified another strand we have traced in Trinidadian involvement with the Internet, the Internet as bypassing the most established educational channels to provide an entrepreneurial rather than a class-based educational vision. Most of those leading this conversion are self-trained, thanks to a commitment to self-sufficiency. This is a college that puts its own computers together from components, making it also a seller rather than a purchaser of computers. If there is a new technical requirement, such as laying down fibre-optic cable, it will only bring in outside consultants once, participating with them in order to gain the skills. The students have 80 online computers available, facilitating anything from downloading text-books to keeping in touch with their families. As a result the college teaches a much wider array of new IT skills and languages than any other Trinidadian institution, and the demand for such courses is quickly overtaking all other courses offered. Its plans for using new bandwidth and satellite technology are in place before these facilities have become available. It provides its own internships for activities such as web development and software engineering, and it is developing full ecommerce with front- and back-end compliancy so that its students have applied as well as theoretical knowledge (not surpris-ingly, there are also inidividual websites associated with the college, for example Plate 7.8).

It is through such developments that it plans its future income generation. Indeed, it claims it is now persuading its 'parent' Andrews College in Michigan to upgrade its IT plans following the Trinidad model. So without any explicit discussion of the religious nature of these changes, the college applies a zealotry to reconstructing itself as an internet and IT institution. Already some people in the State university fear it will become an IT dinosaur by comparison, and there are very few commercial organizations where the Internet has become so foundational to the future, permeating every aspect from its social life to its success in securing employment for graduates. Yet although it is likely to end up equally re-cast in the mould of the Internet as is Elijah Ministries, this is done in the name of pragmatism and finance. It is another case of Trinidadian understanding of skills as embodied and pragmatic, along the lines of exceptional flair in 'car mechanics'. But in this case the skilled practice is also understood as a vocation, and thus part of one's religious mission in life.

Conclusion

The structure of the preceding sections may in one sense be misleading. It might be implied that they are a series of stages in development. One starts with an expansive realization that allows the identity already aspired to by religious groups to be realized through new dynamics of position. One then develops the normative foundations of such communities in the interaction of new forms of freedom and moral authority. Within this the nuances of each technology can be seen as the dynamics of mediation, each facilitating a particular type of communication. Finally, this develops into a full-blooded mode of objectification termed the expansive potential, in which the Internet changes the consciousness of religion itself and of its practice.

This is certainly not the conclusion to be drawn. In this chapter as in our first chapter we have used each case-study to illustrate general points about the production and consumption of the Internet. But, of course, there is considerable overlap between the analytical categories we have developed, most obviously here, where the dynamics of position were seen as the instrument of the expansive realization. We do not intend our general categories to be viewed as an order of development. They are heuristic, intended to promote comparisons. We would not wish them reified. For example, in the final section we can see the importance of the Internet as a sign of totalization. But even this was divided into two stark alternatives: in the case of the Christian Union College totalization was seen as practice, while in the case of the Apostolic Church it was a sign of God.

We oppose the reification of the categories we end with in the same spirit that we opposed the reification of a thing called 'the Internet' as our starting-point. The conclusion of this book is not that there was ever an 'internet' that here has been differentially appropriated because of the diverse forms and contexts in which it is found. We have opposed what might be called the easy positivism of internet studies, which takes this to be a given entity which is then used or appropriated. The Internet only ever existed in the specificity of its use, sometimes as a totality, sometimes as loosely linked technologies rendered as cultural genres. In this chapter the 'Hindu' internet, the 'Catholic' internet, and the 'Apostolic' internet are all equal and legitimate forms.

We have not shied away from acknowledging technology as having effects; and following the recent writings of Latour, the technology has been included as one of the key players in our narratives. We should not be afraid to view technology as an active agency in the social world. But this is always set against prior encounters both with other media and with other idioms. It is this that makes the Internet in one case seem literally preordained, so that an Apostolic Church is enchanted to find something so appropriate to the evolution of its own identity; so that a Hindu community can realize its pressing need for international identity; so that the Catholic Church can retain pastoral links with its Diaspora and exploit new possibilities of mediated spiritual communication.

Ultimately, an ethnography could never be about the Internet where this is considered merely as a series of technologies in particular contexts. The cultural forms we observe comprise technologies already so inextricably linked through normative order, practical constraints and possibilities, metaphor and idiom as to have become forms of practice. For the purposes of any ethnographic study, then, technology always becomes material culture, observed in its context of employment as particular genres, often quite specific Trinidadian genres, which we have attempted both to generalize and to account for. This has been a book about material culture – not about technology. Furthermore, it has been about an integral aspect of people's daily lives: their relationship to their friends and family, part of their identity, their work and in this chapter their religion – not about a virtual world that stands against and defines or supersedes something else called the real. In the case of the Internet we have encountered an extraordinarily dynamic form of material culture. Indeed, the speed of its emergence may leave us breathless; but by appreciating and rendering explicit the nuances of the social practices that account for its manifestation as material culture it may be possible for academics to remain in step.

Appendix:
The House-To-House
Survey

For this survey we were able to return to the districts that Miller (1994) studied during his previous fieldwork. These had been chosen to reflect a very 'ordinary' section of Trinidadian society, comprising four of the main types of housing area, but not including any of the higher-status and wealthier residential communities that are associated with the Western districts of Port of Spain. Given that internet access is an expensive resource in a country that includes areas of considerable poverty, we originally assumed that for this particular study we would have to turn to what are locally referred to as 'up-scale' areas. This would have been a pity, since we would then have lost the ethnographic continuity and background knowledge arising from Miller's eleven years' involvement in the area. Happily, our assumptions proved mistaken. The same four areas contained quite sufficient internet use for our purposes, and indeed this could be said to be a major conclusion of our research: although this may soon be commonplace, we were astonished to find this degree of diffusion to ordinary communities as early as May 1999.

We believe our house-to-house survey provides a clear indication of the actual penetration of internet knowledge and use, complementing other methods and previous research. This is because, as in so much of Trinidadian life, people use a wide variety of informal and highly resourceful means to obtain access that would not be evident in any more formal survey. Information obtained by relevant commercial and state bodies (which is in fact pretty scarce) shows the spread of online computers rather than users, and would have suggested a higher concentration amongst the upper echelons of Trinidadian society. The best available figures come from market research surveys and the subscriptions to the ISPs. The relevant companies were very generous to us in providing commercially sensitive information. Together they suggest that there are between 17,000 and 25,000 online accounts in Trinidad. Overall there are 350,000 households. Those who collect this information are aware that just as newspapers buyers may bear little relation to newspaper readers in Trinidad, a figure of 7 per cent paid internet access by private households is by no means the same as actual usage. Our survey, by contrast, was intended to establish actual usage. Even the figure of 25,000 is impressive when it is considered that only four times that number have access to cable TV, and only around 190,000 households have a telephone.

An account of the four communities surveyed and a justification for seeing them as a reasonable exemplification of Trinidad more generally is given in Miller (1994: 24–50). This is important, since most Trinidadians would assert that this area is unrepresentative. In particular Trinidadians who live in the capital of Port of Spain or along what is called 'the East–West Corridor' look askance at the idea that parts of another town could be selected as representative, especially one in the Central area. Most commonly the town of Chaguanas (best known for its portrait as 1930s Arawak in Naipaul's (1961) *A House for Mr. Biswas* would be regarded as disproportionately 'Indian'. Also, in a country that is numerically dominated by people who regard themselves as middle-class, even the wealthiest area used in this survey was dismissed by some outsiders as 'lower-middle-class'. As was noted in Miller (1994) these dismissals are generally false. To have used Port of Spain or the East–West Corridor would have meant leaving out any sense of the rural populations that make up much of the country and also ignoring the fact that the Indian population is just as large as the African.

Furthermore, the four communities were carefully chosen for particular qualities, which are not those of the Chaguanas town centre. Many Trinidadians live today in new kinds of settlements that have characteristics that are more important than their original locality. As these settlements have developed, the position of Chaguanas as central, as economically vibrant and (barring heavy traffic) only 25 minutes' drive from the capital has led to considerable migration from every other area of Trinidad, so that inhabitants of the four areas are as likely to have been born in the deep South as in Port of Spain. Furthermore, using census data the original study was able to demonstrate (and confirm in the actual house-to-house survey) that the population of the areas chosen reflected the 40 per cent African, 40 per cent Indian and 20 per cent Mixed ethnic identification of the population as a whole.

The fictional names of the areas chosen are:

1. The Meadows – a settlement that exemplifies what in Trinidad are called 'residential areas', which are built as 'up-scale' enclaves.
2. Newtown – an example of the many settlements constructed by the government's National Housing Authority, often dominated by public sector workers or supporters of the previous PNM government.

3. St Paul's – the only one of these four settlements to have existed more than 25 years before this study, comprising a village that has come to be incorporated as the outskirts of the town.
4. Ford – part of an extensive settlement of squatters, one of many such around the country.

For comparison, these areas are discussed in Miller (1994) in the following places: The Meadows, pp. 36–9, Newtown pp. 45–50, St Paul's pp. 30–5, Ford pp. 39–45.

Although we used the same four areas, we did not visit the same households as in Miller's previous survey. The two research assistants who carried out the surveys (students from the University of the West Indies) made some effort to reflect the range of housing within each settlement. Otherwise houses were simply included where someone was at home and able to provide the required information about themselves and what we judged was a reasonable degree of knowledge about other members of that household. We did not count as users those who had only accessed the net once or twice or only as part of a school or college course (which would have added quite a few households), but we did include those whose primary access was their work-place computer or a relative or friend. In addition to the short survey, we carried out more in-depth individual household interviews and informal enquiries in all four areas.

The Four Communities

The Meadows

This is a private housing estate where each leaseholder was originally inter-viewed to establish their suitability, and with many stipulations in the contract limiting commercial use of the house, although these are regularly ignored. In some areas there is a standard housing form, but so many of these have been altered or had plots built on by their owners that the main impression is of heterogeneity, or in some cases awe at the elaborate architecture that may be encountered. Architectural inspiration seems to vary from a mosque, to Gracelands, to neo-classical columned arcades. Several mansions with elaborate decorative conceits have been built in the last decade. Yet most houses remain relatively simple bungalows or upstairs apartments on stilts with one bathroom, and two or three bedrooms, lounge and kitchen (see Plates 2.3). Virtually all houses are surrounded by high fences within which live the ubiquitous guard dogs, though these seem to include miniatures as well as the Rottweilers and Dobermanns. Many also have well-manicured lawns and gardens. Inhabitants tend to the professions, especially teaching but also medicine and law, to the civil service and to medium-scale business operations. Almost every family has relatives living abroad, and many travel to the US with some regularity. The population is ethnically mixed.

Of the 50 households surveyed, 30 included members who used the net. Some 16 of these households had online computers, while a further 3 had offline computers in their homes. A total of 15 households had users who used an online computer for access at their workplace, while 3 specified their school or college as their main place of access and 1 a relative. Of the 61 people who used the net, 33 were males and 27 females (1 record is unclear). Of the 30 households 13 are single-user, 10 have 2 users, 2 have 3 users, 3 have 4 users and 2 have 5 users.

Of the 52 individuals where our evidence of frequency of use seems secure 14 use email every day, 11 several times a week, 19 once a week, and 5 monthly, and only 3 did not use email at all. Some 12 surf every day, 12 several times a week, 12 once a week, 6 once a month and 10 don't surf. Some 13 households and 18 individuals use ICQ or chat, of whom 12 specified having an ICQ or chat numbers. It may be noted that of the 11 users that were under 20 years old (the youngest was 10 years old) 8 use chat, making them a high proportion of the 18 chat users. Indeed, 5 of them use chat everyday. Of those who mentioned contacting relatives living abroad, 9 mentioned the USA, 9 Canada, 6 UK, 2 Other Europe, 1 Mauritius, and 1 Kenya. One person in the overall sample has a personal webpage and also makes webpages for others.

Newtown

At the time of the 1989 survey some 500 units had been built out of what originally had been a much larger scheme, which was viewed with some suspicion by the people of Chaguanas as an attempt to change the political demography of this town, situated in the heartland of what was then the political opposition. Certainly most of the houses went to public sector workers, especially those in uniform, such as police and coastguards. In the last decade the distinction between Newtown and the rest of Chaguanas has become somewhat muted. Areas of the original plan have now been taken up by private companies and developed into new residential areas, either purpose-built, or purchased as lots and then built on by householders in a similar fashion to The Meadows. The fact that this is seen as an attractive possibility is testimony to the point made in Miller (1994: 46) that the original NHA area soon established a reputation as a quiet area striving for respectability. Apart from attempts to differentiate each house from its neighbours there was less evidence that the core housing area has been substantially renovated over the last decade, perhaps suggesting that public sector workers have not seen much increase in their incomes during this period (see Plates 2.4). Less than 10 per cent of the population are Indian according to the 1989 survey.

Of the 50 houses surveyed 15 included at least one internet user; 4 of the households had online computers and one had an offline computer. Two households noted that they had their own online computers at their work-place. Overall 8 said their main access was at work, 1 at a cousin and 1 at school. One individual regularly used a cybercafé and 1 used the public library, which has free internet access for limited periods and uses. Some 9 of the 15 households had only a single user. Where gender was clear there were 10 female and 9 male users. While 7 specified using the net to contact relatives living abroad, these were all in the USA. One person emphasized contacts with friends in the Caribbean. Thirteen households use email: 4 use this several times a week, 5 use it once a week, and 4 less than that. Eleven use the computer for surfing, of whom 7 do this several times a week, and 4 once a week. Five households mentioned the use of their computers for chat; again there was an emphasis on children, one of whom used this everyday and another several times a week.

St Paul's

The character of St Paul's is quite different from that of the other settlements, since they are relatively homogeneous, starting from a recent baseline of similar housing. By contrast, in St Paul's there is much more evidence of the vicissitudes of history, as it has transformed some and left behind others in its wake. As a result St Paul's includes a sprinkling of large mansion-style houses that are not much inferior to those of The Meadows and also clusters of impoverished wooden houses that are much more reminiscent of Ford (see Plate 2.5). The 1989 survey showed this to be the only one of the four settlements where the majority (around 85 per cent) were born within the Central district of Trinidad. Within St Paul's one area seems dominated by a Hindu temple and the community associated with this, but others areas are dominated by groups of limers hanging around the street corners. Overall people see a tendency for the more successful members of the community to move away to more prestigious regions from an area that even its inhabitants tend to see as nondescript; but this is partly belied by the evidence for some successful families that have kept their roots and grown locally. Over 80 per cent of the population is Indian according to the 1989 survey.

Of the 50 households surveyed 10 included an internet user. Two of these only contain a single user; the rest contain several users. Three houses had online computers and 3 more had computers that were not online. Five people noted that their primary access was through their workplace and 3 specified a school or college, while 1 relied on a cybercafé. Where gender was clear there were 9 male and 10 female users. Of the 10 households, all use email, and 5 of them have a person using email every day. All 10 use the net for surfing, and 5 have persons who surf every day. Only 5 households include someone who chats, of whom 3 do so every day. Only 6 mentioned relatives living abroad that were regularly contacted, of whom 4 noted the USA, 1 UK and 1 Canada; but this question was not posed consistently. A measure of the poverty that also exists along with the wealth is that 7 of the 50 households do not have a phone, while this was the case with only a single household in Newtown and The Meadows.

Ford

Ford is part of a densely inhabited and extensive area of squatting. Unlike some of the other squatting areas this is on private land, and so is unlikely to benefit from plans by the state to regularize squatters on government land. People came for reasons of poverty or estrangement from their natal communities. The original houses tended to be made from the remains of boxes used to import car parts, together with corrugated iron. Of all the settlements, however, this one showed the greatest contrast from the 1989 survey. At that time there were no tarmacked roads and little electricity, and crimes such as theft compounded problems caused by cocaine use and AIDS. Today the main entry roads are paved, electricity is in place, and most people have phone access. The main problem of resources is water, which has still not been supplied; and indeed local standpipes had been cut off. In general the area seems quieter and safer, with people feeling more secure about electronic possessions. On very limited evidence we would speculate that cocaine use is more controlled, though AIDS remains unchecked. Most of the original houses have been replaced by brick or concrete structures, although since these are built in stages, often using the traditional 'gayup' system of feeding a group of friends and relatives who come in for a day to complete a particular stage, such as laying the foundations, they are in various states of completion. Today, as in St Paul's, quite reasonable houses nestle among shacks of plywood and corrugated iron (see Plates 2.6). As a result we were less surprised than we might have been to find the occasional user, although very surprised when one turned out to come from one of the most flimsy shacks in the area. What is also evident and has been discussed elsewhere in this volume are the very high levels of information, skill and concern with education, in terms of which Ford seems simply an extension of Trinidadian values in general.

Of the 50 households in Ford 7 had persons who had been online more than once or twice; several more had been online only once or twice usually at school or college. Since there was only one house with a computer, and that was not online, all access is from other sites. Three of these accesses were from a work context, including an oil company and a clothes store, 2 users had their main access at college, and 2 more through relatives and friends. Access might be multiple, as with the person who worked for the oil company, also used the local library at lunchtimes, and would also surf from friends'. Of the 7 users only 2 were male and only one was over 25, while 4 were 20 or under. There was no chatting reported, only surfing and email. We were surprised to find even 7 people using the net in a community where most people don't have access to water, although 30 of the houses do have a phone line. The numbers also fail to reflect the sheer level of knowledge and interest. Several other people reported that they had started computer training courses and would go online as part of that. Apart from the elderly, most people had no difficulty relating to the questions we were asking. Overall the crucial lesson is that people from the poorest districts do not feel intimidated by the idea of the Internet: they did not, as we expected, find our enquiry inappropriate. As far as most young people were concerned it was merely that we had come too early. Sooner or later they expected to have their own experience of the Internet.

Overall Usage and Conclusions

The table below attempts some very broad numerical summaries of the data.. If we use data about average household size drawn from the previous survey (Miller 1994: Table 4.1) we obtain the figures in the first column. The figures are at least equal to more optimistic estimates based on ISP accounts. While the figure of 11.5 per cent of households with online computers is higher than most estimates, it is compounded by the finding that there is substantial usage of Internet access outside the home.

A measure that takes us rather closer to our ethnographic sense of how the Internet relates to everyday usage is that of the 200 households surveyed, 62 contained at least one member who used the Internet to a significant extent. This excludes quite a number of other households that contained people who had only used it once, or only as part of a course. Our figures would place even Ford well above the standard estimates, and confound most commonly held views of Internet diffusion held by Trinidadians. And we believe this is indeed a good reflection of how far the Internet has penetrated into ordinary life.

The figures are made meaningful by being set back into their ethnographic background. In the context of chains of communication in which a single

Table A1. Internet Usage in Four Trinidadian Communities

	No. of individuals using the Internet	No. of households with users	%	No. of households with online computer	%
The Meadows	29%	30	60%	16	32
Newtown	12.5%	15	30%	4	8
St Paul's	7%	10	20%	3	6
Ford	2%	7	14%	0	0
Total	11%	62	31%	23	11.5

household member may be a conduit for email with an extended family or for carrying out research on behalf of friends and neighbours, household access – whether through computers at home, work, library or cybercafé – is the significant figure. These percentages may exaggerate somewhat (there are very few single-person households, for example, and there were many cases where use was restricted to one individual in a household), but they would certainly indicate, firstly, that the Internet has permeated ordinary society to a very significant extent, and that – whether directly or through someone in the household or community – Internet access is not remote even from those living in the most deprived areas. Secondly, the discrepancy between 'households with users' and 'households with online computers' reinforces the important distinction between circulation and readership, or ISP accounts and actual usage. The most likely estimate of numbers of accounts (25,000) suggests a figure of only 7 per cent houses. Our survey suggested 11.5 per cent; but clearly even that figure does not reflect the actual usage, still less the degree of familiarity with the Internet suggested by the evidence that a third of households include an internet user.

These results compare well with estimates in much more developed countries such as the UK (at least before the launch of the free-access ISP Freeserve, which took the usage to an estimate of 1 in 5). Given the huge difference in income levels and the greater logistical difficulties for the Trinidad population this tends to confirm our overall impression that *pro rata* there is a greater level of knowledge and experience already in a country such as Trinidad than in the UK. The UK is the only other place where we have the informal experience to make such a comparison. We would want to add to this picture the huge domestic investments made by private families and individuals (quite apart from government or businesses) in paying for computer training and equipment.

These figures are likely to be out of date almost instantly (certainly by the time of publication), especially in the case of Newtown. As indicated earlier, the government in lifting customs duties on hardware and software and in extending loans for computers to all public-service workers will speed up diffusion hugely. In one ministry the person responsible for such loans told us that fully 50 per cent of employees from the cleaners upwards had taken the first steps to secure one. Although only 1 in 5 households in Newtown had computers almost every household claimed that it intended to purchase one; many of them were waiting until after the Y2K problems had been resolved. Moreover, these loans were sufficient to buy well-specified machines, and indeed everyone treated modems as standard: a computer is a machine that can go online.

There will remain a large component of the population, in areas such as Ford and among those who clearly have not 'made it' in St Paul's, representing perhaps 40 per cent of the overall population, for whom there is little prospect of online access at home. But many of those people will use computer courses, at sometimes good and sometimes dubious colleges, as well as workplaces, the homes of relatives, free access at libraries and paid access at cybercafés, in order to gain some experience of online activity. Even in these areas large numbers of people expressed a degree of informedness, ambition and intention that is likely to find some means to being realized. The exceptions tended to be the elderly rather than the poor.

Glossary of Terms

Chat	The facility to have one's typed sentences appear instantly online in another person's computer window. Most forms allow for both group and private chat.
Chat, random	In ICQ, the facility to chat with people selected by ICQ at random, but usually within parameters such as age-groups or gender.
Doh	Trinidadian for 'don't'.
EDI	Electronic Data Interchange, a pre-Internet protocol.
Email	The primary means by which people send each other messages online.
Flaming, flame wars	Aggressive comments hurled at a member of a newsgroup; by extension, verbal battles within any Internet social setting.
HTML	Hypertext mark-up language. Machine-independent code that is used to produce web-pages.
ICQ	The letters reputedly stand for 'I Seek You', a chat forum that allows a user to know when they log on which of the other people specified are also online at that moment. It then permits both group and individual chat.
IRC	Internet Relay Chat. Online chat system.
ICT	Information and communications technologies.
IMF	International Monetary Fund.
Intranet	A network that uses Internet protocols but restricts access to members of an organization, for internal business.
ISP	Internet Service Providers, to whom one gives payment in order to gain access to the internet.
IT	Information Technologies.
Lime	Originally a group of people meeting at street corners. It then became the term for groups going out for leisure where there was an emphasis on spontaneity. Today it may be applied to almost any time Trinidadians go out together for a leisure activity.
Maco	A person given to minding other people's business, e.g. an anthropologist. Hence 'macotious'.

Maxed out	When Internet Service Providers are unable to cope with the volume of calls from customers trying to log on to the Internet.
MIT	Massachusetts Institute of Technology.
MP3	Compression of recorded music into files small enough to be fairly quickly downloaded or exchanged online. This has created a huge circulation of free and accessible online music.
MUD	Multi User Dungeons/Dimensions. Online facilities allowing synchronous interaction between users, who can carry out role-playing or games.
nicks	Nicknames used on ICQ or other chat systems.
Ole talk	Traditional forms of performative but largely empty banter.
POP	Point of Presence, for local internet access.
SkyBox	A system that provides Trinidadians with a local US address so that they can buy US products at US prices, and then arranges customs and transport into Trinidad for a small sum.
Soca	Orignally the blending of calypso and soul, the word now stands for almost any Trindadian music associated with Carnival.
TIDCO	State-funded organization to promote non-oil enterprises and development; also in effect the main government tourism body.
Trinbagonian	A term intended to include people from Tobago as well as Trinidad, and thus more correct than the term 'Trini'.
TSTT	Telecommunications Services of Trinidad and Tobago. The company runs all phone services and is also an ISP.
Usenet newsgroups	Asynchronous online communication facility, generally organized around interest groups.
UWI	The University of the West Indies campus at St Augustine in Trinidad. The university has other campuses elsewhere in the Caribbean.
WTO	The World Trade Organization, the body that formally adjudicates but also acts as a protagonist for the spread of global free trade.

Bibliography

Abrahams, R. 1983 *The Man of Words in the West Indies*. Baltimore, MD: Johns Hopkins University Press

Alleyne-Dettmers, P. 1998 Ancestral Voices. *Journal of Material Culture* 3: 201–21

Anderson, B. 1986 *Imagined Communities*. London: Verso

Austin-Broos, D. 1997 *Jamaican Genesis*. Chicago: University of Chicago Press

Auty, R. and Gelb, A. 1986 Oil Windfalls in a Small Parliamentary Democracy: Their Impact on Trinidad and Tobago. *World Development* 14: 1161–75

Azzi, A, R. 1999 Islam in Cyberspace: Muslim Presence on the Internet (Malaysia) CSS Internet News 28/8/1999 http://www.brecorder.com/story/S0010/S1002/S1002109.htm

Basch, L., Glick Schiller, N. and Szanton Blanc, C. 1994 *Nations Unbound*. Amsterdam: Gordon & Breach

Bassett, C. 1997 'Virtually Gendered: Life in an Online World', in K. Gelder and S. Thornton (eds), *The Subcultures Reader*. London: Routledge

Baudrillard, J. 1988 *Jean Baudrillard: Selected Writings*. Stanford, CA: Stanford University Press

Bauwens, M. (ed.) 1999 Religion Online / Techno-Spiritualism. *Cybersociology* 7

Boden, D. and Molotch, H. 1995 The Compulsion of Proximity. In R. Friedland and D. Boden Eds, *NOW/HERE*, pp. 257–86. Berkeley, CA: University of California Press

Bourdieu, P. 1977 *Outline of a Theory of Practice*. Cambridge: Cambridge University Press

Bourdieu, P. 1984 *Distinction*. London: Routledge & Kegan Paul

Braithwaite, L. 1975 [1953] *Social Stratification in Trinidad*. Mona, Jamaica: Institute of Social and Economic Research

Brereton, B. 1981 *A History of Modern Trinidad 1783–1962*. London: Heinemann

Butler, J. 1993 *Bodies that Matter: On the Discursive Limits of Sex*. London: Routledge

Cairncross F. 1997 *The Death of Distance*. London: Orion Business Books

Callon, M. 1998 Introduction. In M. Callon (ed.), *The Laws of the Markets*. Oxford: Blackwell

Carrier, J. 1995 *Gifts and Commodities*. London: Routledge

Castells, M. 1996 *The Rise of the Network Society*. Oxford: Blackwell

Castells, M. 1997 *The Power of Identity*. Oxford: Blackwell

Castells, M. 1998 *End of Millennium*. Oxford: Blackwell

Chamberlain, M. 1998 *Caribbean Migration: Globalised Identities*. London: Routledge

Crang, M., Crang, P. and May, J. 1999 *Virtual Geographies*. London: Routledge

Dibbell, J. 1994 'A Rape in Cyberspace; or, How an Evil Clown, a Haitian Trickster Spirit, Two Wizards, and a Cast of Dozens Turned a Database into a Society', in M. Dery (ed.), *Flame Wars: The Discourse of Cyberculture*. Durham, NC: Duke University Press

Dibbell, J. 1998 *My Tiny Life*. New York: Owl Books

Douglas, M. and Isherwood, B. 1979 *The World of Goods: Towards an Anthropology of Consumption*. Harmondsworth: Penguin

Eisenstein, Z. 1998 *Global Obscenities: Patriarchy, Capitalism, and the Lure of Cyberfantasy*. New York: New York University Press

Eriksen, T. 1990 Liming in Trinidad: the art of doing nothing. *Folk* 32: 23–43

Everett, M. 1998 Latin American On-line: The Internet, Development, and Democratization. *Human Organisation* 57: 385–93

Freeman, C. 1998 Femininity and Flexible Labor: Fashioning Class Through Gender on the Global Assembly Line. *Critique of Anthropology* 18: 245–62

Frisby, D. and Featherstone, M. (eds) 1997 *Simmel on Culture*. London: Sage

Furlong, R. 1995 'There's No Place like Home', in M. Lister (ed.), *The Photographic Image in Digital Culture*. London: Routledge

Gell, A.1988 Technology and Magic. *Anthropology Today* 4: 6–9

Gell, A. 1998 *Art and Agency*. Oxford: Oxford University Press

Gilroy, P. 1993 *The Black Atlantic: Modernity and Double Consciousness*. London: Verso

Gupta, A. and Ferguson, J. 1997 Discipline and Practice: the 'Field' as site, method and location in Anthropology. In A. Gupta and J. Ferguson (eds), *Anthropological Locations*. Berkeley, CA: University of California Press

Hakken, D. 1999 *Cyborgs – cyberspace?: An Ethnographer Looks to the Future*. London: Routledge

Hall, S. 1988 'New Ethnicities', in K. Mercer (ed.), *Black Film, British Cinema* (1st edn) London: ICA

Haque, B. 1999 'IDB Country Economic Assessment: Trinidad and Tobago.' Inter-American Development Bank, April 1999. http://www.iadb.org/regions/re3/sep/tt-sep.htm

Haraway, D. and Randolph, L. 1996 *Modest-Witness, Second-Millennium: Femaleman Meets Oncomouse: Feminism and Technoscience*. London: Routledge

Haywood, T. 1998 Global Networks and the Myth of Equality: Trickle Down or Trickle Away? In B. Loader (ed.), *Cyberspace Divide*. London: Routledge

Henry, R. 1988 The State and Income Distribution in an Independent Trinidad and Tobago. In S. Ryan (ed.), *Trinidad and Tobago – The Independence Experience 1962–1987*, pp. 471–93. St Augustine: University of West Indies

Hintzen, P. 1989 *The Costs of Regime Survival*. Cambridge: Cambridge University Press

Ho, C. 1991 *Salt-Water Trinis: Afro-Trinidadian Immigrant Networks and Non-Assimilation in Los Angeles*. New York: AMS Press

Holderness, M. 1998 Who Are the World's Information-poor? In B. Loader (ed.), *Cyberspace Divide*. London: Routledge

Howes, D. (ed.) 1996 *Cross-Cultural Consumption: Global Markets, Local Realities*. London: Routledge

Jaffe, A. 1999 Packaged Sentiments. The Social Meaning of Greeting Cards. *Journal of Material Culture* 4: 115–41

Jameson, F. 1991 *Postmodernism*. London: Verso

Jones, S. (ed.) 1997 *Virtual Culture: Identity and Communication in Cyberspace*. London: Sage

Keane, W. 1997 Religious Language. *Annual Review of Anthropology* 26: 47–71

Khan, A. 1993 What is 'A Spanish'?: Ambiguity and 'Mixed' Ethnicity in Trinidad. In K. Yelvington, (ed.), *Trinidad Ethnicity*. London: Macmillan.

Kirshenblatt-Gimblett, B. 1996 The Electronic Vernacular. In G. Marcus (ed.), *Engagements with Media*. Chicago: University of Chicago Press

Kitchen, R. 1998 *Cyberspace: The World in the Wires*. New York: John Wiley

Klass, M. 1991 *Singing with Sai Baba: The Politics of Revitalization in Trinidad*. Boulder, CO: Westview Press

Lash, S. and Urry, J. 1994 *Economies of Signs and Space*. London: Sage

Latour, B. 1991 Technology is Society Made Durable. In J. Law (ed.), *A Sociology of Monsters*. London: Routledge

Latour, B. 1993 *We Have Never Been Modern*. Hemel Hempstead: Harvester Wheatsheaf

Latour, B. 1996 *Aramis, or the Love of Technology*. Cambridge, MA: Harvard University Press

Latour, B. 1999 *Pandora's Hope*. Cambridge, MA: Harvard University Press

Lejter, N. 1999 A New Eldorado, or A Ticket to the First World. *Cybersociology* 3, http://www.cybersoc.com/magazine

Lieber, M. 1981 *Street Life. Afro-American Culture in Urban Trinidad*. Boston: G. K. Hall and Co

MacKenzie, D. and Wajcman, J. (eds), 1985 *The Social Shaping of Technology*. Milton Keynes: Open University Press

McRobbie, A. 1998 *British Fashion Design: Rag Trade or Image Industry?* London: Routledge

McRobbie, A. 1999 *In the Culture Society: Art, Fashion and Popular Music*. London: Routledge

Malinowski, B. 1922 *Argonauts of the Western Pacific: An Account of Enterprise and Adventure in the Archipelagoes of Melanesian New Guinea*. London: G. Routledge and Sons

Malinowski, B 1935 *Coral Gardens and Their Magic*. New York: American Books Co.

Marcus, G. 1995 Ethnography In/Of the World System: The Emergence of Multisited Ethnography. *Annual Review of Anthropology* 24: 95–117

Markham, A. 1998 *Life Online*. New York: Sage

Marvin, C. 1988 *When Old Technologies Were New*. New York: Oxford University Press

Mauss, M. 1954 *The Gift*. London: Cohen and West

Miller, D. 1987 *Material Culture and Mass Consumption*. Oxford: Blackwell

Miller, D. 1993 Spot the Trini. *Ethnos* 317–34

Miller, D. 1994 *Modernity: an ethnographic approach*. Oxford: Berg

Miller, D. 1997 *Capitalism: an ethnographic approach*. Oxford: Berg

Miller, D. 1998a *A Theory of Shopping*. Cambridge: Polity Press

Miller, D. 1998b A Theory of Virtualism. In J. Carrier and D. Miller (eds), *Virtualism: A New Political Economy*. Oxford: Berg

Miller, D. 2000 The fame of Trinis; websites as traps. *Journal of Material Culture* 5

Mitra, A. 1997 Virtual Commonality: Looking for India on the Internet. In S. Jones (ed.), *Virtual Culture*, 55–79. London: Sage

Munn, N. 1986 *The Fame of Gawa*. Cambridge: Cambridge University Press

Naipaul, V. S. 1959 *Miguel Street*. London: Andre Deutsch

Naipaul, V. S. 1961 *A House for Mr. Biswas*. London: Andre Deutsch

Naipaul, V. S. 1962 *The Middle Passage*. London: Andre Deutsch

Naipaul, V. S. 1987 *The Enigma of Arrival*. London: Viking

Olwig, K. F. 1993 *Global Culture, Island Identity: Continuity and Change in the Afro-Caribbean Community of Nevis*. Chur, Switzerland: Harwood

Paccagnella, L. 1997 Getting the Seats of Your Pants Dirty: Strategies for Ethnographic Research on Virtual Communities. In *Journal of Computer Mediated Communication* 3 (http://jcmc.huji.ac.il)

Peach, C. 1998 Trends in Levels of Caribbean Segregation, Great Britain, 1961–91, in M. Chamberlain (ed.), *Caribbean Migration: Globalised Identities*. London: Routledge

Pearse, A. (ed.) 1988 [1956] *Trinidad Carnival*. Port of Spain: Paria Publishing

Pearson, R. 1993 Gender and New Technology in the Caribbean: Nice Work for Women? In J. Momsen (ed.), *Women and Change in the Caribbean*, pp. 287–95. Kingston: Ian Randle

Pfaffenberger, B. 1990 The Hindu Temple as a Machine, or the Western Machine as a Temple. *Technique et Culture* 16: 183–202

Pfaffenberger, B. 1992 The Social Anthropology of Technology. *Annual Review of Anthropology* 21: 491–516

Porter, M. 1998 *The Competitive Advantage of Nations*. London: Macmillan

Poster, M. 1995 'Postmodern Virtualities', in M. Featherstone and R. Burrows (eds), *Cyberspace, Cyberbodies, Cyberpunk: Cultures of Technological Embodiment*. London: Routledge

Rai, A. 1995 India Online: Electronic Bulletin Boards and the Construction of a Diasporic Hindu Identity. *Diaspora* 4: 31–57

Rao, M. 1999 Bringing the Net to the Masses: Cybercafes in Latin America. *Cybersociology* 4 22/04/99 http://www.cybersoc.com/magazine

Rheddock, R. 1999 Jahaji Bhai: The Emergence of a Dougla Poetics in Trinidad and Tobago. *Identities*: 5: 567–99

Rival, L., Slater, D., and Miller, D. 1998 Sex and Sociality: Comparative Ethnography of Sexual Objectification. *Theory, Cultural and Society* 15 (3–4)

Ross, A. (ed.) 1997 *No Sweat: Fashion, Free Trade and the Rights of Garment Workers.* London: Verso

Ross, A. 1998 *Real Love: In Pursuit of Cultural Justice.* New York: New York University Press

Ryan, S. (ed.) 1988 *Trinidad and Tobago: The Independence Experience 1962–1987.* St Augustine: Institute for Social and Economic Research

Ryan, S. (ed.) 1991 *Social and Occupational Stratification in Contemporary Trinidad and Tobago.* St Augustine: Institute for Social and Economic Research

Sahlins, M. 1999 Two or Three Things I Know About Culture. *Journal of the Royal Anthropological Institute* 5: 399–421

Sanpath, N. 1997 *Mas'* Identity: Tourism and Global and Local Aspects of Trinidad Carnival. In S. Abram, J. Waldron and D. V. L. Macleod (eds), pp. 149–70. *Tourists and Tourism: Identifying with People and Places.* Oxford: Berg

Singh, C. 1989 *Multinationals, the State and the Management of Economic Nationalism: The Case of Trinidad.* New York: Praeger

Slater, D. 1998 Trading Sexpics on IRC: Embodiment and Authenticity on the Internet. *Body and Society* 4 (4)

Slater, D. (in press a) Consumption Without Scarcity: Exchange and Normativity in an Internet Setting, in P. Jackson, M. Lowe, D. Miller, and F. Mort (eds), *Commercial Cultures.* London: Berg

Slater, D. (in press b) 'Political Discourse and the Politics of Need: Discourses on the Good Life in Cyberspace, in L. Bennett and R. Entman (eds), *Mediated Politics.* Cambridge: Cambridge University Press

Smith, R. T. 1988 *Kinship and Class in the West Indies.* Cambridge: Cambridge University Press

Smith, R. T. 1995 *The Matrifocal Family.* London: Routledge

Springer, C. 1996 *Electronic Eros: Bodies and Desire in the Postindustrial Age.* Austin, TX: University of Texas Press

Stein, J. 1999 The Telephone: Its Social Shaping and Public Negotiation in Late Nineteenth- and Early Twentieth-century London. In M. Crang, P. Crang and J. May, *Virtual Geographies*, pp. 44–62 London: Routledge: 44-62

Stewart, J. 1986 'Patronage and Control in the Trinidad Carnival', in V. Turner and E. Bruner (eds), *The Anthropology of Experience.* Urbana, IL: University of Illinois Press

Thomas, N. 1999 Becoming Undisciplined: Anthropology and Cultural Studies. In H. Moore (ed.), *Anthropological Theory Today.* Cambridge: Polity

Turkle, S. 1995 Life on the Screen: Identity in the Age of the Internet. New York: Simon and Schuster

Vertovec, S. 1992 *Hindu Trinidad.* London: Macmillan

Wakeford, N. 1999 Gender and the Landscapes of Computing in an Internet Café. In M. Crang, P. Crang and J. May (eds), *Virtual Geographies*, pp. 178–201. London: Routledge

Waters, M. 1995 *Globalization*. London: Routledge

Weber, M. 1958 *The Protestant Ethic and the Spirit of Capitalism*. New York: Charles Scribner's Sons

Wilk, R. 1995 Learning to be Local in Belize: Global Systems of Common Difference. In D. Miller (ed.), *World's Apart: Modernity through the Prism of the Local*. London: Routledge

Williams, E. 1942 *Capitalism and Slavery*. Durham, NC: University of North Carolina Press

Williams, E. 1969 *Inward Hunger: The Education of a Prime Minister*. London: Andre Deutsch

Wilson, P. 1973 *Crab Antics*. New Haven, CT: Yale University Press

Wresch, W. 1998 Information Access in Africa: Problems with Every Channel, *The Information Society* 14:4

Yelvington, K. (ed.) 1993 *Trinidadian Ethnicity*. London: Macmillan

Yelvington, K. 1995 *Producing Power*. Philadelphia: Temple University Press

Yelvington, K. 1996 Flirting in the Factory. *Journal of the Royal Anthropological Institute*. 2: 313– 33

Index